# Enhancing
# Faculty Careers

*Jack H. Schuster*
*Daniel W. Wheeler*
*and Associates*

# Enhancing
# Faculty Careers

*Strategies for*
*Development*
*and Renewal*

 J o s s e y - B a s s   P u b l i s h e r s

San Francisco   •   Oxford   •   1990

ENHANCING FACULTY CAREERS
*Strategies for Development and Renewal*
by Jack H. Schuster, Daniel W. Wheeler, and Associates

Copyright © 1990 by:  Jossey-Bass Inc., Publishers
350 Sansome Street
San Francisco, California 94104
&
Jossey-Bass Limited
Headington Hill Hall
Oxford OX3 0BW

**Library of Congress Cataloging-in-Publication Data**

Schuster, Jack H.
    Enhancing faculty careers : strategies for development and renewal/
Jack H. Schuster, Daniel W. Wheeler, and associates.
        p.      cm.—(Jossey-Bass higher education series)
    Includes bibliographical references.
    ISBN 1-55542-210-1
    1. Universities and colleges—United States—Faculty.   2. College
teaching—Vocational guidance—United States.   I. Wheeler, Daniel
W., date.   II. Title.   III. Series.
LB2331.72.S37      1990
378.1'2'0973—dc20                                        89-39666
                                                          CIP

Manufactured in the United States of America

The paper in this book meets the guidelines for
permanence and durability of the Committee on
Production Guidelines for Book Longevity of the
Council on Library Resources.

JACKET DESIGN BY WILLI BAUM

FIRST EDITION

*Code 9018*

The Jossey-Bass
Higher Education Series

# Contents

This book is dedicated to Howard R. Bowen. His extraordinary career exemplifies the very best of scholarship and academic leadership; his fervent caring for the teacher-scholars who make up the faculty has been for us a source of inspiration.

# Preface

During the 1960s and 1970s, as campuses rapidly expanded and concern about teaching grew apace, the need for faculty development captured the attention of those in American higher education. In consequence, campuses by the hundreds initiated programs to assist faculty members to do their jobs more effectively. Theorists and practitioners quickly identified three major elements critical to faculty development programs. Of the three, only activities to improve instructional development were widely implemented; unfortunately, the other two elements—personal and organizational development—have often languished. Thus much of the original promise of faculty development remains unfulfilled at a time when, arguably, the need for fully elaborated programs has never been greater. Even so, at least some campus programs can be found that address comprehensively the needs of individual faculty members and their institutions.

The unevenness of faculty development efforts, viewed against the backdrop of gradually deteriorating conditions for many American professors, provided the basis for the present collaboration by the authors. Arising out of a deepening awareness of faculty and institutional needs, and predicated on the recognition that suitable "techniques" for faculty development already exist, this volume addresses the task of disseminating the "good news": excellent models—both of full-blown faculty development programs and of more narrowly focused efforts—are already operational, and they can be adapted to the needs of campuses committed to maintaining a vital faculty. The chief prerequisite, in our judgment, is a campus's commitment and will; with leadership and a modicum of resources—for excellent faculty development programs need not be

terribly costly—programs can be developed that will respond effectively to faculty and institutional needs.

We have sought to assemble in these pages practical guidelines and illustrative models of effective developmental programs.
The result, we believe, is a compilation of resources and strategies
that will be useful to those seeking to institute or expand faculty
development efforts.

The overall purpose of this volume is to enhance the quality
of faculty life and, thereby, to enrich the educational process for
faculty members and their students. This admittedly ambitious goal
is grounded in the twin convictions that some vital aspects of faculty life go largely ignored in many (probably most) campus settings *and* that relatively modest interventions can lead to improvements. These interventions should embody the concept of
"enhanced faculty development"—a concept described briefly here
and addressed more fully later, especially in the concluding chapter.

In this book we advocate a more comprehensive—or holistic—conception of faculty members and academic careers. We argue
that a broader, more integrated view of professional and personal
development—what we have labeled "enhanced faculty development"—not only is more sensitive and humane but is closely linked
with a college's or university's ability to achieve its missions. Indeed, we see it as a given that an engaged, committed, lively faculty
is a prerequisite to achieving any measure of institutional success.
Yet the conditions that shape faculty careers these days, as described
especially in Part One of this book, require fresh approaches to
faculty development—stretching beyond the limited attainments of
the past several decades.

### Audience

The audience we envision includes all who are concerned
with improving the conditions of faculty life. Thus the prospective
readership encompasses diverse campus populations: campus and
departmental academic administrators, faculty leaders, and those
who administer faculty development programs—in a word, all who
are responsible for the design, implementation, and support of programs intended to assist faculty in the many facets of their careers.

## Overview of the Contents

Toward that end, we have organized *Enhancing Faculty Careers* into four parts. Part One, comprising the first three chapters, sets forth the historical and conceptual context for faculty development, presents a view of the developmental nature of academic careers, and reviews the extensive literature on faculty development concepts and programs. It is within this framework that more specific programs and strategies, described in the remaining chapters, must be understood.

Part Two (Chapters Four through Eight) illustrates strategies that address an array of issues impinging upon faculty careers. Some programs—wellness and faculty assistance programs, for instance—were either unknown before or have so recently sprouted on the academic scene that they need to be viewed in the broader context of faculty or professional development. The five chapters in Part Two span the faculty career continuum, from the preparation of prospective faculty members to programs that facilitate early retirement.

Part Three, consisting of Chapters Nine through Thirteen, depicts program strategies as developed on four very different campuses, as well as an interinstitutional program instituted by one multicampus consortium. The objective of Part Three is to illustrate success stories of campuses that have evolved a broader vision of faculty life and have invested the requisite resources to facilitate faculty growth in "new" ways. Each of these programs, whose particular focus and accomplishments are familiar to the authors, emphasizes the personal and/or organizational aspects of development, in contrast to the more traditional preoccupation with instructional development. We selected programs for inclusion on the basis of three criteria: the program's capacity for illustrating an important aspect of faculty development (other than instructional development), the program's established track record over a period of time, and the reputation of the campus development specialists. Each program demonstrates a strong *campuswide* commitment to professional growth and development. The common thread running through these diverse settings and strategies is the apparent organizational will to move beyond familiar, conventional, nar-

rowly bounded approaches in order to address faculty needs in a
more comprehensive—and, we argue, more realistic and more productive—manner.

Part Four sets forth recommendations for campuses—approaches to faculty development that are grounded in the concept
of enhancement. Given the diversity of higher education institutions, we refrain from proffering a prescription to fit all campuses.
However, we firmly believe that there are orientations and principles, derived from observably successful programs, that can be
molded to the idiosyncratic circumstances of a given campus to
enrich the faculty's professional development. We stress here the
urgency of strong administrative and faculty leadership. Initiators
of campus programs, we contend, must recognize the necessity of
adapting specific activities to the ever-changing developmental
needs of faculty members. We encourage conceptualizing broadly
and moving step by step toward building comprehensive programs.

In sum, *Enhancing Faculty Careers* endeavors to link the
theoretical and the practical. This volume also seeks to span the
length of an academic career, from professional preparation to retirement. The segments outlined above provide a conceptual framework within which faculty members' efforts to adapt to a volatile
environment can be viewed. The book's primary objective is to provide concrete illustrations of campus activities—focused programs
as well as integrated campuswide strategies—designed to promote
faculty vitality. Through such efforts to enhance faculty careers,
colleges and universities can come closer to fulfilling their institutional missions in an era replete with challenges and pitfalls.

### Acknowledgments

Our collaboration began in February 1987 at a meeting of the
Association for the Study of Higher Education, when the two principal authors began to share perceptions about the conditions of
faculty life and the role—potential as well as actual—of professional development. In the ensuing months, many people helped
bring this project to fruition. Most important are the chapter con-
tributors. We sought out the most accomplished authorities, and
they responded with competence and good humor—despite incon-

venient deadlines and the press of other priorities. We are proud to be associated with all of them as colleagues in this endeavor.

We are grateful for the support and encouragement provided by TIAA-CREF, in particular by Peggy Heim. That support facilitated the authors' collaboration across half a continent. Our thanks go also to Gale Erlandson of Jossey-Bass and to the reviewers of our manuscript; their careful reading and helpful suggestions have wrought numerous improvements on our initial efforts.

We acknowledge with appreciation the tireless and painstaking work of office secretaries—especially Fay Rulau in Claremont and Cheryl Ross in Lincoln. They neither flinched nor faltered when confronted with yet another version of the manuscript.

Finally, to our spouses, Diane Tickton Schuster and Betty Jo Wheeler, both professionals who know the joys and frustrations of academic writing, we say thank you for tolerating our preoccupation with this project. We owe you!

*January 1990*                                          Jack H. Schuster
                                                        *Claremont, California*

                                                        Daniel W. Wheeler
                                                        *Lincoln, Nebraska*

# The Authors

Jack H. Schuster is professor of education and public policy and head of the graduate program in higher education at the Claremont Graduate School. Before joining the faculty there in 1977, he was legislative assistant, then administrative assistant, to Congressman John Brademas. He served from 1970 to 1977 as assistant to the chancellor at the University of California, Berkeley, and as lecturer in political science. He has been a visiting scholar at the University of Michigan's Center for the Study of Higher Education and a guest scholar in governmental studies at the Brookings Institution.

He received his B.A. degree (1959) from Tulane University in history, his J.D. degree (1963) from Harvard Law School, his M.A. degree (1967) from Columbia University in political science, and his Ph.D. degree (1977) from the University of California, Berkeley, in higher education.

Schuster is coauthor with Howard R. Bowen of *American Professors: A National Resource Imperiled* (1986), for which they received the Association of American Colleges' Frederic Ness Book Award. He is coauthor with Lynn H. Miller and Associates of *Governing Tomorrow's Campus* (1989). One of his articles, "The Politics of Education in a New Era" (1982), received a 1983 Distinguished Achievement Award from the Educational Press Association of America. Schuster received the Research Achievement Award from the Association for the Study of Higher Education in 1989.

Schuster is a member of the Council and the Executive Committee of the American Association of University Professors and chair of Committee T on campus governance issues. He is a member of the American Council on Education's National Leadership Group.

Daniel W. Wheeler is associate professor and coordinator of professional and organizational development at the Institute of Agriculture and Natural Resources, University of Nebraska, Lincoln. Previously he was a faculty career consultant at Nebraska's Teaching and Learning Center. Wheeler received his B.A. degree (1962) from Antioch College in biology, his M.S. degree (1964) from Cornell University in conservation and science education, and his Ph.D. degree (1971) from the State of University of New York, Buffalo, in foundations of education and curriculum development.

At Nebraska, Wheeler has been involved as director or associate director of several major faculty development efforts, including NUPROF, A Faculty Renewal and Redirection Program; NUPAGE, New Partnerships in Agriculture and Education in the College of Agriculture; and a national study, which will soon be published as *The Academic Chairperson's Handbook.*

Wheeler previously served in program and administrative roles with the Omaha Teacher Corps Project at the University of Nebraska, Omaha, and was the developer and coordinator of the Fredonia-Hamburg Teacher Education Center in Hamburg, New York. He has also taught elementary and high school science.

Wheeler has been involved in the Professional and Organizational Development Network since its inception. He is currently a member of the Core Committee and the Executive Committee. He has been a consultant to various higher educational institutions, particularly on career development and the role of the chairperson in facilitating faculty growth and development.

Robert G. Baldwin is assistant professor of higher education at the College of William and Mary. His principal research interests are faculty career development and the academic work environment. Baldwin received his B.A. degree (1969) from Hiram College in psychology, his M.A. degree (1973) from Cornell University in counseling and student personnel administration, and his Ph.D. degree (1979) from the University of Michigan in higher education.

Carole J. Bland is associate professor in the Department of Family Practice and Community Health at the University of Minnesota Medical School. Selected as an American Council on Education Fellow, she is serving in the offices of the president and the provost of the University of Minnesota for 1989-90. Bland received her B.A. degree (1968) from Augustana College in psychology, her M.A. degree (1970) from Drake University in experimental psychology with a specialist's degree in behavior modification, and her Ph.D. degree (1974) from the University of Minnesota in educational psychology. Her main research activities have been in faculty development and have resulted in articles and books, including *Faculty Development Through Workshops* (1980) and *The Successful Academician: The Essential Skills and How to Acquire Them* (1988, with others).

Jay L. Chronister is professor of higher education and, until recently, was associate dean for administration in the Curry School of Education at the University of Virginia. His research activities and publications in recent years have centered on faculty personnel policies in higher education. He received his B.S. degree (1956) from West Chester State College in education, his M.Ed. degree (1961) from the Pennsylvania State University in counselor education, and his Ed.D. degree (1967) from the University of Pittsburgh in higher education.

Ted E. Hartung is associate vice-chancellor of the Institute of Agriculture and Natural Resources and former dean of the College of Agriculture at the University of Nebraska, Lincoln, where he is also professor of food science and technology. He received both his B.S. degree (1951) and his M.S. degree (1953) from Colorado State University in poultry husbandry and poultry nutrition, respectively, and his Ph.D. degree (1962) from Purdue University in food technology.

Barbara H. Hill has worked for the Loyola University of Chicago Career Development Program since its inception in 1978, as assistant to the director (1978-83), as director (1983-87), and now as consultant and workshop leader. She is president of Career Resources, Inc., a career consulting firm in Northbrook, Illinois, since 1983, serving higher education, business, and individuals. She received her B.A. degree (1959) from DePauw University in psychology and education and her M.A. degree (1980) from Northeastern

Illinois University in guidance and counseling. She coauthored
*Backyard Vacation* (1980, with C. Haas and A. Cole) and has written
extensively for her own programs. Along with E. Wells, she is currently revising the workbook *Integrating Professional and Personal
Growth* for publication in 1990.

Elizabeth P. Hosokawa is director of the Employee Assistance Program at the University of Missouri, Columbia, and also
assistant director of the University Counseling Services. She received her B.S. degree (1961) from the University of Illinois in occupational therapy, her M.A. degree (1975) from Southern
Methodist University in social psychology, and her Ph.D. degree
(1986) from the University of Missouri, Columbia, in counseling
psychology. She has written on various aspects of employee assistance programming and coedited *Employee Assistance Programs in
Higher Education: Alcohol, Mental Health and Professional Development Programming for Faculty and Staff* (1984, with R.
Thoreson).

William K. Jackson is associate director of the Office of Instructional Development at the University of Georgia. He received
his B.S. (1967) and M.S. (1968) degrees from the University of South
Carolina in physics and his Ed.D. degree (1981) from the same institution. Before coming to the University of Georgia in 1983, he
served for fourteen years on the faculty and administrative staff of
Presbyterian College.

Ann F. Lucas is chair of the Department of Managment and
Marketing at Fairleigh Dickinson University, where she is also the
founder and former director of the Office of Professional and Or-
ganizational Development, a member of the Core Committee of the
Professional and Organizational Development Network in Higher
Education, and department chair consultant for the American
Council on Education's Center for Leadership Development in
Higher Education. A licensed psychologist and diplomate in the
American Board of Professional Psychology, Lucas is a consultant
for both higher education and industrial organizations. She received

her B.S. degree from Seton Hall University in psychology and her M.A. and Ph.D. degrees from Fordham University in psychology.

Joyce Povlacs Lunde is an educational development specialist and associate professor of agricultural education at the University of Nebraska, Lincoln. She is currently co-director of New Partnerships in Agriculture and Education (NUPAGE), a curriculum project funded by the W. K. Kellogg Foundation. From 1978–1989 she was an instructional consultant with the university's Teaching and Learning Center. She is associate editor of *Face to Face: A Sourcebook of Individual Consultation Techniques for Faculty/Instructional Developers* (1988). She received her B.A. degree (1959) from Kent State University in English and her M.A. (1960) and Ph.D. (1970) degrees from the University of Minnesota, also in English.

John W. Munson is an associate dean in the College of Professional Studies and head of the School of Health, Physical Education, Recreation and Athletics at the University of Wisconsin, Stevens Point. He is the chief architect of the university's well-known professional preparation program in health promotion/wellness. Munson currently serves as vice-president of the Association for Fitness in Business, Region IV, and is highly active in developing life-styles, health behavior change strategies, and programs. He received his B.S. degree (1967) from the Ohio State University in physical education and health, his M.S. and C.A.G.S. degrees (both in 1970) from Springfield College, Massachusetts, in physical education and athletic administration, and a Ph.D. degree (1979) from the Ohio State University in physical education and education administration.

Joan DeGuire North is dean of the College of Professional Studies at the University of Wisconsin, Stevens Point. She previously held administrative positions at the University of Alabama, several private colleges, and a Washington, D.C., consortium. An early leader in the faculty development movement, she was founding director of the Professional and Organizational Development Network in Higher Education. Her current research interests are in stress management, group decision making, and faculty-staff wellness programs. She received her B.S. degree (1964) from Spring Hill College in English, her M.A. degree (1967) from the University of Alabama, also in English, and her Ph.D. degree (1974) from the University of Alabama in educational administration.

Constance C. Schmitz is an evaluation specialist in the Office of Research and Evaluation in the General College at the University of Minnesota. A doctoral candidate there in educational psychology, she received her B.A. degree (1972) from Bennington College in visual arts and literature and her M.A. degree (1984) from the University of Minnesota in curriculum and instructional systems. From 1984 to 1987 she was project manager for a national study in family medicine faculty development. She is the author of *The Successful Academician: The Essential Skills and How to Acquire Them* (1988, with others).

Ronald D. Simpson is professor of science education and higher education and director of the Office of Instructional Development at the University of Georgia. He received his B.S. (1960) and M.S. (1964) degrees from the University of Tennessee in biological science and his doctorate (1970) from the University of Georgia in science education. Before assuming his current position, he was head of the Department of Mathematics and Science Education at North Carolina State University.

Neil R. Wylie, until recently vice-president of the Great Lakes Colleges Association, is executive officer for the Council of Presidents, New England Land-Grant Universities. He previously served as an American Council on Education Governmental Fellow and as a tenured faculty member in psychology, department chair, and assistant academic dean at Cornell College. He received his B.A. degree (1962) from the University of Minnesota in psychology and zoology and his M.A. (1963) and Ph.D. (1969) degrees from Temple University in psychology.

# Enhancing
# Faculty Careers

 *PART ONE*

# Faculty Careers
# in a Time
# of Transition

Part One establishes a context—both historical and conceptual—within which to view the need for enhanced faculty development programs.

In Chapter One, Jack Schuster describes the contemporary faculty condition and argues for new approaches to renewal. With an aging faculty at one end of the demographic "pipeline" and a projected burgeoning cohort of new faculty at the other, faculty development programs must now utilize strategies to address their contrasting needs. The chapter argues that considerable know-how is available to those who seek it but is unknown or neglected on campus after campus. It concludes with a challenge: Do sufficient will and commitment exist to develop comprehensive developmental programs?

Chapter Two sets the stage for grasping the essential link between faculty careers and faculty members' continuous evolution as adults. Roger Baldwin makes the case that the adult development literature, particularly that which is grounded in stage development, provides a basic conceptual framework and useful "handle" for understanding faculty needs and issues. Each of the stages he describes—career entry, early career, midcareer, and late career—presents its distinctive challenges. The author points out that faculty interests often change; at midcareer, in particular, faculty circumstances may cry out for creative interventions. An overall concern is expressed that higher education institutions "fail to acknowledge the developmental nature of careers" and tend indiscriminately to establish the same expectations and policies for virtually all faculty members.

Chapter Three provides a comprehensive survey of the faculty development literature over the past two decades. Carole Bland and Constance Schmitz divide faculty development activities into three segments: institutional aspects, the department/college setting, and individual faculty members or administrators. The authors note a trend moving from an emphasis on *individual* faculty vitality toward "faculty and institutional vitality," in which the individual is seldom "considered independently of the institutional context."

1

# The Need for Fresh Approaches to Faculty Renewal

*Jack H. Schuster*

The quality of higher education and the ability of colleges and universities, of whatever kind, to perform their respective missions is inextricably linked to the quality and commitment of the faculty. That assertion is perhaps a truism, but as institutions of higher education continue to struggle with a challenging environment and an uncertain future, it is important to recognize the implications of that central proposition. The faculty comprise the core of the institution. To be sure, faculty members cannot begin to perform their tasks without adequate support from innumerable others. And the teaching faculty cannot accomplish much of what their jobs require unless there are also students who possess at least a threshold aptitude for, and interest in, learning. Nonetheless, successful teaching and learning cannot be achieved in the absence of a faculty that is caring, competent, committed. That proposition is the ideological point of departure of this volume.

A second basic proposition advanced in these pages contends that colleges and universities, for whatever reasons, have been neither sufficiently alert to the ever-changing circumstances of their instructional staffs nor adequately resourceful about meeting their changing needs for professional development. It is indeed striking how much has been written about faculty growth and renewal (see, for instance, the overview of research in Chapter Three) and how few campuses have seen fit to develop comprehensive, systematic programs. As suggested below, splendid conceptual models are available; adequate *programs* have not taken seed.

A final proposition—the one around which this book is organized—holds that campuses can accomplish much to enhance faculty careers (and thereby enable colleges and universities to more effectively carry out their missions) without Herculean efforts and enormous expenditures. Effective strategies to promote faculty renewal are neither as elusive nor as costly as some may imagine. Effective campuswide approaches can be fashioned at reasonable costs, so long as campus leadership is prepared to make a serious commitment.

This book is designed to show how the issues that impinge on a vital faculty can be better conceptualized, and how particular programs have been and can be organized to respond creatively and constructively to faculty needs for interlinked professional and personal growth. Its scope encompasses the entire span of an academic career, from preparing for the profession (see especially Chapter Four) to disengaging from it (see especially Chapters Five and Eight).

Toward that end, the present chapter is intended to establish a framework within which the ensuing chapters can be viewed. Its tasks are fourfold: (1) historical, to provide a capsulized account of how faculty development programs have evolved over the past quarter-century; (2) descriptive, to depict succinctly the changing conditions of the American faculty and to suggest implications for future professional development; (3) evaluative, to argue that colleges and universities have been remiss in not thinking more resourcefully about professional development needs and opportunities; and (4) advocative, to outline in preliminary fashion the kind of institutional mindset necessary to preserve and enhance the faculty resource over the years ahead.

## The Evolution of Faculty Development

Faculty competence and vitality surely have been a concern of institutions of higher learning for about as long as universities have existed. In the United States, for instance, sabbatical leaves of absence—said to be the oldest form of organized faculty support—

can be traced to Harvard in 1810 (Eble and McKeachie, 1985, p. 5). Only in the last quarter-century, however, has faculty development emerged as a systematic campus priority, giving rise in many settings to a campuswide strategy for promoting faculty competencies (Blackburn, Pellino, Boberg, and O'Connell, 1980, p. 32). During that time the faculty development "movement" emerged and crystallized, gaining momentum from the late 1960s to the mid 1970s, while spawning a literature throughout the 1970s rich in diagnoses and prescriptions.

Before the 1960s, faculty development "programs" were a rarity (Centra, 1976, cited in Blackburn, Pellino, Boberg, and O'Connell, 1980, p. 32), and the pertinent literature was decidedly sparse. Bergquist and Phillips described the limited agenda of faculty development efforts prior to the mid 1960s as consisting of "additional research possibilities, reduced teaching loads, lower student faculty ratios, sabbaticals and leaves of absence" (1977, p. 4). Institutional commitments to facilitate professional development began to accelerate in the mid 1960s. Even so, as noted by Stordahl, "prior to 1970 faculty development was of little concern to either college and university faculties or to their administrations. On most campuses development was limited to such things as orientation of new faculty, sabbatical leaves, visiting professorships, and, perhaps, reductions of class loads. A survey of literature in that period would have turned up a limited number of articles on the topic" (1981, p. 1). This is not to suggest that institutions ignored the need to stimulate research and scholarship. Within that corridor of context specialization, many institutions had long been active. As Lindquist has pointed out, faculty development's overriding concern had been the promotion of "new contributions to knowledge"; this, he emphasized, was "the traditional meaning of professional development prior to 1960" (1981, p. 734).

The 1970s saw significant changes in faculty development programs. Momentum continued to build rapidly. Eble and McKeachie set the stage: "Faced with declining and changing enrollment patterns, increased requirements for accountability, declining financial resources, and a faculty adversely affected by these and other conditions, many colleges and universities in the 1970s turned to faculty development as a major responsibility" (1985, p. 3). A great deal of attention was lavished on the improvement of teaching—a laudable objective—and campus centers designed to facilitate more effective teaching sprang up by the score, if not the hundreds, across the higher education landscape. This gentle revolution was spurred on by the generous support of major foundations—perhaps most notably Lilly, Kellogg, and Danforth—and by the catalytic activities of many of the higher education associations, including the discipline-based associations.

Indeed, so much progress had occurred in so short a time that Bergquist and Phillips, in the third volume of their remarkable series of handbooks on faculty development, were moved to declare that "the field of faculty development reached maturity in the late 1970s" (1981, p. 3). They cited evidence to support their claim: "Colleges and universities now teach courses about and conduct research on faculty development activities—a sign of respectability, even of middle age. There is a national association, the Professional and Organizational Development Network in Higher Education, which devotes much of its collective attention to faculty development matters. This organization publishes a quarterly journal [now an annual book of readings] and holds well-attended national conventions. Specific schools of thought and even statements of dogma now are found on the field, giving it the appearance of stability and discipline" (p. 3). The discussion by Bland and Schmitz in Chapter Three attests to the explosion of attention paid to faculty development since 1970.

Faculty development had indeed progressed markedly in the span of little more than a decade. And few scholars or practitioners have contributed as handsomely to the development of this field as have Bergquist and Phillips. However, the present volume is predicated on a quite different perspective on the status of faculty development programs. Yes, faculty development may have "matured" in some respects as a field, but on the whole, campus programs designed to assist faculty are almost always too narrowly conceived and even more narrowly implemented. A "mature" program to enhance professional and personal development must exist above all as an integrated, systematic program. In that respect, faculty development must take more fully into account the changes visited upon the instructional staff in recent years.

## The Changing Faculty Condition

Many developments over the past two decades have combined to alter the faculty's condition and thereby their needs. This, in turn, has created a new set of challenges for those members of the academic community committed to enhancing and revitalizing faculty members' careers. The litany of changes in the academic environment is familiar and need not be recited in detail in these pages. We are not contending that faculty have been engulfed in crisis or that American higher education is coming undone. There is considerable evidence to the contrary. Indeed, it is no exaggeration to suggest that American higher education, entering upon the 1990s, remains the envy of much of the world. On the whole, the record shows that the faculty itself has persevered and has remained committed to its tasks. In fact, the current faculty is almost surely the best qualified in American history (Bowen and Schuster, 1986).

Even so, the point to emphasize here is that developments in recent years have harmed rather than helped the faculty, have made their jobs more difficult. These developments need to be acknowledged before appropriate countervailing measures can be mounted. Accordingly, some understanding of eight "megatrends" is important for understanding the context within which programs designed to enhance faculty careers must now operate. Moreover, we submit that campuses can influence, to a greater or lesser degree, how each of these developments (except the national academic labor market) will affect local faculty conditions. Synopses of these eight developments follow.

- *Working conditions* for faculty members have deteriorated. Although that deterioration is not easy to measure, evidence abounds that the quality of the academic workplace has suffered (Austin and Gamson, 1985). The indicators are numerous, ranging from reduced secretarial and clerical support to cramped office space, from diminished (sometimes negligible) travel funds to badly outmoded research instrumentation, from billions of dollars of accumulated deferred maintenance to increasing proportions of ill-prepared students with whom faculty members must contend.

- *Compensation* for faculty has faded badly since its peak year, 1972–73. True, losses in the faculty's real earnings have abated over the past several years and, indeed, modest gains vis-à-vis standard measures of inflation have been realized each year since 1982–83 (Kasper, 1989). Nonetheless, since 1970 the faculty has lost about 10 percent of its earning power, turning the faculty into the biggest losers among all major occupational groups in the nonagricultural sector. The faculty, in fact, have absorbed losses in real income on a considerably bigger scale than, for example, government employees, blue-collar workers, and even elementary and secondary school teachers, who are often perceived to have fared so poorly in recent years.
- The academic *labor market* has been inhospitable to most faculty members. Of course, the market in the aggregate is made up of numerous submarkets. In a few fields, blessed by growth, faculty members find themselves in demand, and the marketplace for them is fluid, sometimes even flourishing. Computer science, electrical engineering, and marketing come most readily to mind. They are the exceptions, however, for the academic labor market in most disciplines has been weak, bordering on inert in some of the humanities. While harbingers of an eagerly awaited thaw in marketplace conditions are now evident (Bowen and Sosa, 1989), there remains, at least until the mid 1990s, little faculty mobility among campuses, compared to the strong seller's market that prevailed from the mid 1950s into the early 1970s. That earlier condition—in which the demand for faculty exceeded supply—fostered considerable movement among campuses and, consequently, upward mobility. As demand for the faculty's talents tapered, many faculty members in recent years have reported feeling "stuck," dead-ended in professional cul-de-sacs.
- More perplexing, the faculty often find themselves caught in a crossfire of *conflicting expectations*. Tight budgets, the demands for efficiency and accountability, and shifting campus values result in faculty members sometimes being asked to juggle a bewildering variety of roles: to deepen their own research and scholarship, to enliven their teaching, to restore cohesion and integrity to a curriculum pulled asunder by the twin forces

of rampant specialization and student fixation on careerism, to link instruction more closely to industry's needs for a trained workforce, to expand access and fashion curricular remediation for marginally prepared students while at the very same time imposing more rigorous academic standards (Schuster, 1986). It is little wonder that faculty members are sometimes confused and discouraged by these crosscutting pressures.

- The faculty is also "congealing," which is to say growing *older* and increasingly more *tenured in*—at a rate of 66 percent in 1985 (U.S. Department of Education, 1987b)—and is bunching up in the senior ranks. Among the tenure-track ranks of professor, associate professor, and assistant professor, the proportion of assistant professors has been steadily diminishing while, correspondingly, the proportion of full professors has been climbing, now accounting for about 38 percent. In the mid 1970s, assistant professors were the modal rank; by the mid 1980s, a flip-flop had occurred, and professors are now the most numerous (based on HEGIS survey respondents, U.S. Department of Education, 1987a, p. 11):

|  | *1976–77* | *1985–86* |
|---|---|---|
| A.  Professors | 30.5% | 37.9% |
| B.  Assistant professors | 37.2% | 29.8% |
| Ratio of B to A | 1.22:1 | 0.79:1 |

With relatively little hiring in well over a decade and with mandatory retirement ceilings now lifting, faculty members are far more likely to find themselves embedded in a single institution for years longer than their predecessors, as noted above. This development is examined in greater detail below.

- *Shifting values* on campuses leave considerable numbers of faculty members feeling frustrated and undervalued. Given the tight academic labor market, campuses of all kinds have been able to hire well-trained faculty members. Many of them—having obtained their degrees from universities with very pronounced research orientations, but unable to find jobs at similar campuses—"filtered down" to institutions that had traditionally prized good teaching far more than original research. As a response to these developments, many of those campuses have resorted to raising expectations of their faculty by elevating the importance of research and scholarship to new heights. The faculty reward structure, accordingly, has been altered, and many midlevel and senior faculty members, having been hired in a previous era of teaching-focused expectations, perceive themselves as caught in the lurch—unappreciated and penalized in the keen competition for promotion and merit pay (Schuster and Bowen, 1985). One indicator of this and related phenomena is that nearly seven of ten faculty members at four-year institutions report, "In my department it is very difficult to achieve tenure without publishing": 69 percent said so in 1984, up sharply from 54 percent in 1976 (Boyer, 1987, p. 130).

- Compressed *career ladders* in academe have often been criticized as inhibitors to motivation. As noted, many faculty—currently the highest proportion ever—find themselves at the top rank with no formal rung in the career ladder remaining to scale. Many others perceive themselves as stuck on the associate professor rung with little prospect for promotion unless they find the wherewithal to adapt to shifting, research-oriented campus values. Those who progressed rapidly to the top rung encounter a different kind of psychological challenge: they typically find themselves facing decades in which in some basic sense there is little or no room for upward movement. Consider also in this regard that perhaps 13 to 14 percent of all full-time faculty members hold no differentiated academic rank (mostly in two-year colleges); in such instances, salary increases are often a function solely of seniority. For them the absence of any normal career ladder can have a dampening impact on motivation.

- As a function of these changing conditions, *faculty morale* generally has not been good; many faculty members are said to be dispirited. Ennui and disengagement are by most accounts far from uncommon. According to the 1984 national survey conducted by the Carnegie Foundation for the Advancement of Teaching (1985), 38 percent of faculty members asserted that they may leave academe within the next five years (pp. 32–33). To be sure, an exodus on such a large scale has never before materialized (and will not now); whatever their grievances, faculty members have consistently opted to remain on their campuses. Nevertheless, the fact that almost two of every five faculty members chose to send such a message is a signal of shaky morale. Moreover, significant numbers—about 40 percent of the 5,000 faculty members who were surveyed—reported that they were "less enthusiastic about their work now than when they began their academic careers" and that morale in their department "is worse today than five years ago" (p. 32). Contributing further to faculty malaise is the perception by many faculty members that they are unable to participate effectively in the governance process; they often report feeling thwarted in efforts to exercise a reasonable degree of control over their professional destinies (Schuster and Bowen, 1985; Boyer, 1987).

Two aspects of the changing faculty condition require further comment: the faculty's heterogeneity and the emerging age-related phenomenon of a "bipolar" faculty.

*Varieties of Academic Life.* Heterogeneity is increasingly the hallmark of the faculty. Consider: the number of campuses continues to grow (to nearly 3,400), and the total number of faculty has reached about 710,000. Women now comprise close to 30 percent of the faculty, and racial minorities comprise about 10 percent. The proportion of part-timers continues to rise: 35.8 percent in 1985, compared to 21.9 percent in 1970. And the proportion of faculty employed in four-year colleges and universities continues to dwindle: 70.4 percent in 1985, compared to 80.6 percent in 1970 (U.S. Department of Education, 1987b, pp. 158–159).

In a great many respects, faculty are faculty; they tend to share many basic values (Bowen and Schuster, 1986). But subtle differences abound, for innumerable faculty subcultures are arrayed across different types of institutions and academic pursuits. The details need not be spelled out here; an overview must suffice. Perhaps no one has portrayed this diversity of faculty as vividly as Burton Clark, when he muses, "Who can fathom an econometrician when he or she is in full stride, let alone a high energy physicist, a molecular biologist, an ethnomethodologist newly tutored in semiotics, or an English professor determined to deconstruct literary texts" (1987, p. *xxi*). More prosaically, he cautions us that "grasping the sheer magnitude of the differentiation and the tangledness of the academic domain is a necessary step in the triumph of realism over romanticism in understanding American academic life" (p. *xxix*). This, by way of caveat, is to posit that institutional responses to the needs of faculty members cannot be forged without taking fully into account the powerful reality of faculty diversity.

*The Bipolar Faculty.* A second condition bears particular scrutiny—namely, the changing demographics of the instructional staff, which will result in an age-polarized—or "bipolar"—faculty. The new conditions? A faculty characterized simultaneously by relatively young *and* relatively old cohorts appears to be emerging, almost surely to an unprecedented extent. This development, although transitory, will pose extraordinary challenges to college and university policy makers for a number of years. Consider first the older, then the younger faculty.

At one end of the age continuum, faculty are growing not just older but old. The implications of a "graying professoriate" have been debated vigorously in recent years. The current distribution of faculty by age, combined with the limited opportunity for new hires in the proximate future, ensures that the faculty as a whole will be growing older well into the 1990s. The faculty's average age has already shot up over the past decade, and while projections vary, the modal age range of tenured faculty, by at least one estimate, will soar to between fifty-six and sixty-five by the turn of the century (Eble and McKeachie, 1985, p. 3).

The consequences of landmark federal legislation, enacted in 1986, that will soon lift the cap off mandatory retirement ages—it will take effect for faculty members in January 1994—are not now known. Important recent research suggests that retirement patterns may not depart significantly from currently prevailing practices, despite the faculty's legal entitlement to continue teaching beyond the traditional time for retirement (Petrovich, 1985; Lozier and Dooris, 1987; Kellams and Chronister, 1987). What in fact will be the response of faculty, in 1994 and beyond, to their legal right to continue in their jobs, depends on many factors. Perhaps primary among them will be the faculty members' estimates of their postretirement standard of living, which in turn will be linked to such highly unpredictable factors as inflation rates and income generated by faculty pension plans. Meanwhile, the National Research Council, at the behest of Congress, is examining the implications of eliminating age-based retirement rules for faculty.

Even assuming that future retirement patterns will be similar to current practices, any number of situations will inevitably arise in which faculty members, some of them well past their prime, choose to remain in their jobs. McKeachie (1983) and others have demonstrated that older faculty members are not necessarily less productive. At the same time, colleges and universities have not yet found themselves in a situation in which a not-negligible proportion of the faculty—perhaps 2 or 3 percent—*may* opt to continue beyond age seventy or seventy-five. Such developments are destined to trigger some very awkward, sometimes bitter, confrontations as administrators, and perhaps faculty colleagues, seek to make room for new hires.

The other cohort that helps to create a "new ballgame" is the anticipated influx of large numbers of young faculty members. This is new in the sense that colleges and universities have not had the problem/luxury of absorbing large numbers of new faculty members for two decades. Is it consistent to express concern simultaneously about *both* an aging faculty that may be inclined to overstay its welcome (thus limiting the number of new appointments) *and* a burgeoning cohort of youthful appointees? Yes, it is, for both phenomena can and *will* occur in consequential proportions by the mid 1990s. (The challenges of acquainting new faculty members with the norms of the academic profession are explored in Chapter Four.)

The proximate future is likely to bring more of the same kinds of pressures. Although the academic labor market will loosen and compensation may continue its recovery, overall there is no indication that resources for colleges and universities (or the faculty's share of them) are likely to improve significantly in an era of budgetary constraints. Demands upon the faculty surely will continue to be acute and multiple. And external pressures on campuses almost surely will continue to mount, affording even less buffering from accountability-oriented policy makers. In sum, the careers of faculty members today are evolving in circumstances that cry out for more effective ways to facilitate faculty commitment and reinvigoration.

## Paradox of the Academic Profession

A curious paradox confronts the observer of college and university efforts in the realm of professional development. On the one hand, colleges and universities—perhaps especially the research universities—are unparalleled repositories of knowledge about the management and development of human resources. Research and teaching in behavioral, social, and organizational studies commonly explore issues germane to the development of human potential, both in people's capacities as employees and in the more personal aspects of human endeavor.

Yet few would argue that institutions of higher education do an admirable—or even an adequate—job of supporting their professional (and nonprofessional) staff except in the limited (although essential) area of research and scholarship. In that area, faculty members at many campuses routinely attend and present at professional, discipline-based meetings; take advantage, on occasion, of sabbatical leave programs; receive stipends—often very modest—to support research; and so forth. But these concerns about research and scholarship have traditionally been addressed outside the scope of systematic, campuswide "faculty development" programs.

With so differentiated an array of colleges and universities, as one would expect there are many variations in institutional commitment to the support and revitalization of faculty. Some institutions have made substantial commitments, and considerable progress undoubtedly has been made in recent years as these campuses' collective consciousnesses have been raised about the decline in the quality of academic life and as academic personnel standards and procedures have been clarified.

However, as is far more commonly the case, other campuses appear to have accorded faculty development a barely visible priority. Some critics suggest that campus accomplishments in enhancing professional development, beyond the traditional concentration on research and scholarship, on the whole tend to be very poor indeed. Critics maintain that the professional development agenda at most campuses neglects to view faculty members in more comprehensive terms. That is to say, most campuses do little if anything to help faculty members (or nonacademic staff) move toward self-actualization except in the most narrow professional sense. They routinely fail to conceive of, and respond to, faculty members as human beings whose needs and abilities are relevant to the workplace but extend beyond the honing of such task-related competencies as writing grants, using computers, and leading classroom discussion. Moreover, campuses in general appear to have failed to take into adequate account the changing demographic and environmental factors that shape faculty careers.

These contentions will take on more meaning as successful "enlightened" programs are described in subsequent chapters. The point here is that a confluence of forces now sets the stage for a fresh look at campus approaches designed to assist faculty members in their professional and personal development.

### Enhanced Faculty Development

As I suggested above, change has been the hallmark of the faculty development movement for the past two decades. While some might argue that the movement has stagnated in recent years—or at least has not advanced to a more prominent, widely accepted role on campuses—the fact is that a "movement" did emerge in the mid to late 1960s where none had existed much before.

*A Delineation of Objectives.* More than that, the chroniclers and advocates of the movement, as it evolved, identified three more-or-less-distinctive areas or targets for improvement. By the mid 1970s, Gaff had categorized these facets of development as professional and personal development, the improvement of instruction, and organizational development (1976). At about the same time, Bergquist and Phillips had distinguished among the "personal," "instructional," and "organizational" dimensions (1975). (Bergquist and Phillips have provided a useful discussion of models for faculty development in the second volume of their handbook, 1977, pages 3–12.) Accordingly, the three major components of a comprehensive approach to faculty revitalization have been articulated and espoused for some time. But what does it take to put such a program in place and to make it work?

*Known Techniques.* In some important respects, the *how* to enhance faculty careers is reasonably well known. This is not to suggest that all the answers are in place. But a great deal, in fact, *is* known, if not perfectly at least sufficiently to suggest that successful models exist for the various elements of a comprehensive campus approach to maintaining a vital faculty—including ventures into such relatively new realms (for campuses) as wellness, employee assistance, and faculty career consulting programs. Much of what has been garnered from experience, yielded by considerable trial and error, simply was not well understood when the faculty development movement was emerging in the mid 1960s and 1970s. The ensuing chapters will, we think, underscore the point that much is now known about what works, and toward that end various programs and strategies are described.

This is not to suggest that every idea proffered in the following pages is wonderful, or that, given the idiosyncratic characteristics of each campus, an approach that works well in one setting will work equally well in another. Nor do we contend that enlightened approaches to faculty development can by themselves offset basic structural problems where they exist. The point is simply this: the obstacles to a successful, integrated program lie *not* in the technology of how to make a program work reasonably well but rather in marshaling the requisite organizational will, or commitment, to make faculty renewal a priority. As is illustrated in the following pages (especially in Part Three) and summarized in the final chapter, with genuine campus commitment much can be accomplished to enhance faculty careers and to promote faculty vitality. Without such a commitment the prospects for faculty renewal are illusory.

*Organizational Culture.* At base, it is the organizational culture that is salient, for that will determine whether an adequate faculty development program can take root and even flourish over time. As the following chapters will demonstrate, the campus culture must feature a shared commitment on the part of administrative and faculty leadership to provide conditions conducive to faculty growth and renewal. Doing more of the same likely will not accomplish much (for there are few comprehensive programs in place); instead, campus efforts must be systematic and continually evolving in order to adapt to evolving conditions. Academic careers must be viewed differently, in the light of changing career realities. Concurrently, there must be a more realistic conceptualization of longstanding career features. Thus new notions of career models are essential—models that encourage different kinds of pathways within and outside the institution.

Enhanced faculty development encompasses many things. As is spelled out in Chapter Fourteen, the concept entails career reconceptualization, career facilitation, and a basic commitment to link professional and personal development. But most crucially, an enhanced approach to faculty development involves a willingness to look afresh at academic careers and to mount the serious organizational commitment to enhance those careers. This new commitment, this new mindset, is a prerequisite for infusing academic careers with a new vitality.

## References

Austin, A. E., and Gamson, Z. F. *Academic Workplace: New Demands, Heightened Tensions.* ASHE-ERIC Higher Education Report, no. 10. Washington, D.C.: Association for the Study of Higher Education, 1985.

Bergquist, W. H., and Phillips, S. R. "Components of an Effective Faculty Development Program." *Journal of Higher Education,* 1975, *46*, 177–209.

Bergquist, W. H., and Phillips, S. R. *A Handbook for Faculty Development.* Vol. 2. Washington, D.C.: Council for the Advancement of Small Colleges, 1977.

Bergquist, W. H., and Phillips, S. R. *A Handbook for Faculty Development.* Vol. 3. Washington, D.C.: Council for the Advancement of Small Colleges, 1981.

Blackburn, R. T., Pellino, G., Boberg, A., and O'Connell, C. "Are Instructional Improvement Programs Off-Target?" In *Current*

*Issues in Higher Education.* Washington, D.C.: American Association for Higher Education, 1980.

Bowen, H. R., and Schuster, J. H. *American Professors: A National Resource Imperiled.* New York: Oxford University Press, 1986.

Bowen, W. G., and Sosa, J. A. *Prospects for Faculty in the Arts and Sciences: A Study of Factors Affecting Demand and Supply, 1987 to 2012.* Princeton, N.J.: Princeton University Press, 1989.

Boyer, E. L. *College: The Undergraduate Experience in America.* New York: Harper & Row, 1987.

Carnegie Foundation for the Advancement of Teaching. "The Faculty: Deeply Troubled." *Change,* 1985, *17* (5), 31-34.

Centra, J. A. *Faculty Development Practices in the United States and Canada.* Princeton, N.J.: Educational Testing Service, 1976. (Cited in Blackburn, Pellino, Boberg, and O'Connell, 1980.)

Clark, B. R. *The Academic Life: Small Worlds, Different Worlds.* Princeton, N.J.: Carnegie Foundation for the Advancement of Teaching, 1987.

Eble, K. E., and McKeachie, W. J. *Improving Undergraduate Education Through Faculty Development: An Analysis of Effective Programs and Practices.* San Francisco: Jossey-Bass, 1985.

Gaff, J. G. *Toward Faculty Renewal: Advances in Faculty, Instructional, and Organizational Development.* San Francisco: Jossey-Bass, 1976.

Kasper, H. "High Education Goals: Low Salary Increases. The Annual Report on the Economic Status of the Profession, 1988-89." *Academe,* 1989, *75* (2), 3-21.

Kellams, S. E., and Chronister, J. L. "Life After Early Retirement: Faculty Activities and Perceptions." Paper presented at annual meeting of Association for the Study of Higher Education, Baltimore, Md., Nov. 1987.

Lindquist, J. "Professional Development." In A. W. Chickering and Associates, *The Modern American College: Responding to the New Realities of Diverse Students and a Changing Society.* San Francisco: Jossey-Bass, 1981.

Lozier, G. G., and Dooris, M. J. "Is Higher Education Preparing for Faculty Shortages?" Paper presented at annual meeting of Association for the Study of Higher Education, Baltimore, Md., Nov. 1987.

McKeachie, W. J. "Older Faculty Members: Facts and Prescriptions." *AAHE Bulletin,* 1983, *36* (3), 8–10.

Melendez, W. A., and deGuzman, R. M. *Burnout: The New Academic Disease.* ASHE-ERIC Higher Education Research Report, no. 9. Washington, D.C.: Association for the Study of Higher Education, 1983.

Petrovich, J. "Focus on Faculty: Campuses Respond to Uncapping of Retirement Age." *Higher Education and National Affairs* (American Council on Education), Sept. 16, 1985, pp. 5, 7.

Schuster, J. H. "Faculty Vitality: Observations from the Field." In R. G. Baldwin (ed.), *Incentives for Faculty Vitality.* New Directions for Higher Education, no. 51. San Francisco: Jossey-Bass, 1985.

Schuster, J. H. "The Faculty Dilemma: A Short Course." *Phi Delta Kappan,* 1986, *68* (4), 275–282.

Schuster, J. H., and Bowen, H. R. "The Faculty at Risk." *Change,* 1985, *17* (5), 13–21.

Stordahl, B. "Faculty Development: A Survey of Literature of the '70s." *Research Currents,* Mar. 1981 (entire issue).

U.S. Department of Education. "College Faculty Salaries, 1976–1986." *Bulletin OERI.* Washington, D.C.: Center for Education Statistics, U.S. Department of Education, 1987a.

U.S. Department of Education. *Digest of Education Statistics, 1987.* Washington, D.C.: U.S. Government Printing Office, 1987b.

2

# Faculty Career Stages and Implications for Professional Development

*Roger G. Baldwin*

A brief stroll down a corridor of "Old Main" reveals the seasons of academic life. In one office sits a new professor frantically preparing notes for her afternoon lecture. The chair of the faculty senate hurries from the next office as he races to catch a plane. Tomorrow morning he will deliver a paper on an exciting new research project. The door to the third office is closed for the day. By 2:00 P.M. its occupant, a midcareer professor, is up to the eighth green of the local golf course. The last office before the elevator belongs to one of the university's senior professors. He is having coffee with a younger colleague while helping him with a complex statistical procedure.

A casual observer of faculty lounges or committee meetings can divide the academic career into a series of loosely ordered stages. Research design specialists might take issue with this "soft" methodology, yet most academics would agree that—while exceptions abound—professors change as they progress through the faculty ranks and as their careers gradually place different demands on them. Typically, however, colleges and universities fail to acknowledge the developmental nature of faculty careers. They maintain basically the same expectations and apply the same policies to all professors, regardless of their age or career stage. By viewing all faculty members synonymously, higher education institutions overlook some basic facts of academic life, and in so doing they forgo important opportunities to fashion policies that could benefit faculty members and their institutions.

Colleges and universities that wish to maintain a vital professional workforce must be cognizant of the powerful developmental forces that influence faculty members. Faculty development policies and practices, such as those described in this book, should accommodate the varying needs of professors at successive points in the academic career. Effective strategies to renew faculty and enhance their performance must take into account the special character of each phase of the academic life cycle.

### Growth and Change During Adulthood

People change through the course of their lives and careers in fairly predictable ways. The adult years may be viewed as a series of stages characterized by changing developmental tasks, concerns, activities, values, and needs (Hall, 1976). Focusing on academic life through a developmental lens can reveal subtle, but important, differences among professors at successive stages.

Development theorists portray adulthood as a variegated and dynamic phase of life. Erik Erikson defines the adult years in terms of three sequential objectives: intimacy, generativity, and ego integrity. The young adult seeks intimacy, meaning involvements and commitments beyond oneself. Establishment of meaningful interpersonal relationships and choice of a vocational role, for example, help to satisfy the natural drive for connections with the larger world. Erikson views the core years of adulthood as a quest for generativity. The goal at this stage is to produce or create things (such as children, theories, buildings, new scholars) of enduring value. The task of late adulthood is a drive for ego integrity. The individual at this stage seeks a feeling of fulfillment, of satisfaction with life. This assessment phase permits the late adult to disengage from life's commitments with a sense of closure. Erikson's framework broadly illustrates the varying forces that exert themselves at different points of life and significantly shape the concerns and behavior of adults (Erikson, 1963).

Levinson (1984; and others, 1978) describes the adult years as a series of alternating stable and transitional periods. During a stable period the basic task is to pursue clearly defined priorities and goals and enhance one's life within that framework. However, after seven to ten years of one life-style, "we are propelled by certain psychological forces to assess what . . . we are doing with our lives" (Bardwick, 1986, p. 110). Hence the adult moves into a transitional phase (lasting four to five years). The task during transition is to evaluate the existing life structure, explore alternatives, and make some initial commitments that will form the basis of a new, more satisfactory life plan. According to Bardwick, this assessment always reveals some disparity between reality and a person's expectations or dreams. Internal negotiation and compromise are often necessary before one can establish new or revised objectives for the next stable phase of life. Frequently these adjustments are not made easily or without pain. For this reason, transitional periods sometimes become major life crises.

This sequence of stable and transitional periods repeats itself regularly. According to Levinson and others (1978), the cycle never becomes routine. Each season has its special character and presents distinctive tasks to be completed.

Most academic careers begin near the end of Levinson's early-adult era and continue until the transition into late adulthood. Early adulthood is a time for choices and initial commitments. This is a period of heavy burdens as the young person struggles to form a vocation, marry, and start a family, often concurrently. The settling-down period, which in Levinson's scheme concludes early adulthood, is strongly achievement-oriented. During this period one often feels pressured to accomplish specific goals (for example, tenure, senior partnership) on a certain timetable (often by the age of forty). Essentially, the objective is to earn recognition, to become a full-fledged member of a valued segment of the adult world.

No matter how successful a person may be, however, the onset of midlife triggers another transitional phase. Levinson calls it the midlife transition; the popular media label it the midlife crisis. Bardwick says that this is the point at which the future no longer seems endless, and at which it seems to extend with a "frighteningly unvarying script" (1978, p. 131). At this stage there is a sudden realization: "This is your work; this is your spouse; this is your place; this is your level; this is your life" (Bardwick, 1978,

p. 132). Long-neglected parts of the self seek expression during the midlife transition. For example, artistic interests and nurturing drives overshadowed by career demands may suddenly reemerge (Levinson and others, 1978). The task of the adult in midlife transition is to work through anxieties about aging, to set priorities, and to define new goals that will form a more satisfactory life structure.

The outcome of the midlife transition influences the subsequent course of life. A flawed life structure (composed of unrealistic ambitions, unsatisfying relationships, and so on) can cause some people to decline in midlife. For many, however, middle adulthood can be "the fullest and most creative season in the life cycle" (Levinson and others, 1978, p. 62). Mature men, for instance, are less driven by the illusions, passions, and ambitions of youth and are freer to become deeply attached to others (Levinson and others, 1978).

Evidence suggests that the sequence of stable and transitional stages continues to the end of the life cycle (Levinson, 1986). Reassessment and revision are repeatedly necessary as one adapts to the changing demands of relationships and careers. Satisfactory adjustments can lead to fulfillment at any stage of life. Failure to adapt to changing circumstances can promote disappointment, despair, even withdrawal from major life roles.

Stage models of adult development should be applied with caution. Critics object, for example, to the rigid sequence of age-related stages that schemes such as Levinson's present. Models that conceptualize the adult years as a routine series of common tasks may oversimplify the complexities and diverse forms of postadolescent life. Levinson's theory, based on a small sample of men only, no doubt fails to portray the distinctive developmental experiences of women and other groups not adequately represented in his research. (This omission should be partially remedied soon, however. Levinson has been studying the adult development of women and is scheduled to publish *The Seasons of a Woman's Life* in the near future.)

Yet in spite of these valid criticisms, theories of adult development offer an enlightening perspective from which to examine faculty. Contrary to the popular myth, college and university professors do not reside in an ivory tower. They are subject to the same psychosocial forces as are other adults. Alternating periods of goal seeking and reassessment are common as academics proceed through their careers. Higher education should acknowledge the changing character of these periods and help professors travel through them successfully.

## The Evolving Career

The work career is a major anchor of adult life. Especially for highly job-involved professionals, work is an important component of identity and a vehicle for pursuing dreams (Levinson and others, 1978).

The career consists of "a sequence and combination of roles a person plays during the course of a lifetime" (Super, 1986, p. 96). Like other aspects of adulthood, the career follows a developmental path. Even when an individual continues in the same broadly defined occupation, qualitative changes usually occur over time in workplace, status, and meaning and mode of work (Levinson and others, 1978). Hence career stages can help to explain the different attitudes and behavior of people in complex organizations such as universities (Hall, 1976).

Career stages and their associated tasks have been conceptualized by many occupational theorists (Voydanoff, 1980). Each model views the career development process slightly differently, but a comparable evolutionary process emerges from the various schemes. Most careers progress from an initial entry and establishment period to a period of growth and advancement. Eventually careers cease to expand; they level off to a stable plateau in a maintenance stage. Finally they move into a disengagement phase, during which people's involvement with their occupation decreases in anticipation of retirement. Each career stage poses distinctive challenges that significantly influence the concerns and performance of workers.

*Career Entry.* The initial stage of any career is a time of learning and socialization. The novice learns the basic rules and expectations of the profession or organization and is judged in terms of long-term potential (Bailyn and Schein, 1976). Career entry can be a stressful experience. Research with young AT&T managers, for example, has shown considerable concern for "career safety." Typically the new professional wishes to achieve competence, establish him- or herself securely in the organization, and receive some preliminary recognition from superiors or higher-ranking colleagues (Hall and Nougaim, 1968).

Substantial changes in a person's self-image, attitudes, and aspirations can occur during the early years of a career. Often these changes are negative rather than positive. To prevent a negative outcome, efforts to make career entry a satisfying experience are desirable (Hall, 1976).

*Early Career.* Further learning occurs during the early-career phase as the individual tries to master the organization or profession. But this stage is qualitatively different from career entry. The experienced worker is more capable of functioning fully and of performing meaningful work (Bailyn and Schein, 1976). This is a good period for creativity and innovation; junior members of an organization tend to be work-engaged and unbridled by years of habit and tradition. Advancement and promotion are often dominant concerns of the early career (Glaser, 1964). Bardwick (1986) describes this phase of life as a time of "full-out striving, grabbing for long-range opportunity" (p. 10). This is an exciting period in a person's work life as he or she strives to carve out an area of specialization, move up professionally, and make a name.

*Midcareer.* The midpoint of a career represents a watershed for many, especially for highly career-involved professionals. It is the point at which an individual feels established and has achieved perceived mastery of his or her work (Hall, 1986a). This is the period of maximum productivity and greatest influence for persons in many occupations. Yet it may also be the time when the career begins to ebb, when the limits of one's achievements come into view. At this stage the need or opportunity to compete may decrease (Hall, 1976). For many, midcareer brings the onset of a career plateau of few new challenges or creative achievements.

Midcareer is a time for reexamination of personal values and needs as well as professional concerns (Rabinowitz and Hall, 1981). Questions about the future and what it has to offer naturally emerge. According to Hall (1986a), the issue of balance between one's work roles and personal roles becomes more salient. He suggests that careers often become less of a priority as one ages and assumes additional life roles. This may necessitate some reordering of priorities. The reassessment process can be uncomfortable, but it is necessary in order to redefine one's relationship with work and to identify new goals for a rewarding future.

*Late Career.* The final years of a career present their own challenges. Senior members of an organization or profession are usually beyond the point of maximum productivity, but their knowledge and experience enable them to continue making valuable contributions (Bailyn and Schein, cited in Voydanoff, 1980). Two primary tasks dominate the late-career period: concluding the career in a personally satisfactory manner and preparing for retirement. Termination of a career requires considerable adjustment— especially for professionals, who must accept a significantly altered identity. The central emotional need is to achieve a sense of personal integrity—the feeling that one has achieved worthwhile goals, that one's work truly mattered (Hall, 1976). Often there is a strong desire to leave some kind of legacy that will have value in the future. The latter years of a career can be very fulfilling, if one is given the opportunity for stimulating work and satisfying professional relationships. Alternatively, if one's professional life is stale and the future is uncertain, this can be a devastating period.

*Career Plateau.* The career plateau is a developmental phenomenon that deserves special attention here, because it is common in the academic profession. A plateau is "a stage in work or life where there is no growth or movement" (Bardwick, 1986, p. *vii*). Career plateauing is most common at midlife, but it can occur whenever work becomes routine and is no longer engrossing. Once the sensation of progress ceases, motivation, commitment, and productivity may well decline (Bardwick, 1986). A person who feels stuck gradually withdraws psychologically from work in search of other sources of gratification (Kanter, 1977).

Faculty members are susceptible to two forms of plateauing: structural and content. Structural plateauing results when opportunities for advancement are constrained by the organization's hierarchical arrangement. The faculty career ladder from assistant to full professor provides only a short path for formal career development. Thus professors quickly plateau structurally, often by the age of forty (Bardwick, 1986).

Content plateauing is a more serious problem. It occurs when work is mastered, when there is nothing new to learn. In *The Plateauing Trap* Bardwick (1986) claims that it is difficult to maintain a sense of growth if work remains essentially the same for more than three years. She estimates that after five years of the same responsibilities, a sense of mastery turns into a feeling of boredom. Professors who continue teaching the same course or studying the same narrow research questions are easy victims of content plateauing.

Fortunately, plateauing is not an irreversible phenomenon. Hall (1986b) recommends that "flat" organizations, such as universities, identify alternatives to promotion that provide opportunities for genuine professional growth. Bardwick (1986) advocates that people alter their work responsibilities often enough to sustain a continuous sense of challenge and learning: "When people have the opportunity to engage in new work, be creative, and make things happen, enormous amounts of psychic energy can be released so that they work well and feel good" (p. 82).

## Sources of Variation in Development

Developmental concepts and models enhance understanding of major forces that shape the concerns and behaviors of adults, including college and university professors. Theories of adult and career development describe common life patterns. However, much latitude exists within the models for individual and group differences. Development during the adult years does not follow a uniform, unvarying course. Levinson (1986; and others, 1978), for example, believes that certain developmental issues emerge in a set chronological sequence, yet his stages occur over flexible age ranges, not at fixed points for everyone. Other models are even more flexible than Levinson's, suggesting that adult and career development are contextual processes that are significantly influenced by individual attributes and intervening circumstances. Career timing, for one thing, may affect the development process. Hall (1986a) suggests that the pattern of work life influences when various career stages occur. A person with an uninterrupted career will experience a mid-career transition sooner and in a different way than a person whose career has followed an irregular course. Career stages may even recur, depending on how often work responsibilities change and then become routine again.

The length and dynamics of career stages may also vary by occupation (Voydanoff, 1980). Obviously the prime of professional life is different for football players and orchestra conductors. Similar variations may occur within the academic ranks. Blackburn (1985) reports that "career advancement differs across disciplines and even within subspecialties in the same field" (p. 69). Variation most likely occurs for faculty in different types of higher education institutions as well. Nuclear physicists at Berkeley and philosophers at Oberlin do not progress professionally in the same ways or at the same pace.

Gender is another major source of variation in the development process. Women's development has received scant attention from researchers, but theorists presume significantly different life patterns. Women's occupational development is often more complex than men's. Clark and Corcoran (1986) report that women find it more difficult than do men to locate sponsors and mentors to facilitate their career advancement. Similarly, Clark and Corcoran observe that women's marital and family roles affect their professional work engagement much more than men's work is affected by their marital and family roles. Women in American society are more likely than men to have interrupted careers due to family obligations. Also, transition stages for women may occur in a somewhat different manner than those for men. The biological clock can prompt women to confront life's basic issues at different times than men confront those issues. Theorists suggest that men and women start at opposite ends of a psychodynamic continuum but gradually move closer together. With age, men become more involved in their internal psychological needs and less driven by external career demands. Women, on the other hand, become more externally oriented as their relational commitments decrease (Bardwick, 1980). Frequently this trend includes a greater interest in careers.

Life confronts both genders with many of the same tasks, but the distinctive nature of each sex in this society surely influences the manner in which they respond to these challenges. The demands of academic life in theory are identical for women and men, yet the timing of major career events (for example, job entry, onset of a career plateau) may vary significantly for professors from the two genders. Hence the salient professional issues concerning male and female faculty members may sometimes differ in qualitative ways that affect career orientation and job performance.

Distinctive career patterns may be true for individuals from different ethnic groups as well. The developmental forces that shape adults' identity and behavior may vary in significant ways according to ethnic origins. For instance, the growing presence of Asian Americans and the diminishing presence of black males on college campuses suggest that their respective backgrounds do not position people of those backgrounds equally well for successful careers in the academic profession. The relative availability of role models, mentors, and peers from similar origins is among the factors that may account for developmental differences among faculty from distinctive sociological subgroups.

Developmental models provide a valuable lens that enhances understanding of academic life. Within the developmental framework, however, there is wide latitude for individual and group differences. Together, these sources of variation account for the rich diversity that exists within the overall developmental pattern that characterizes members of the academic profession.

## Developmental Research on Faculty

Developmental research on faculty has identified notable differences among professors at successive ages and career stages. For example, interest in various faculty roles seems to vary among professors with different levels of experience. Scholars have found among older faculty a decreased interest in research (Baldwin, 1979; Fulton and Trow, 1974; Ladd and Lipset, 1976a) and an increased enthusiasm for teaching (Fulton and Trow, 1974; Ladd and Lipset,

1976a) and institutional service (Baldwin, 1979). Several studies report differing time allocations among the principal faculty roles. Apparently teaching responsibilities require less of experienced professors' time (Durham, Wright, and Chandler, 1966; Thompson, 1971; Baldwin, 1979), while institutional service activities require more (Mortimer, 1969). Professors' perceived strengths and weaknesses also seem to differ over the academic career. A study of liberal arts college faculty, for instance, revealed greater comfort with teaching and institutional service at successively higher academic ranks but less comfort with scholarly activity (Baldwin, 1979). Limited research also suggests that faculty problem solving and professional development behavior differ at successive career points. Senior professors appear more likely to solve problems independently than do their junior colleagues, for example, and they are less likely to participate in formal professional development activities (Baldwin, 1979).

Blackburn (1985) concluded from several studies that faculty research productivity seems cyclical. Research productivity appears to follow a complex developmental pattern, with alternating periods of increased and decreased achievement common among professors. This recurring phenomenon, in Blackburn's view, supports the contentions of adult development theorists.

The relationship between professional and personal life appears to vary over the career cycle as well. A study at a major research university found that assistant professors reported more negative "spillover" (that is, they reported that feelings associated with work directly influenced life outside of work, and vice versa) between work and family life and between work and leisure activities than did associate and full professors. Junior faculty in the study reported "conflicts between time and energy for work and for spouses, children, dual careers, and commuter marriages" (Sorcinelli and Near, 1987, p. 18). They also noted the lack of time for pleasure reading, exercise, and social and civic activities. This study suggests that balance between professional and personal roles is most difficult to achieve during the early years as a faculty member.

Evidence on faculty satisfaction also reveals noteworthy differences across the academic career. Some researchers (Eckert and Williams, 1972; Ladd and Lipset, 1976b) have reported that career satisfaction increases steadily with age. Baldwin and Blackburn (1981) likewise found that satisfaction was greatest among senior faculty, but they also found some evidence of decreased satisfaction at transition points in academic life.

More comprehensive research is needed to clarify the developmental nature of the academic career. To date, few national studies of the professoriate have been completed that are representative of the range of academic disciplines and institutions (Blackburn, 1985), yet available evidence on faculty across the career is sufficiently compatible with developmental theory to justify a close look at the stages of academic life.

### Faculty Career Stages

It is possible to translate various developmental schemes into a sequential model of the academic career. This generic view of academic life covers at least four distinct phases from the time of career entry to retirement. In some (perhaps many) cases the career surely follows an even more differentiated course. As has been noted, the pattern may vary for professors from different fields, institutions, genders, and ethnic groups. The framework outlined here is thus not a definitive model of academic life; many successful academic careers do not fit this precise developmental pattern. Still, because the model addresses developmental issues common to many professors throughout higher education, it provides a basic foundation for understanding the evolving interests, activities, and development needs of college and university faculty members.

*Novice Professor: Getting into the Academic World.* Beginning an academic career is a complex and demanding process. The new professor's major concern is competence. How can he or she learn quickly to perform all the duties of a college teacher? With so many things to do at once, how does a person set priorities and balance these new roles successfully? This entry period (lasting from one term to several years) is a time of intense pressure and considerable growth.

Numerous tasks must be completed as the new professor establishes a solid base for a successful career. The novice must design several courses in a brief period of time. Often these cover subjects in which the individual has limited expertise. More fundamentally, the beginner must develop a repertoire of teaching skills. It is one thing to lead a small discussion section as a graduate assistant; it is considerably more demanding to have full responsibility for lecturing, sequencing assignments, designing examinations, and motivating students with diverse needs. Not surprisingly, developing effective teaching skills is perhaps the most immediate concern of the new professor.

Early learning tasks extend beyond the classroom, however. The novice must gain knowledge of the institution's resources and support services. He or she must also become acquainted with the formal policies of the institution and, more importantly, with its mores and expectations. It would be regrettable, for example, if a new college teacher failed to hear of the instructional development center on a campus, and it could be fatal for a beginning professor to remain ignorant of the values and manners of his or her department or institution.

Successful career entry also requires attention to the scholarly dimensions of academic life. The new teacher must avoid becoming so consumed by instructional responsibilities that professional development and research are neglected.

Initiation to the academic ranks presents many competing demands. Young professors are often juggling new family responsibilities and related financial obligations in addition to a full menu of professional duties. Unfortunately, if the early years as a professor are unsatisfying, they can diminish enthusiasm and create a negative attitude that may persist throughout the career.

The distinctive demands of entering the academic profession call for special efforts on the part of the institution to smooth this important transition. Work assignments should acknowledge the extra time required of a new teacher—time to design new courses and take on other new roles. It is unrealistic to assume that a beginning professor can effectively carry the same range of duties as a veteran professor. Some reduction of normal teaching, advising, or committee work is appropriate at this stage. Similarly, formal orientation to the new institution is desirable. Information on policies and services relevant to a professor's diverse responsibilities should be shared systematically rather than in a haphazard fashion. A well-planned orientation strategy can facilitate adjustment to the institution and reduce initial career anxiety. Finally, sensitive guidance from established professionals may be the most effective way to ease the initial career transition. A supportive department chair or senior colleague willing to give advice and respond to questions can remove many hurdles confronting a new professor. Higher education institutions should foster mentoring relationships of this nature to promote the rapid adjustment of new faculty members. Well-planned strategies to meet the unique needs of new professors can promote the feeling of competence so important at the beginning of a career.

*Early Academic Career: Settling Down and Making a Name.* Achievement and confirmation are the dominant themes of the early-career years—that is, the period between career entry and full membership in the academic ranks. These objectives are especially manifest in the academic profession, where full membership status is awarded only after a lengthy probationary period. Although the early-career years are substantially different from the initial entry period, they also have a make-or-break quality to them. A professor at this stage wishes to master the principal faculty roles, and some kind of meaningful achievement (deserving of recognition within one's institution or broader discipline) is usually a prominent goal as well. The desire for publication of respected articles, chapters, or a book, or for acquisition of a major research grant, often focuses the efforts of an early-career professor. This is a task-oriented phase with concrete goals. Beneath the stability offered by a clear sense of purpose, however, may linger a nagging concern about the future. The early-career professor recognizes that denial of tenure could provoke a major transition in his or her life.

The clear objectives of the early career demand much of the junior academic. On the basis of initial experience in the classroom, courses must be redesigned and teaching strategies refined. Participation in institutional service must be increased; more time must be allotted to meeting with committees and preparing reports. The quest for confirmation often demands involvement in external scholarly communication networks, professional associations, and editorial boards, in addition to research and writing. The press of fixed responsibilities leaves little time to stay broadly informed of developments in one's field or to plan for an uncertain future. Stress at this career stage is an everyday experience.

Higher education institutions should acknowledge the special burdens of the early academic career. It is in their best interest to help junior faculty members prosper. Support should be available to facilitate young professors' teaching and research endeavors. (A small number of institutions even provide sabbatical leaves for non-tenured, junior faculty. This provides an opportunity to organize one's research agenda when it is most needed.) Perhaps most important, academic administrators should be willing to adjust faculty assignments during the early-career years to help professors accomplish their highest professional priorities. Keeping the demands of the early career manageable can prevent burnout and preserve fragile faculty morale.

*Midcareer: Accepting a Career Plateau or Setting New Goals?* Reaching midcareer (the long period after one feels established but before the career disengagement process begins) signals another major phase in the academic life cycle. This is often a very productive and rewarding phase, a time when professors enjoy maximum professional influence. Extrinsic goals, such as promotion to full professor, may direct faculty efforts during the early years of this period. Likewise, the desire for true senior status within one's institution and discipline is common among midcareer faculty members.

For many, it is also a transitional phase. Interests and concerns that were dormant during the intense early-career years may bubble to the surface. The midcareer professor may become aware that family obligations have been shortchanged and hobbies or recreation neglected. Midlife increases one's awareness that time is finite. This realization may provoke some effort to achieve more balance among life's competing roles.

Frequently, midcareer parallels the onset of a career plateau. After many years in the classroom or laboratory, a professor may begin to note a monotonous sameness about his or her work. A fear that professional challenge and growth have ended may develop. Worries about falling behind in one's field and about potential obsolescence are also common at this stage. Additionally, the professor who has reached a plateau lacks the concrete goals and clear sense of direction that make the early career so exciting.

Even for professors who have not reached a plateau, one pervasive question of midcareer is, What should I do with the rest of my professional life? For many academics, midcareer stimulates a period of assessment; priorities and goals are reexamined. Do I want to continue teaching full time? Would I make a good administrator? Is it too late to learn to use the computer? Could team teaching with the new member of our department help me catch up with new developments in my field? Ideally, this process of assessment should identify new goals that can energize subsequent phases of a professor's career.

The costly toll of faculty "deadwood" is sufficient reason for higher education institutions to devote special attention to midcareer professors. Veteran faculty need opportunities to review and redefine career goals from time to time. Career planning workshops may benefit some, while formal growth contracts outlining new goals and development strategies may help others. Sometimes an informal conversation with the dean or department chair can enable a midcareer professor to define new career challenges. Regardless of the method employed, professors need periodically to examine their careers and identify exciting new paths for the future.

Acceptance of this point of view has implications for faculty policies and work assignments also. Policies must be sufficiently flexible to foster professors' growth in new directions. For example, sabbatical plans that require faculty members to conduct research in their established area of specialization may be too rigid to meet the distinctive needs of midcareer professors. In addition, colleges and universities must be willing to revise work assignments to maintain a spark of variety and challenge in professors' careers. It must be acknowledged that a lifelong career in higher education is not the best course for everyone. Policies that make career change and early retirement feasible alternatives can help some midcareer academics leave campus for other types of work that they may find more invigorating.

*Late Career: Leaving a Legacy.* The last phase of an academic career (the years prior to retirement, when gradual disengagement from work ordinarily occurs) can be filled with paradox. Senior professors express considerable satisfaction with their careers (Eckert and Williams, 1972; Ladd and Lipset, 1976b; Baldwin and Blackburn, 1981). Many enjoy a respected position in their institution and can look with pride at the achievements of a long life in higher education. Concurrently, however, a professor nearing retirement may feel increasingly out of touch with developments in a rapidly changing field. As one of the oldest members of a department, this individual may have little in common with younger colleagues and feel isolated and somewhat irrelevant. On many campuses, shifting values—a new emphasis on research productivity over teaching, for example—leave senior faculty members feeling neglected and underappreciated. These feelings are sometimes reinforced by the effects of market-driven salaries that favor young faculty members in "hot" fields. Concerns about retirement security—both financial and psychological—may likewise trouble a person whose identity is closely tied to the work role. This combination of positive and negative factors can leave a senior professor feeling ambivalent about the end of his or her career and anxious about what lies ahead.

The final stage of academic life need not be a mixed bag, however. In fact, from the perspective of overall faculty morale, it ought to be a gratifying period, and an institution can do much to ensure that it is. Helping faculty prepare for a secure retirement is one way to reduce their stress at concluding a career. Retirement planning assistance well in advance of the actual separation date is essential. Such assistance should address personal and psychological aspects of retirement as well as financial considerations. Individual counseling and group discussion sessions in addition to informative seminars can ease the adjustment process. Phased retirement, which enables a faculty member to reduce work commitments gradually, is another way to smooth the path to emeritus status.

Senior professors should be treated as full-fledged faculty members, not as old-timers waiting to be put out to pasture. They deserve challenging teaching assignments and support for their professional development. Professors approaching retirement have much to offer their institution and the academic profession. Roles that capitalize on seasoned professors' special skills and their natural desire to leave a legacy can be particularly satisfying to senior faculty. For example, academic veterans are uniquely qualified to orient new colleagues to academic life. Some are well prepared to lead workshops on teaching strategies, while others can help novice scholars with research methodology or committee duties. Such opportunities for junior and senior colleagues to work together can bridge generational barriers and provide both generations with avenues for exciting professional growth. Special service to the department or institution is another way senior professors can make a lasting contribution before retirement: work with important task forces, the admissions or alumni offices, or the president can offer stimulating challenges for the last years of an individual's professional life. Meaningful work that is recognized and respected by others is important at *all* stages of work life, of course, but it may be *essential* in bringing a long academic career to a satisfying conclusion.

### Conclusion

The academic profession does not lend itself to neat classification schemes. Professors comprise an exceptionally diverse occupational group; they differ by field and by institution as well as by age and career stage, and they represent both genders and many ethnic groups. Above all, they are individuals who possess unique interests, talents, and expertise.

Yet a shared value system and a spirit of community pervade the academic ranks. As Bowen and Schuster (1986) conclude from a nationwide study, "Despite the variety that exists in academe, it is appropriate for many purposes to treat the professoriate as a closely knit social group and not merely as a collection of disparate individuals or unrelated small groups" (p. 13). Widespread socialization practices and similar work roles help to unify the profession. So does the developmental process common to academic life.

The developmental framework outlined in this chapter clarifies major themes and events that dominate successive seasons in the careers of many faculty members. It suggests why a new college teacher with superb credentials can be scattered and ineffective. It indicates why a prolific young scholar may become the sedentary campus curmudgeon. It helps to explain why a professor on the verge of retirement spends his weekends working in the laboratory with a new colleague.

A developmental model of the faculty career sensitizes higher education to the changing demands of academic life. It helps colleges and universities to define policies and work assignments in light of differing professional circumstances rather than by a rigid standard. It enables a dean or department chair to offer faculty development support when it can be most beneficial.

No model can fully capture the rich variety that exists within the professoriate. No two academic careers are identical, and professors deserve to be treated as the talented *individuals* they are. A developmental frame of reference, however, illuminates powerful forces that influence many faculty members at different points of the career. This insight can empower higher education to serve more effectively the distinctive needs of individual professors. Ideally, it will help to extend the most creative phases of academic life and abbreviate unproductive career plateaus.

## References

Bailyn, L., and Schein, E. "Life/Career Considerations as Indicators of Quality Employment." In A. D. Biderman and T. F. Drury (eds.), *Measuring Work Quality for Social Reporting*. Beverly Hills, Calif.: Sage, 1976.

Baldwin, R. G. "The Faculty Career Process—Continuity and Change: A Study of College Professors at Five Stages of the Academic Career." Unpublished doctoral dissertation, Center for the Study of Higher Education, University of Michigan, 1979.

Baldwin, R. G., and Blackburn, R. T. "The Academic Career as a Developmental Process: Implications for Higher Education." *Journal of Higher Education*, 1981, *52* (6), 598–614.

Bardwick, J. M. "Middle Age and a Sense of Future." *Merrill Palmer Quarterly*, 1978, *24* (2), 129–138.

Bardwick, J. M. "The Seasons of a Woman's Life." In D. G. McGuigan (ed.), *Women's Lives: New Theory, Research, and Policy*. Ann Arbor: University of Michigan Center for the Continuing Education of Women, 1980.

Bardwick, J. M. *The Plateauing Trap.* New York: AMACOM, 1986.

Blackburn, R. T. "Faculty Career Development: Theory and Practice." In S. M. Clark and D. R. Lewis (eds.), *Faculty Vitality and Institutional Productivity: Critical Perspectives for Higher Education.* New York: Teachers College Press, 1985.

Bowen, H. R., and Schuster, J. H. *American Professors: A National Resource Imperiled.* New York: Oxford University Press, 1986.

Clark, S. M., and Corcoran, M. "Perspectives on the Professionalization of Women Faculty: A Case of Accumulative Disadvantage?" *Journal of Higher Education,* 1986, *57* (1), 20–43.

Durham, R. E., Wright, P. S., and Chandler, M. O. *Teaching Faculty in Universities and Four-Year Colleges.* Washington, D.C.: U.S. Office of Education, 1966.

Eckert, R. E., and Williams, H. Y. *College Faculty View Themselves and Their Jobs.* Minneapolis: College of Education, University of Minnesota, 1972.

Erikson, E. H. *Childhood and Society.* (2nd ed.) New York: Norton, 1963.

Fulton, O., and Trow, M. "Research Activity in American Higher Education." *Sociology of Education,* 1974, *47* (1), 29–73.

Glaser, B. G. *Organizational Scientists: Their Professional Careers.* Indianapolis, Ind.: Bobbs-Merrill, 1964.

Hall, D. T. *Careers in Organizations.* Pacific Palisades, Calif.: Goodyear, 1976.

Hall, D. T. "Breaking Career Routines: Midcareer Choice and Identity." In D. T. Hall and Associates, *Career Development in Organizations.* San Francisco: Jossey-Bass, 1986a.

Hall, D. T. "Introduction: An Overview of Current Development Theory, Research, and Practice." In D. T. Hall and Associates, *Career Development in Organizations.* San Francisco: Jossey-Bass, 1986b.

Hall, D. T., and Nougaim, K. "An Examination of Maslow's Need Hierarchy in an Organizational Setting." *Organizational Behavior and Human Performance,* 1968, *3,* 12–35.

Kanter, R. M. *Men and Women of the Corporation.* New York: Basic Books, 1977.

Ladd, E. C., and Lipset, S. M. "The Aging Professoriate." *The Chronicle of Higher Education,* 1976a, *12* (13), 16.

Ladd, E. C., and Lipset, S. M. "What Do Professors Like Best About Their Jobs?" *The Chronicle of Higher Education,* 1976b, *12* (5), 10.

Levinson, D. J. "The Career Is in the Life Structure, the Life Structure Is in the Career: An Adult Development Perspective." In M. B. Arthur, L. Bailyn, D. J. Levinson, and H. A. Shepard, (eds.), *Working with Careers.* New York: Center for Research in Career Development, Columbia University, 1984.

Levinson, D. J. "A Concept of Adult Development." *American Psychologist,* 1986, *41* (1), 3–13.

Levinson, D. J., and others. *The Seasons of a Man's Life.* New York: Knopf, 1978.

Mortimer, K. P. "Academic Government at Berkeley: The Academic Senate." Unpublished doctoral dissertation, School of Education, University of California, Berkeley, 1969.

Rabinowitz, S., and Hall, D. T. "Changing Correlates of Job Involvement in Three Career Stages." *Journal of Vocational Behavior,* 1981, *18,* 138–144.

Sorcinelli, M. D., and Near, J. P. "Relations Between Academic Work and Personal Life: Conflicts and Strategies for Change." Paper presented at annual meeting of American Educational Research Association, Washington, D.C., Apr. 1987.

Super, D. E. "Self-Realization in Work and Leisure." In D. T. Hall and Associates, *Career Development in Organizations.* San Francisco: Jossey-Bass, 1986.

Thompson, R. K. *How Does the Faculty Spend Its Time?* Seattle: University of Washington, 1971. (Mimeographed.)

Voydanoff, P. "Work-Family Life Cycles Among Women." In D. G. McGuigan (ed.), *Women's Lives: New Theory, Research, and Policy.* Ann Arbor: University of Michigan Center for the Continuing Education of Women, 1980.

3

# An Overview of Research on Faculty and Institutional Vitality

*Carole J. Bland*
*Constance C. Schmitz*

The literature in faculty vitality is impressive, both in terms of quantity and of eloquence. Yet what is empirically "known" about the professional vitality or renewal of faculty is less abundant. The knowledge we have, for the most part, has been gained not by experimental test but by discussion, by personal experience, and by the culling of collective experience through systematic review, evaluation, and consensus.

### What Is Known and How We Know It

With the exception of Levinson-Rose and Menges's (1981) meta-analysis of research on the effectiveness of teaching improvement programs, there are few empirical studies (other than surveys and literature reviews) and few studies documenting impact (for exceptions, see Hoyt and Howard, 1978; Rice, 1985; Eble and McKeachie, 1985; Friedman and Stomper, 1983).* The literature does not, therefore, reveal conclusive evidence of the effect of programs, or even a final summative judgment regarding their outcomes.

*An extensive bibliography, containing the references for this chapter and keyed to Tables 3.1 and 3.2, appears as the Resource (at the end of this book).

Still, much of the existent literature is insightful in analyzing the phenomena of personal and professional development of faculty, and thoughtful in its documentation of various efforts to promote and sustain development. In search of wisdom on the engineering of faculty or institutional vitality, we reviewed the faculty development literature from 1965 to mid 1985 (Bland and Schmitz, 1988). In the fall of 1987 we updated this review to include 1985 to 1987. In both cases we searched ERIC, Psych Abstracts, Sociology, and Medline, using the key words "faculty development" and other phrases incorporating *faculty* and *institutional vitality*. We confined the search to activities taking place at universities, four-year colleges, and professional schools in the United States. We rejected articles unpublished or available only on microfiche. Books frequently referenced in articles were inspected also.

To be included in our final collection, the source had to offer specific strategies or recommendations for developing full-time faculty members, departments, or institutions. This criterion excluded opinion pieces, research on professional or career development, and how-to information on administration or organizational development. Through this process we found a lively assortment of records (315 in total), which include the following:

- Illuminating reports "from the field" (for example, Nelsen and Siegel, 1980; Bedsole, 1983)
- Detailed case studies (for example, Sikes and Barrett, 1976; Alexander, 1982; Levine, 1985)
- Reports (for example, Rice and Davis, 1979) and evaluations (for example, Eble and McKeachie, 1985; Rice, 1985)
- Important surveys of practice (for example, Centra, 1978a; Belker, 1983; Merwin and others, 1983; Sorcinelli, 1985; Garbee, Strother, and Ferraro, 1986)
- Literature reviews (Stordahl, 1981; Stritter, 1983a)
- Discussions of primary concepts such as "vitality" (for example, Eble, 1971; Maher, 1982; Clark, Boyer, and Corcoran, 1985) and "renewal" (for example, Gaff, 1976b)
- Models for designing professional or faculty development programs (for example, Buhl, 1978; Lindquist, 1978a; Connell and others, 1976–77; Hipps, 1982)

- Handbooks of strategies, lists of prescriptions or admonitions (for example, Bergquist and Phillips, 1975b, 1979; Hammons and Wallace, 1976; Baldwin, 1981)
- Guides to resources (for example, Gaff, Festa, and Gaff, 1978; Inglis and Scholl, 1982)

Virtually all (93 percent) of this literature has been published since 1976; almost half of it was published between 1981 and 1987. By 1985 the literature had become more synthetic; books and monographs outnumbered individual articles. In considering the writings collected in the Resources we are led to ask the following questions:

1. What underlying concepts and issues over the last two decades have given rise to renewal efforts?
2. What have faculty renewal programs been designed to do, and how should they do it?
3. What specific strategies have been used to promote faculty renewal?

In addressing these questions, we hope to provide an overview of what is known about renewal efforts and some of the challenges associated with them.

### Concepts and Issues Underlying Renewal Efforts

Before describing the purpose of programs or the methods by which they attempt to renew faculty, we need to clarify the concepts and issues underlying renewal efforts. Just what is it that these programs and strategies are designed to influence?

What they are designed to influence is "vitality," a concept that suffers from ambiguity and vagueness but that has powerful intuitive appeal. Clark and Lewis, in *Faculty Vitality and Institutional Productivity* (1985), devote an entire chapter to the meaning of this concept, noting that *"vitality . . . is widely used but infrequently defined."* Generally, *vitality* refers to those "essential, yet intangible, positive qualities of individuals and institutions that enable purposeful production" (p. 3).

One reason that *vitality* defies precise definition is that its meaning varies with the context. Behaviors considered indicative of vitality are defined and measured in various ways, depending on the mission of the institution. For example, "purposeful production" in a community college describes activities that are not as highly valued in a research university. Maher (1982, p. 3) recognized this when he said, "The quest for vitality . . . focus[es] on the capacity of the college or university to create and sustain the organizational strategies that support the continued investment of energy by faculty and staff both in their own career and in the realization of the institution's mission."

Just as the definition of vitality varies according to the institutional context, the threats to vitality—the forces that weaken either the individual faculty member's or institution's ability to sustain vitality—vary according to context and historical time period. On one hand, we presume that faculty must continually develop and adapt to meet their primary obligations to develop and disseminate knowledge. This is a given in the best as well as worst of times. Thus personal and professional renewal of faculty is a necessary, cyclic process to be nurtured, regardless of circumstances. On the other hand, certain external pressures on the academy (for example, retrenchment, financial exigency, and changes in the workforce) increase the threats to vitality by removing many of the natural conditions that support renewal, such as opportunities for job change, the hiring of new faculty, and expansion of programs. Accordingly, concerns and strategies for faculty vitality during periods of institutional growth and economic security differ markedly from those seen in times of duress.

In the early writings on faculty development (those before 1975), vitality was defined narrowly as a faculty issue. The underlying "problems" that strategies such as workshops and leaves were designed to address were teacher fatigue, outmoded teaching skills, and lack of protected time for scholarship. It was commonly assumed that if seminars on pedagogy were offered and sabbaticals and leaves were increased, vitality would take care of itself. Faculty members were held responsible for their own productivity and motivation; all that the administration had to do was leave faculty alone and provide minimal support.

Since then the academy has become more sophisticated in its understanding of vitality and what it entails. Today's vitality "problem" lies not just with individual faculty members and such issues as their lack of teaching skills or protected research time. Rather, the threats to vitality are increasingly seen to lie with tenured-in departments, with new student populations, with "marketing" problems and outmoded curricula, with the lack of "opportunity structures" in academe, with the decline in real earnings, and with a deteriorating work environment. Everything that affects faculty morale, whether its source is internal or external, enters into the vitality equation.

For this reason, faculty vitality is rarely considered independently of its institutional context in contemporary thinking. "Faculty and institutional vitality" has replaced the narrower concept of "faculty development." Thus there are two key points to consider when thinking about programs and strategies to enhance vitality:

1. Vitality involves an interplay of faculty qualities and institutional factors.
2. Whether faculty activities are considered productive (vital) or not depends on whether they relate both to the faculty member's personal and professional goals *and* to the institution's mission.

These two points require elaboration. First, in regard to the interplay involved, which faculty qualities *do* relate to productivity? Numerous studies outline the characteristics of successful faculty researchers and teachers (for example, Creswell, 1985; Bland and Schmitz, 1986). They include such factors as intelligence, training, commitment, and socialization. Fortunately, today's faculty possess these characteristics in abundance. Current faculty are perhaps the most highly trained, intelligent, and socialized group the United States has ever had (Bowen and Schuster, 1986). If hours devoted to work or willingness to accept lower salaries signifies commitment, current faculties score high there also. Still, even the best-prepared and highly qualified faculty can get burned out, fall behind in their field, or require new teaching tools to meet new demands in teaching. Thus faculty have a responsibility to remain current in their field, to challenge their own thinking, to redesign courses or begin new lines of research, to engage in professional organizations, and so on.

Which institutional factors affect vitality? Organizational factors, more than individual faculty characteristics, are thought to influence vitality and productivity. Blackburn (1979, p. 25) found that *"the institution determines to a high degree a faculty member's productivity*—faculty at some colleges and universities produce appreciably more than faculty at other institutions, and this differential rate is independent of place of preparation, ability, workload, and prior places of work." He goes on to say that "nearly every positively correlated factor [with research productivity] resides in administrative hands and hence can be fostered by the organization" (p. 26).

Similarly, in their review of characteristics of productive researchers, Bland and Schmitz (1986, p. 28) concluded that "institutional and organizational characteristics affect, pehaps even control, faculty members' productivity. . . ." In his investigation of research groups in six countries, Andrews (1979) found organizational factors to be primary determinants of productivity. These factors include such things as material resources, internal communication processes, and quality of group climate, leadership, and decision-making processes. Finally, as discussed in Chapter Two of this book, common values, purposes, and a sense of collegiality greatly affect faculty morale and productivity. Thus organizations have a responsibility to create environments that reinforce such ideals and actual behaviors on the part of faculty and staff.

The second essential point to consider is that vitality occurs when there is a match between an institution's mission and the faculty members' goals. As many of the authors in our review observed, if any of the links between institutional and faculty "goals, performance, rewards, and desires" are broken, the system will not be effective (Chait, 1979, p. 45). Programs that meet individual needs unrelated to the institution's priorities seem doomed from the outset. At the same time, programs that ignore faculty goals and interests quickly become "paper programs." They exist in documents but have no real existence or impact on faculty.

In summary, then, vitality is the underlying concept that is both the trigger and the goal for renewal efforts. It is an innately desirable concept for academics. A stimulating intellectual environment and the opportunity to be curious and to engage in lifelong learning are what attracts bright, talented people to academe. Exactly how vitality is conceived and defined, however, varies with the institutional culture and the historical time period. Theoretically, vitality is related to four complex factors: (1) faculty characteristics, (2) institutional features, (3) faculty goals, and (4) institutional mission. Thus programs to improve faculty and institutional vitality must take each of these factors into account.

## The Design and Use of Renewal Programs

The literature on faculty renewal programs reflects the ambiguous, elastic meanings of vitality discussed in the previous section. Earlier programs focused on teaching skills, largely because advancements in instructional technology and educational research highlighted the widespread neglect of teaching in the preparation of most faculty. The focus on teaching also developed because of the sheer repetition involved with this faculty role. Faculty members began to acknowledge publicly the challenge of maintaining enthusiasm for teaching a specialized area of knowledge over a long period of time, particularly in the face of declining student preparation. The potential for burnout among even highly motivated teachers led to strategies such as workshops and seminars, faculty evaluation, centers for instructional development and media assistance, and educational consulting.

Later programs expanded to address a much broader range of needs. Department cutbacks led to department retreats, increased hiring of adjunct faculty, various cross-department teaching assignments and shared teaching positions, organizational consulting, and program self-studies. Tenured-in departments led to buyouts, early retirement, innovative career-change arrangements within and beyond academe, and special recruitment programs for new, especially talented Ph.D. graduates. The threat of institutional insolvency led to the redefinition of mission and goals, alternative personnel policies, massive curriculum renovation, and other strategies (see next section). Basically, all of these attempts to renew faculty and "solve" problems can be seen as attempts to empower faculty to fulfill the mission of the institution and to meet their own goals.

The lessons learned from over twenty years of faculty renewal provide both general advice and examples of specific strategies from which to draw when building a faculty vitality program. First, let us summarize the advice. In reviewing the literature, we recorded 178 specific recommendations from over 141 authors and grouped them under 20 recommendations (see Table 3.1). These 20 recommendations span several categories, including institution and faculty roles, advice on program design, and intangible considerations relevant to faculty renewal.

The most frequent recommendation we encountered in the first category (institution and faculty roles) addressed the critical, delicate link (discussed above) that needs to be forged between institutional missions and policies and faculty renewal strategies. For example, Chait (1979, p. 45) says, "Determine what faculty and staff, as individuals, seek and value. . . . [M]ake certain that the performance to be rewarded supports institutional goals. . . . Ensure that institutional rewards reinforce individual desires. None of the links between goals, performance, rewards, and desires can be broken for the system to be effective." Bedsole and Reddick (1978, p. 75) similarly observe that "the individual must frame personal developmental goals within institutional goals. . . . The institution must create an environment conducive to faculty. . . . [meeting the goals]."

Underlying this type of recommendation is the understanding that faculty vitality and institutional vitality are the responsibility of faculty and administrators alike. Both parties must agree to common organizational goals. Furthermore, they must accept responsibility for, and acknowledge their role in, maintaining individual and institutional vitality so that together they can meet those goals. Two other recommendations in this category also address the roles of institutional members. One of them reminds us that it is necessary for both faculty and administrators to take and feel ownership of any faculty development program. The other states that faculty should be expected to allocate specific time to their continued development and vitality.

Many authors discussed elements of effective renewal programs. The element most often mentioned was the importance of

Table 3.1. Recommendations for Faculty and Institutional Vitality
Programs (with Cross-References to Authors in the Resource).

1. Link and balance individual development plans and activities with organizational needs and objectives (1, 7, 19, 22, 27, 33, 73, 76, 87, 92, 99, 121, 130, 135, 136, 149, 156, 163, 182, 192, 199, 224, 226, 230, 245, 253, 254, 258, 263, 291, 295, 300, 302, 315).
2. Expect faculty to spend time on their own faculty development and encourage faculty members' long-range planning (83, 164, 226, 277, 284).
3. Ensure faculty ownership and planning in a faculty vitality program (1, 65, 107, 131, 134, 154, 156, 163, 164, 197, 230, 254, 258, 264, 277, 295, 305, 315).
4. Reward participation in faculty development activities; tie in promotion, tenure, compensation (65, 214, 258, 295, 296, 305).
5. Place the primary faculty development administrator high in the campus organization; select an administrator who is a tenured associate or full professor, a competent teacher and scholar, and an expert in culture of the institution, and who is involved in political decision making and has an active internal and external network for ideas, support, and materials (32, 72, 89, 118, 134, 156, 197, 214, 254, 296, 315).
6. Make faculty development an integral, ongoing, visible, specifically budgeted, important, explicit part of the institution (3, 36, 69, 81, 92, 106, 107, 151, 154, 214, 224, 230, 254, 258, 271, 277, 284, 295, 296, 305).
7. Provide a variety of vitality strategies to meet varying career needs of individual professors (16, 32, 65, 92, 100, 107, 118, 154, 156, 197, 199, 213, 214, 224, 227, 254, 266, 291, 295, 296, 300).
8. Train leaders (chairs, deans, others) in promoting vitality—including how to design, implement, and evaluate a faculty development program (36, 54, 73, 99, 224, 227, 244, 271, 296).
9. Manipulate institutional policies, rewards, and resources to stimulate academic work and career variety (16, 65, 73, 87, 131, 176, 197, 231, 253).
10. Decide whether or not to link faculty development with faculty evaluations (10, 59, 134, 154, 155, 163, 230, 231, 296, 305).
11. Develop a comprehensive program that addresses instructional, personal, and organizational aspects of vitality (3, 32, 78, 91, 137, 140, 149, 164, 191, 199, 210, 226, 230, 232, 258, 279, 296, 300).
12. Tailor vitality programs to individuals and their institution (19, 26, 36, 59, 92, 151, 163, 213, 230).
13. Start with the influential opinion leaders of the institution (163, 197).
14. Make participation in specific programs or activities voluntary (156, 284, 296).
15. Support research on faculty careers, on faculty and institutional vitality, and on ways to improve them (1, 154, 156, 196, 258, 295, 306).
16. Take into account the knowledge and experience of others before starting a faculty vitality program (10, 214).
17. Develop a thorough plan for faculty and institutional vitality before specific faculty development activities are planned or begun (1, 32, 107, 111, 134, 140, 163).

Table 3.1. Recommendations for Faculty and Institutional Vitality
Programs (with Cross-References to Authors in the Resource), Cont'd.

18. Guarantee that traditional programs of faculty support (for example,
    leaves, sabbaticals) will not be abandoned (163, 176).
19. Address and reaffirm institutional values and mission as well as aca-
    demic values and purpose (127, 163, 192, 226, 253, 314).
20. Broaden the definition of a faculty career (too often thought of as struc-
    tured, inflexible, predicated on a one-life, one-career expectation) and
    provide opportunities for faculty members to achieve a more broadly
    defined career (20, 36, 93, 130, 179, 214, 254, 284, 291, 301).

making any development program an integral and influential part
of the institution by using such strategies as recruiting a highly
regarded tenured faculty member to direct the program, placing the
faculty development director high in the organization, and ear-
marking substantial funds for vitality efforts. This recommendation
complements the "delicate link" described above, operationalizes
the administration's role and commitment to faculty vitality, and
acknowledges the ongoing nature of faculty vitality efforts. No
longer, then, will such efforts be seen as tangential programs designed to meet transient problems. Rather, they will be seen as an
essential part of an enduring, healthy organization.

Other recommendations related to program planning and
design were more specific. Frequently authors stated that renewal
programs should be comprehensive; they should attend to the organizational, personal, and professional dimension of renewal; and
they should provide a host of diverse strategies to meet various
faculty needs and institutional problems. Comments by Clark, Corcoran, and Lewis (1986, p. 179) exemplify the considerable scope
that current writers propose for faculty vitality programs. Such programs should "include value-added, quality-associated concerns
with careers over the long-term in organizations; skill-development
at different career stages; internal opportunities for both vertical
and lateral mobility; relationships that promote both the psychological sense of community or collegium and sponsor-mentor
generative activity; and participation in shaping the direction of
one's unit or the institution at large." Given this broad scope, it is
critical to attend to the previous recommendations—that is, to link

vitality strategies to institutional missions and common goals and to appoint an able director who can see that such a multifaceted, comprehensive approach does not become fragmented, unfocused, or unwieldy.

The final set of recommendations concerns the symbolic or intangible features of renewal programs. Several writers stressed the importance of traditional academic values and called for a return of the rituals and rites of the academy to celebrate (renew) historic values. Other authors believed that renewal programs should help faculty redefine what it means to be a faculty member. Renewal efforts, it was said, should challenge the one-life, one-career imperative and find innovative ways to employ faculty.

These last two recommendations alert us to a subtle but powerful facet of faculty development: many faculty draw significant motivation and satisfaction from the traditional beliefs of academe and from being a member of the academic community. Rice (1983a, p. 56) puts it eloquently: "Nowhere in the contemporary world do socially constructed fictions have more power than in the professions and there is no profession where a socially constructed, professional imagery dominates more thoroughly than among faculty." Socially constructed fictions include beliefs such as the following: research is the primary focus of academic life; only in the academy can knowledge be pursued for its own sake; an academic career is a lifetime calling. Buhl (1982) goes so far as to say that it is these academic assumptions and prevailing ethics that most affect (both positively and negatively) faculty growth and development.

Thus a faculty development program will benefit from attending to how these traditional values and beliefs contribute to (or detract from) faculty members' satisfaction and productivity. Particularly if alternative careers are a part of the faculty development effort, care will have to be taken to build bridges between these new options and the traditional assumptions that faculty have used to find meaning in their work.

## Specific Strategies for Promoting Faculty Renewal

The current decrease in faculty development efforts in higher education (Centra, 1985) does not stem from a lack of documented approaches. We identified forty-nine separate strategies in our review of the literature. As Table 3.2 shows, strategies for development fall under three headings: the institution, the department/college, and the individual faculty member or administrator. These three headings indicate the object or entity targeted for development. Although it is logical to expect individual development to influence the institutional climate as a whole, or (conversely) for institutional or departmental development to benefit individual faculty members, strategies still seem to imply a primary target. The selection of the target is important, for it dictates the organizational level at which development is initiated and reflects underlying assumptions about the origin of developmental areas requiring attention.

Although the recent literature we surveyed emphasized quite persuasively the institution's role in sustaining faculty productivity, strategies aimed at developing the individual were mentioned much more frequently. In fact, individual strategies were discussed eight times more frequently than department-level strategies and six times more frequently than institution-level strategies. This finding reveals that early definitions saw vitality as being basically a faculty issue. Development activities were aimed most often at the individual faculty member and least often at the department or college, because vitality was usually considered a faculty "problem." Of all strategies reviewed (including those targeted at institutions, departments, and individuals), the most frequently mentioned were workshops (listed in eighty sources), sabbaticals and leaves (fifty-six sources), evaluation of faculty (fifty-three sources), and growth contracts or professional development plans (forty-five sources). The strategy cited most often in recent years (1985–1987) was alternative personnel policies (thirteen sources).

Focusing on the *institutional level,* alternative personnel policies were again the most frequently mentioned strategy during the period 1965–1987. Examples of alternative policies include mid-career change (either to another career or to new duties), early retirement and buyout options (Patton, 1978; AAHE Task Force on Professional Growth, 1984; Holden, 1985), flexible benefits (Nelsen and Siegel, 1980), early recruitment of faculty from graduate school (Clark, Corcoran, and Lewis, 1984), flexible staffing patterns (Gaff,

Table 3.2. Faculty Development Strategies Directed at Institutions,
Departments/Colleges, and Individual Faculty Members or Administrators
(with Cross-References to Authors in the Resource).

I. *Institution*

1. Redefinition of mission, goals (3, 17, 136, 137, 139, 163, 182, 193,
   210, 222, 242, 244, 255, 267, 269, 277, 283, 284, 285, 292, 309).
2. Academic planning, systemwide replanning (3, 9, 36, 107, 130, 134,
   136, 187, 193, 197, 242, 244, 253, 255, 314).
3. Internal centers for instructional and professional development (1,
   24, 32, 34, 86, 105, 106, 107, 134, 137, 140, 144, 161, 163, 197, 198, 199,
   247, 282, 294, 314).
4. Interinstitutional consortia, programs (29, 34, 71, 99, 102, 107, 134,
   139, 196, 198, 251, 255, 282, 294, 299, 303).
5. Alternative personnel policies (1, 20, 23, 27, 37, 57, 64, 68, 74, 91, 92,
   94, 100, 106, 107, 128, 129, 130, 135, 136, 137, 157, 163, 169, 178, 210,
   213, 219, 224, 237, 238, 244, 254, 275, 289, 301).
6. Institution-wide practical support (libraries, day care, parking) (19,
   59, 88, 100, 214, 244, 266, 277, 287).
7. Planned institutional research (50, 99, 105, 134, 138, 178, 196, 197,
   198, 232, 242, 277, 284).
8. Readjustment/rethinking of reward system (12, 20, 50, 73, 87, 106,
   131, 176, 231, 244, 254, 288, 289).

II. *Department/College*

1. Organizational development (31, 32, 45, 65, 71, 73, 107, 134, 153, 163,
   164, 191, 196, 197, 198, 199, 232, 243, 244, 254, 285, 303, 308, 314).
2. Faculty retreats (34, 36, 55, 65, 89, 96, 107, 139, 142, 160, 164, 196, 197,
   221, 232, 255, 277, 303, 308).
3. Intra- and interdisciplinary curricular reform (1, 8, 32, 34, 39, 81,
   107, 134, 136, 139, 160, 191, 193, 196, 197, 203, 242, 255, 257, 279, 292,
   303).
4. Evaluation of departmental programs and processes (3, 32, 36, 65,
   85, 86, 105, 107, 139, 140, 197, 214, 255, 283, 308, 314).
5. Department-wide practical support, technical assistance, computers, library, research, teaching, and assistants (20, 46, 55, 59, 65, 88,
   134, 148, 177, 196, 197, 214, 266, 277, 290).
6. Differential staffing patterns (16, 20, 106, 160, 203, 214, 242, 272,
   314).

III. *Individual Faculty Member or Administrator*

1. Sabbaticals and leaves (1, 12, 16, 20, 23, 27, 32, 59, 65, 70, 74, 79, 81,
   84, 86, 88, 89, 100, 106, 111, 129, 130, 131, 134, 136, 139, 151, 157,
   163, 182, 185, 196, 198, 199, 205, 214, 222, 224, 227, 249, 255, 260,
   263, 266, 267, 277, 283, 285, 287, 288, 289, 303, 305, 314).
2. Professional conferences, organizations, meetings, travel, networking (12, 16, 19, 20, 27, 65, 71, 84, 86, 88, 89, 99, 107, 134, 139, 163,

Table 3.2. Faculty Development Strategies Directed at Institutions,
Departments/Colleges, and Individual Faculty Members or Administrators
(with Cross-References to Authors in the Resource), Cont'd.

176, 182, 185, 190, 196, 197, 198, 199, 205, 214, 224, 227, 232, 255, 266, 267, 277, 285, 288, 292).

3. Self-instruction: materials, media, study rooms (12, 32, 36, 55, 65, 106, 107, 134, 137, 139, 140, 146, 148, 177, 185, 186, 194, 196, 197, 232, 233, 255, 262, 277, 287).

4. Faculty and staff education regarding development opportunities and institutional needs (35, 50, 65, 71, 79, 81, 89, 107, 122, 139, 172, 185, 214, 232, 243, 277, 303).

5. Seminars, symposia, forums, brown-bag lunches (1, 16, 20, 35, 65, 71, 84, 86, 88, 89, 91, 97, 105, 106, 111, 134, 139, 142, 148, 163, 170, 186, 190, 195, 196, 197, 199, 201, 205, 218, 220, 221, 232, 233, 255, 272, 277, 287, 288, 303, 308, 314).

6. Workshops: residential and short-term (1, 11, 20, 23, 31, 36, 41, 42, 43, 45, 48, 49, 55, 59, 65, 71, 81, 84, 86, 89, 95, 96, 103, 104, 106, 107, 111, 120, 125, 129, 131, 134, 139, 142, 151, 158, 163, 168, 183, 189, 190, 191, 194, 195, 196, 197, 199, 205, 214, 221, 224, 227, 232, 233, 234, 250, 255, 263, 267, 270, 274, 277, 281, 292, 299, 306, 308, 312, 314).

7. Skills training: courses, microteaching (1, 32, 51, 65, 107, 119, 123, 134, 142, 148, 165, 171, 184, 188, 194, 196, 197, 205, 221, 226, 263, 267, 277, 303, 305, 309).

8. Course redesign (12, 16, 65, 71, 81, 86, 125, 129, 168, 182, 186, 197, 205, 221, 275, 279, 285, 292).

9. Study in a second discipline (1, 12, 20, 55, 65, 107, 111, 128, 190, 199, 214, 222, 267, 308).

10. Expert consultation in teaching, research, or curriculum design (1, 13, 31, 32, 34, 43, 51, 55, 65, 71, 84, 86, 88, 89, 105, 107, 116, 126, 129, 134, 139, 148, 163, 172, 173, 175, 185, 186, 196, 197, 198, 205, 221, 232, 233, 234, 236, 247, 255, 259, 277, 290, 307, 308).

11. Team teaching, guest lecturers, cross-department teaching (1, 25, 31, 32, 36, 65, 89, 106, 107, 111, 115, 134, 214, 227, 310).

12. Special-service assignments (task forces, ad hoc committees) (1, 16, 19, 20, 65, 88, 178, 266, 284, 285).

13. Endowed chairs, professorships (65, 134, 214).

14. Visiting scholars (20, 59, 65, 81, 84, 86, 89, 106, 107, 110, 129, 205, 214, 215, 260, 289).

15. Faculty consulting (external) (1, 60, 61, 65, 74, 131, 132, 203, 214, 285).

16. Professional activity other than consulting (editing a professional journal, serving as program chair or grant reviewer) (1, 12, 16, 65, 173, 178, 203, 285, 289).

17. Growth contracts (1, 22, 27, 31, 32, 36, 51, 65, 74, 79, 80, 84, 86, 88, 99, 107, 131, 134, 137, 144, 151, 159, 164, 167, 196, 197, 211, 222, 224, 227, 230, 232, 254, 277, 285, 311, 314).

**Table 3.2. Faculty Development Strategies Directed at Institutions, Departments/Colleges, and Individual Faculty Members or Administrators (with Cross-References to Authors in the Resource), Cont'd.**

18. Retraining (1, 16, 20, 58, 64, 92, 99, 107, 129, 136, 137, 203, 210, 213, 214, 219, 222, 223, 237, 254, 275, 277, 283, 314).
19. Career counseling, life planning (1, 20, 23, 31, 32, 36, 84, 86, 96, 97, 99, 106, 107, 129, 131, 134, 137, 139, 163, 205, 214, 224, 237, 254, 289).
20. Release time (12, 32, 36, 46, 59, 65, 78, 79, 84, 86, 88, 89, 106, 107, 111, 125, 130, 139, 148, 163, 186, 196, 197, 205, 214, 222, 224, 227, 232, 255, 266, 272, 277, 287, 289, 308, 314).
21. Nonacademic internships and midcareer change programs (1, 16, 20, 23, 64, 65, 91, 96, 129, 130, 131, 134, 137, 139, 157, 163, 196, 224, 238, 288, 289, 311).
22. Faculty exchanges (1, 16, 20, 59, 65, 80, 106, 107, 113, 129, 137, 163, 196, 214, 227, 238, 254, 263, 275, 313).
23. Academic opportunities abroad (36, 107, 214).
24. Student-faculty colleagueship (25, 50, 65, 106, 107, 227).
25. Orientation for new faculty (32, 55, 78, 79, 81, 84, 86, 106, 134, 139, 142, 211, 217, 229, 279).
26. Socialization to faculty role (36, 46, 50, 92, 211, 216, 217).
27. Administrator development (1, 3, 12, 20, 36, 53, 54, 65, 105, 134, 163, 222, 224, 232, 246, 293).
28. Mentors (1, 25, 36, 46, 56, 81, 84, 86, 100, 106, 134, 148, 162, 163, 211, 214, 267).
29. Institutional awards for excellence, recognition (2, 20, 32, 46, 84, 86, 87, 88, 106, 185, 205, 214, 243, 255, 267, 272, 289).
30. Grants and special funds (1, 2, 16, 20, 25, 59, 65, 71, 81, 84, 86, 88, 89, 99, 105, 106, 107, 120, 125, 130, 133, 134, 151, 163, 168, 186, 194, 195, 196, 197, 205, 214, 224, 227, 228, 255, 260, 267, 277, 289, 311, 312, 314).
31. Fellowships (12, 21, 44, 49, 71, 94, 107, 165, 166, 186, 194, 197, 202, 232, 251, 268, 272, 289).
32. Informal, nontraditional publishing and other publications (1, 16, 19, 55, 88, 107, 135, 137, 196, 224, 227, 232, 234, 265, 277, 282, 285, 287).
33. Inter- and intradepartmental collaboration by individual faculty (1, 16, 65, 107, 139, 148, 203, 205, 214, 267, 284, 288, 289).
34. Evaluation of faculty (1, 16, 25, 30, 31, 32, 50, 63, 65, 78, 81, 82, 84, 85, 86, 89, 106, 107, 112, 114, 117, 120, 123, 128, 129, 134, 137, 139, 140, 145, 167, 168, 174, 188, 194, 196, 197, 204, 205, 209, 214, 224, 230, 232, 235, 260, 261, 274, 280, 282, 287, 289, 296, 297, 310).
35. Teaching consultation with faculty peers (1, 13, 16, 25, 32, 59, 65, 75, 79, 84, 85, 86, 107, 109, 115, 120, 129, 133, 134, 137, 147, 168, 171, 172, 189, 196, 197, 205, 218, 277, 313).

1985), time-shared positions (Toombs, 1983), and combinations of
these (Smith, 1978; Furniss, 1981a, 1981b). Bruss and Kutina (1981)
demonstrated how computer modeling and projections of income
and personnel could guide promotion and hiring. Others discussed
arguments for revising policies governing tenure, promotion, retirement, pension, incentive pay, and payment schedule (Gaff, 1976b;
Bedsole and Reddick, 1978; Rice, 1985).

Perhaps the most difficult institutional strategy we found
was that of redefining mission and goals. Gaff and others (1976–77)
and Gaff (1985) cited examples of numerous small liberal arts colleges involved with comprehensive change, such as redrawing the
boundaries between liberal and professional education and recruiting new student populations. Rice and Davis (1979) described how
an "institutional goal survey" helped newly merging "cluster" colleges fit into the University of the Pacific's revised mission and
goals.

Two of the most innovative institutional strategies found
were interinstitutional consortia and institutional research centers
(to guide planning and development and to contribute to the intellectual vitality on campus). Lindquist (1978a and 1980) was illuminating and convincing on both of these topics.

Turning to the *department level,* the most frequently cited
strategies were organizational development and curricular reform.
Grasha (1968), Buhl and Greenfield (1975), Lindquist (1980), and
Peterson (1984a) provided the conceptual framework for various
organizational development strategies. Wurster and McCartney
(1980), Whitcomb and Beck (1981), and Lanphear and Cardiff (1987)
also gave clear examples of organizational development procedures.
Administrator development was addressed by Nordvall (1979) and
Booth (1978). Curricular reform was well described by both Armstrong (1980) and Gaff (1985). Small, private liberal arts colleges
appeared to be the most active in curricular reform and organizational development, although some state university campuses used
these strategies as well.

Both early (Eble, 1971) and very recent writings (Mortimer
and others, 1985) emphasized the need for departments and colleges
to think more creatively about the assignment of faculty through
the use of flexible and differentiated staffing patterns. The depart-

mental strategies listed most frequently in recent articles (1985–1987), however, were organizational development, curricular reform, and practical support. Readers should note that practical support can occur both on the institutional level (for example, improved parking lots and library facilities) and on the departmental level (for example, clerical help, research assistants, computers, editorial or grant-writing assistance, supplies).

Finally, at the *individual level* workshops were clearly the strategy most commonly mentioned for any type of professional or personal development. Historically, workshops were practically synonymous with faculty development. More recently, however, many creative alternatives to the workshop have been found. Most frequently mentioned were strategies to reward and promote recognition of faculty (Chait, 1979). Other innovative, individual-level strategies included the use of mentors (Graham, 1968; Centra, 1972), peer consultation (Winsted, 1983a; Becker, 1981), expert consultation that involved traditional contingency management procedures (Boice, 1984a), socialization of new faculty (Bogen, 1978; Mauksch, 1982), faculty exchange (AAHE Task Force on Professional Growth, 1984; Worley, 1984–85), cross-department teaching (Nelsen, 1983b), and retraining (Patton, 1978; Rice, 1985). Hagberg (1981) and Maher (1981) and the AAHE Task Force on Professional Growth (the "Faculty Opportunities Audit," 1984) called for exploration of new roles, new definitions of faculty careers.

In summary, a broad array of strategies for faculty development have been suggested, and many have been implemented. Our review documented faculty renewal activities in 174 institutions across the country (63 colleges, 79 universities, and 32 professional schools). An additional 40 sponsors representing interinstitutional consortia, professional associations, and other organizations were also cited in the literature. (Certainly this documentation is not exhaustive, however. The lists of strategies and of recommendations are limited to the time period 1965–1987 and are confined to the sources in our review.)

### A New Focus in the Literature

Since 1965 the concept of vitality has evolved from a focus on the individual faculty member to a focus on the organization. The target for development strategies has also shifted accordingly. A trend in the most recent literature (1985–1987) suggests that a further shift has occurred: the most recent focus is on the country's entire professoriate and on higher education institutions as a whole. This shift in the target for development is accompanied by parallel changes in thinking about (1) the responsible parties for continued faculty and institutional vitality and (2) the types of appropriate strategies.

For example, Bowen and Schuster (1986) consider faculty morale to be of national concern, because of the strategic role faculty members play in our society. Accordingly, these authors consider this problem to be the responsibility of national entities and call for substantial corporate, foundation, and government programs to recruit and retain qualified scholars. They recommend the following: (1) funding grants to universities for recruiting new faculty during the current short-term decline in student enrollment, (2) early recruitment of potential faculty during their graduate training, (3) adjustments in tenure codes to decrease the risk of tenuring faculty and to increase opportunities for more faculty to achieve tenure, (4) support for personal development of midcareer faculty, and (5) increased faculty salaries.

Similarly, Lipetz, Bussigel, and Foley (1986, p. 141) consider faculty and institutional vitality a state responsibility. They describe a faculty exchange program proposed by the Illinois Board of Higher Education. Its aims were "(i) maintaining the vitality of faculty and academic programs through exchange, retraining, and updating skills, and (ii) contributing to the economic revitalization of the state." The authors continue: "As it seeks to integrate institutional and state needs with those of individual faculty members, the Illinois proposal broadens the concept of faculty development. Underlying the proposal is the assumption that if the State of Illinois is to remain competitive, it must attract new industry and retain present industries, both of which require well-trained and technically qualified personnel. This in turn requires that college and university faculty members be able to develop and maintain curricula that will produce a technically competent labor force. And this requires state assistance and encouragement."

Two other characteristics of the most recent literature should be mentioned. First, the literature suggests that an important key to faculty vitality lies in subtle elements of the work environment: a sense of community, a unique culture, opportunities for participation in governance, productive colleagues, pleasant surroundings, sensitive administration. Mention of these elements is scattered among earlier writings, but recently they are more persistently listed. Second, recent publications suggest that faculty vitality can be affected by upgrading "concrete" aspects of faculty lives, such as salaries, office facilities, classroom conditions, and laboratory buildings. The decline in faculty salaries and university structures has been frequently described in general writings on the state of the professoriate, but only recently have writers strongly suggested that these material aspects are affecting faculty vitality. In Bowen and Schuster's words (1986, p. 114), "The decline in either monetary conditions or working conditions alone would have been bad enough, but both together have been extraordinarily disquieting." Addressing both these subtle elements and these concrete aspects of faculty vitality calls for creative strategies not included in the tables in this chapter.

## Conclusion

Professors comprise the heart of the academic enterprise. In many respects a college or university is its faculty. The excellence of a higher education institution is inseparable from the excellence of its faculty. Hence the character of a college or university depends heavily on the vigor and commitment of its professors. An institution cannot offer a quality educational product without high-caliber, dedicated professors—in other words, a vital faculty.

Of course, this is true of many institutions, not just those of higher education. Many businesses—3M, IBM, Apple, and Rand, to name just a few—employ professionals, sometimes called "gold-collar workers," whose creativity, inventiveness, and enthusiasm determine the profit margin of their companies (Kelly, 1985). Still, no industry is as dependent on its human capital for excellence as is higher education. Thus faculty vitality—employee vitality—is of paramount importance for higher education.

The importance of a vital faculty is not a new revelation. As this chapter shows, vitality is a recurring "concern." The issue is especially timely and significant at present, however, because of current trends that threaten the morale and performance of professors on many college and university campuses.

Fortunately, the literature on faculty and institutional vitality has much to tell us about how to maintain productivity. In addition, several other bodies of literature provide new insight into the phenomena of faculty and institutional vitality. For example, the well-mined research on faculty careers (particularly on the careers of researchers) has much to tell us about the conditions that promote productivity (Pelz and Andrews, 1966; Andrews, 1979; Creswell, 1985). The business literature on "excellent companies," particularly those staffed by "gold-collar workers," provides generalizable insights into vital organizations (Kanter, 1983; Peters and Waterman, 1982). Finally, the literature on career development and professional development in higher education, and on organizational development, also has findings that apply to faculty and institutional vitality (Baldwin, 1979) and professional socialization (Lortie, 1975; Corcoran and Clark, 1984).

As Maher (1982, p. 6) notes, "In the quest for vitality, it may be that we are seeking an elusive chemistry that catalyzes a rare integration of individual and institutional energy, commitment, and creativity. . . . For the sake of quality in our institutions and effectiveness in our educational programs, however, we had best renew the quest."

The quest for personal, professional, and institutional vitality to which Maher commands us is surely difficult and probably never-ending. No longer can we take the vitality of our faculty or of our higher education institutions for granted. Faculty and administration must purposefully design an organizational climate to support personal productivity and institutional vitality.

As Gardner (1987, p. 17), a founding thinker in self-renewal, reminds us, "Life is endless trying, and the human organism is well designed to deal with it." Persons charged with maintaining faculty and institutional vitality who draw on this innate ability of faculty members, and on the lessons from past vitality efforts, will be well armed for the task.

**References**

Works referenced in Chapter Three are included in the bibliographical Resource at the end of the book.

 *PART TWO*

# Programs and Strategies for Professional, Personal, and Organizational Renewal

Part Two describes five very different program areas or activities designed to improve the quality of faculty careers through enhanced approaches to professional development. The emphasis in this part is on emerging, rather than traditional, aspects of faculty development and renewal. For each of the five topics presented, examples are cited of campuses that have implemented activities successfully.

The first of these chapters raises the critical issue of the need for fresh approaches in preparing new professors. Given the impending need to appoint hundreds of thousands of new recruits over the next two decades, Jack Schuster makes the case that graduate schools, in conjunction with academic departments and faculty development offices, must shoulder greater responsibility in preparing this enormous new cohort. He argues that the traditional discipline-bounded emphasis on preparation must be supplemented by systematic attention to effective teaching and to the norms of the academic profession.

In Chapter Five Daniel Wheeler describes a process designed to facilitate faculty in examining their careers. Of particular concern is an aging professoriate, many of whose members made an *early* decision, if a definite decision at all, to enter academic life. The author suggests that conditions of academic life have changed and that in many cases the individual faculty members have altered their priorities. The resulting disjunction sometimes necessitates a reexamination of the original career decision. In addition, career consulting, which can be a catalyst for continual growth and development, can help demoralized professors become "unstuck" by initiating the necessary steps to regain professional vitality.

Chapter Six describes a health-oriented movement that was initially seen as somewhat of a fad in academe. Joan North and John Munson demonstrate that "wellness" gained acceptance in corporate settings because increased attention to health promotion activities proved to be cost-effective: the investment in wellness activities actually appeared to save money. More recently, a number of colleges and universities learned that wellness programs can benefit the institution and its staff. Steadily gaining acceptability, the wellness orientation provides an opportunity to respond to faculty members' personal needs within a larger professional-organizational context.

Employee assistance programs (EAPs) are described by Elizabeth Hosokawa in Chapter Seven. Originally begun in the business world to counteract a decrease in employee effectiveness attributable to substance and alcohol abuse, many assistance programs have been broadened to combat other psychological problems and, in some cases, to address career issues as well. A growing number of campuses have tailored the EAP concept to their particular needs. The resulting activities, known generically as faculty assistance programs (FAPs), are among the most recent innovations in the realm of faculty development.

Chapter Eight presents early retirement as a strategy for providing organizational flexibility as well as a graceful way for faculty to depart the campus. Jay Chronister asserts that while faculty often choose to retire for financial reasons, they also opt for retirement because of a lesser attachment to their work. Although some critics foresee the exodus of too many talented faculty members, that appears not yet to be the campus experience. One key finding: most faculty who have chosen early retirement indicate satisfaction with that decision. The author concludes that "faculty renewal cannot be achieved solely through a process of faculty replacement" and that early retirement programs should be used in conjunction with other strategies.

4

# Strengthening Career Preparation for Prospective Professors

*Jack H. Schuster*

The topic of faculty development focuses, naturally enough, on the needs and activities of faculty members—junior faculty, senior faculty, in-between faculty; part-time faculty, women faculty, minority faculty; engaged faculty, disengaged faculty, disengaging faculty. Sometimes the faculty development topic extends to others—principally, spouses of faculty members. Often the topic encompasses the role of administrators in the development or revitalization process. But overlooked in the exploration of faculty development is a critically important population: those who are about to *become* "the faculty"—the prospective professors.

Most of these future faculty members at some time will be graduate assistants. How they are prepared and imbued with attitudes about their future academic careers undoubtedly influences, perhaps powerfully, the attitudes, knowledge, and skills that they subsequently will bring to their faculty assignments. More amenable than veteran faculty members, these trainees stand to benefit handsomely from well-conceived *pre*faculty development programs.

The apprentice faculty members exist in large numbers, are concentrated in relatively few institutions, and are quite readily identifiable. They are almost universally enrolled in doctoral programs (except those who will teach in two-year institutions) and are often employed as graduate assistants—specifically, as teaching assistants or research assistants. Many of them—the substantial majority, in many fields—are aspiring to become regular, full-time, tenure-track faculty members. Other graduate assistants appear to have no such ambition, and studies clearly establish the high proportions, especially in fields such as psychology and chemistry, who elect employment in nonacademic settings. Nonetheless, most faculty members, at least at four-year institutions, do hold doctorates and in the course of their training most of them were employed as graduate assistants of some sort, for a semester or even for several years.

No one knows precisely what proportion of current professors once participated in some form of graduate assistantship as part of their preparation for an academic career. That question apparently has not been asked in national faculty surveys since the early 1970s, when a survey of faculty members was conducted by the American Council on Education. Based on 42,345 usable responses from faculty members actively teaching in 1972–73, that survey provides the best estimates of faculty members' participation in graduate teaching and research assistantships (Bayer, 1973, p. 5). Two items on that questionnaire asked, respectively, whether the respondent had "ever held a student teaching assistantship" or a "student research assistantship" (appendix C).

Slightly under half of all faculty members actively teaching at that time, in institutions of all types, reported that they had "held a student teaching assistantship." The frequency was much lower for research assistantships (p. 27):

|  | All Institutions | | |
| --- | --- | --- | --- |
|  | *Men* | *Women* | *Total* |
| Teaching assistantship (TA) | 48.9% | 34.1% | 45.9% |
| Research assistantship (RA) | 31.9% | 15.3% | 28.6% |

The extent of these experiences, as would be expected, progressed from modest but by no means negligible levels among faculty members at two-year colleges (nearly one-third) to somewhat more than half of all university faculty members:

|      | Two-Year Colleges | | | Four-Year Colleges | | | Universities | | |
|------|-------|-------|-------|-------|-------|-------|-------|-------|-------|
|      | *M* | *W* | *Tot.* | *M* | *W* | *Tot.* | *M* | *W* | *Tot.* |
| TA   | 32.8% | 24.1% | 30.7% | 49.7% | 34.2% | 46.3% | 54.5% | 40.3% | 52.1% |
| RA   | 14.0 | 9.4 | 12.9 | 29.1 | 14.5 | 25.9 | 41.3 | 20.0 | 37.8 |

It is evident that much smaller proportions of women in all institutions were afforded assistantships, especially research assistantships. This is explained in part by the fact that twice as many faculty men as women had earned a Ph.D. or Ed.D.: 36.9 percent compared to 18.2 percent.

Based on the same data, Drew (1985) subsequently reported the frequencies for academic scientists. The responses are provided by three categories of universities: research universities 1 and 2 (based upon the Carnegie classification scheme) and "second- and third-tier universities." The results show very high levels of participation in TA and RA programs (pp. 84, 88, 92):

|                            | Research Univ. 1 | Research Univ. 2 | 2nd-/3rd-Tier Univ. |
|----------------------------|------|------|------|
| *Teaching Assistantships*  |      |      |      |
| Chemistry                  | 87%  | 84%  | 89%  |
| Mathematics                | 76   | 76   | 85   |
| Physics                    | 68   | 76   | 79   |
| *Research Assistantships*  |      |      |      |
| Chemistry                  | 81   | 85   | 77   |
| Mathematics                | 62   | 60   | 49   |
| Physics                    | 79   | 86   | 83   |

In fact, Drew's figures show a dramatically higher frequency of assistantships among these scientists than do Bayer's figures for all faculty.

Various estimates confirm that in the mid 1980s, large proportions of graduate students—and hence future faculty members—passed through the graduate assistant portal (see Sell, 1987, pp. 1-2;

Stokely, 1987, p. 310). A more recent estimate finds that among students receiving doctorates in 1987, 70 percent of those in the arts and humanities and 55 percent of those in the social sciences had held teaching assistantships (Bowen and Sosa, 1989, p. 174). Given the increasing proportion of faculty members who hold doctorates (compared to 1972-73), perhaps 70 to 75 percent of arts and sciences faculty members at all four-year institutions, including liberal arts colleges, were once TAs or RAs. Probably the rate is lower—maybe 50 to 60 percent—among professional school faculty, fewer of whom entered upon academic careers directly from graduate school programs. A lower proportion still—perhaps 20 or 25 percent—would apply to community college faculty members, relatively few of whom trained in doctorate-granting programs.

Thus, by any reckoning, the percentage of today's faculty members who once served as TAs or RAs must be substantial at the four-year institutions. Because it will be necessary to appoint hundreds of thousands of persons to faculty positions during the next several decades (Bowen and Schuster, 1986), the efficacy of such programs will be an important factor in preparing future cohorts of faculty.

Arguably, the most intensive "development" of faculty members—the experience with the most enduring effects in shaping professional attitudes and behaviors—takes place during this apprenticeship phase. As the late Joseph Katz was fond of noting, the strongest influence on academics, next to mother, is graduate school. And that is probably not much of an exaggeration, if any.

In sum, because very high proportions of future professors will experience some sort of graduate assistant training, and because so many new professors must be hired in the foreseeable future, the quality of the graduate assistant experience will be critical—more critical than usual—to the ability of colleges and universities to perform their missions effectively. Accordingly, this chapter seeks to develop two central propositions, each focusing on the role of graduate schools in preparing future generations of faculty members. The first holds that although academic departments today bear the primary role—indeed, virtually the exclusive role—in preparing future professors, graduate schools (or divisions) *should* play a more prominent role in their preparation. Second, graduate schools *can* make a much more substantial contribution in preparing future professors than they typically do—*if* they are willing to exert their potential influence.

## The Case for Intensifying Graduate Schools' Involvement

Research universities are the filters through which most future faculty members pass. As is noted frequently, these institutions function as "the training ground for new faculty members" and, in so doing, they establish the norms for the academic profession (Burke, 1987, p. 200).

However, within the university, graduate schools have assumed a very limited role—indeed, an excessively narrow role—in the preparation of future professors. The reality, as I previously noted, is that American professors almost universally experience intensive graduate or professional school training. Professors are prepared, socialized, and acculturated during their graduate student years. Jules LaPidus, president of the Council of Graduate Schools, has put it succinctly: "The scholarly nexus through which interested students become faculty members is the graduate schools" (1987, p. 6). However, there is little evidence to suggest that graduate *schools* (or, for that matter, individual graduate *programs*—that is, academic departments) normally see the preparation of professors as one of their more important roles—despite their purview of graduate education (Sell, 1987). Indeed, eighty-two administrators of graduate school and academic affairs offices surveyed in 1986 (at 200 universities) ranked "developing TAs as future faculty" twelfth in importance among twenty-four activities and issues (pp. 8–11). Simply put, the historical preoccupation of graduate schools has been the promotion of scholarship. As Oleson and Voss (1979, p. 15) have noted, "Their distinctive purpose was to develop productive scholars and scientists."

The argument that graduate schools *should* play a prominent role in the preparation of those who aspire to become faculty members is predicated on three premises:

1. Graduate education succeeds admirably in providing cohorts of would-be professors with essential content in their fields and

training in the ways of doing research. They provide, too, although very unevenly, models of what professors actually do in their multifaceted professional lives.

2. Yet graduate education does a poor job in two crucial respects: facilitating effective preparation for teaching and, more neglected still, providing perspective about the values and norms of academic life.

3. Accordingly, many neophyte faculty members are inadequately prepared to teach, and fewer still have an informed vision of the academic profession and the complex institutions in which professors practice.

Indisputably, academic *departments* play the dominant role in transmitting the body of knowledge and appropriate research methodologies vital to a graduate student's preparation. Lindquist (1981) speaks to the salience of specialization in the process of becoming a professor: "We learn what professors and administrators do, what constitute college teaching and learning, by experiencing higher education for a good eight to ten years as students. . . . [We] get channeled quickly into a major field. . . . Our professors drill us in their subjects and instill in us the norms and values of the academic profession. . . . A central feature of this system is the future professor's becoming an increasingly specialized scholar and researcher" (pp. 732–733).

But beyond that salient departmental role, what is accomplished to prepare future cohorts of teacher-scholars? On most campuses the answer appears to be "very little," especially in two critical domains: preparing graduate students to become effective teachers, and familiarizing them with the normative issues of academic organization and the academic profession. In these crucial areas, campus endeavors in general—and graduate school efforts in particular—appear to be badly inadequate.

*Teaching.* First, consider the matter of teaching. A national graduate teaching assistant/associate survey by Syracuse University researchers establishes a point of departure: "Teaching assistants are not only responsible for a major portion of undergraduate lower division instruction at most major research universities, but they are also the potential faculty members of tomorrow. Unfortunately, there is a general perception that the teaching performance of many teaching assistants is poor" (Diamond and Gray, 1987, p. 1).

It is unfortunate that a problem so important, and one so widely acknowledged, receives relatively little attention from administrators campuswide or at departmental levels. Academics *do* decry the unevenness of preparation for teaching—a situation that has existed for perhaps as long as higher learning. (John of Salisbury complained about poor teaching at the University of Paris almost a millennium ago.) Contemporary students complain regularly about poor teaching, and horror stories occasionally surface.

At least two state legislatures have intervened. The Illinois legislature has enacted a statute mandating that foreign students must possess adequate English language skills prior to obtaining teaching assistantships. And the California legislature passed two multifaceted resolutions in 1987. The first (Assembly Concurrent Resolution 39) presses public colleges and universities to pay substantially greater attention to the quality of teaching (Secter, 1987). The second (ACR 41) focuses on the training, supervision, and evaluation of TAs; among the measure's several provisions designed to ensure more effective teaching assistants is this clause: "In cases where a prospective teaching assistant is unable to demonstrate competence in oral communication, he or she should be required to improve fluency and communication skills through courses, workshops, or programs specifically designed for this purpose before classroom teaching begins . . ." (California State Legislature, 1987). It seems likely that other states will follow suit if universities fail to upgrade the language competence of foreign teaching assistants or, more broadly, fail to address the general issue of teaching assistant preparation.

This is not to suggest that all or even most teaching assistants and new faculty members are less than adequately prepared. The evidence suggests otherwise: that most of them, in fact, do reasonably well in meeting their demanding mix of responsibilities. As Jencks and Riesman concluded two decades ago, "While the teaching assistants who fill in for those senior men who flee the classroom are often deprecated by status-conscious undergraduates, they frequently know more than senior faculty and in the better places may also care more" (1968, p. 512). At the same time, the evidence strongly establishes that the need exists for substantial improvement—a proposition supported by the Syracuse study.

This study, the most ambitious of its kind, surveyed 4,230 teaching assistants at eight major research universities (Diamond and Gray, 1987, p. 5). Six of the institutions were public (Oregon State University, Texas A & M University, the University of California, Davis, the University of California, Los Angeles, the University of Nebraska, and the University of Tennessee); two were independent institutions (Stanford University and Syracuse University). Responses were received from 1,357 teaching assistants, constituting a 32 percent response rate. (Response rates by campus ranged from 26 to 47 percent.) Even though more needs to be known about this study before we judge how representative its findings may be, the results deserve close attention.

- 75 percent of the responding TAs reported that they planned to teach in a college or university after graduation. The interest in academic careers was widespread among respondents. As Diamond and Gray note, "With the exception of Architecture (40%), Communications (48%), and Law (17%), over 50% of the respondents of every discipline planned to teach after receiving their degrees . . ." (pp. 5, 17).
- One-fifth of the teaching assistants reported that they were not getting adequate guidance and supervision from the department or college in which they taught (pp. 36–41).
- Just over one-fifth (21 percent) of the respondents indicated that they were not given enough time to adequately fulfill their teaching responsibilities (pp. 30–33).
- High proportions of the teaching assistants reported (pp. 52–53) that they desired more training in such areas as evaluating oneself as a teacher (72%), evaluating one's course (71%), lecturing (60%), conducting classroom discussion (55%), using media (54%), and preparing tests (53%).

In all, the evidence strongly suggests that preparation for teaching is at best uneven and leaves considerable room for improvement.

*Professionalization.* Graduate training inevitably provides a strong measure of socialization to the *discipline*—to the so-called "invisible college." But that process obscures the importance of the larger, too-often-neglected socialization experience—namely, acculturation to the more general norms of the academic profession. As LaPidus has observed, "In most cases the relationship to the discipline . . . is inherent; that to the university is incidental" (1987, p. 3). There are many elements of academic life that bear examination in graduate school. While the "invisible college" affords a rigorous course of *intra*discipline instruction and provides, in part through osmosis, an introduction to the norms of the academy, that is not enough. There is much that professors-to-be can and should become familiar with during their period of preparation—matters, as suggested below, that transcend the boundaries of academic departments. There is much more to becoming a professor than simply becoming a competent anthropologist, engineer, historian, microbiologist.

The barriers to a more generic socialization process are several, including doubts about both content and method. As to content, the academy remains highly dubious of the proposition that there is a corpus of useful, relevant information and concepts about the academy and about academic careers that *should* be passed on to novitiates. Doubts about methods for doing so contribute further to the resistance as skepticism undermines the notion that such matters as academic norms *can* be conveyed sensitively, usefully, effectively. The skeptics' biases are not without foundation; the task of transmitting insights about the nuance-rich academy and about academic careers is not easily accomplished. But the study of higher education has produced a wealth of relevant material, and that material *can* be conveyed in useful ways to would-be professors. In sum, useful models do exist for teaching about the institutions and careers in which the majority of these TAs will be spending much, if not all, of their professional lives.

*Countermeasures.* What might be done to redress these shortcomings? Graduate schools should assess the extent to which problems exist and then help to initiate programs designed to partially offset the problems. Some graduate schools already have significant programs in place; most do not. Some campuses have instructional centers that appear to meet these needs effectively. The University of Georgia (see Chapter Nine) and the University of California, San Diego come readily to mind. But most campuses have not developed effective programs. Thus, assuming that no other unit on campus is already playing a major campuswide role, the graduate school should initiate a coordinated program designed to help better prepare prospective professors.

What, then, are the desirable elements of such a program? Consider six aspects of a systematic effort: assessment, a campuswide strategy, specific interventions, "certification," evaluation, and recruitment.

1. *Assessment of teaching assistant preparedness.* Campuses should make a serious effort to assess the effectiveness of their teaching assistants and to identify specific problems for which help is needed. Such an effort might utilize the questionnaire developed for the national study of teaching assistants referred to earlier, or an even more detailed survey recently developed at the University of California. (Existing faculty development programs may already be performing this task.) In any event, efforts should be made to determine whether teaching assistants have adequate access to whatever teaching improvement facilities exist on campus.

2. *Formulating a campuswide strategy for intervention.* Much is already known about the generic needs of current faculty members and, accordingly, about those who aspire to faculty careers. This gives rise to two opposing campus strategies. Specifically, graduate schools will need to balance the readily available opportunity to draw on well-established principles for developing effective TA programs against the "political" reasons on a particular campus to start anew—perhaps beginning with a needs assessment of sorts—in order to enable that campus (especially the faculty) to claim ownership of programs ultimately proposed.

3. *Interventions.* No "right way" to organize a proper development program for teaching assistants has emerged. Given the differences among institutions, there may be doubts about whether a single strategy would fit divergent institutions. But campuswide intervention is not likely to occur unless the graduate school/division takes some initiative. There are a host of proposals and models

from which to choose (Chism, 1987). These range from more radical approaches—for instance, the utilization of an internship-residency sequence patterned after programs for training physicians—to straightforward seminars that require minimal organizational upheaval (Jencks and Riesman, 1968, pp. 537–539). Most appear to agree that ongoing supervision, especially by experienced TAs, coupled with the teaching of essentials of effective teaching, works best (Stokely, 1987).

Whether the organizational response is substantial or modest, it is important that the institution develop special seminars for prospective faculty members. Such seminars probably ought to be required of all new TAs and be open to others who are contemplating academic careers. Model seminars come in many forms. These include, for example, a seminar offered by the Teaching Resource Center and required for foreign TAs at the University of California, Davis, and a four-course interdepartmental specialty in college teaching offered, as an outside minor, at Florida State University.

The content of such seminars ought to address major issues in the teaching-learning process. Useful topics might include lecturing, guiding classroom discussion, counseling and advising, evaluation, test construction, ethical issues, teaching critical thinking, and so forth. But that is not nearly enough. Such seminars should seek also to acquaint participants with basic information about American higher education and the academic profession. This effort might include modules on the history of American colleges and universities and the evolution of their missions, on the basic elements of organization and governance, on the differences among types of institutions, and on the academic profession itself. These seminars should address some of the major policy statements of the American Association of University Professors that establish principles of academic freedom and shared governance. Other segments might broach such topics as the financing of higher education, the relationship of the public policy process to postsecondary education, and the rudiments of the academic labor market.

I believe that a great many *faculty* members are largely unfamiliar with many of these matters, sometimes to an appalling degree, and that ignorance on these topics is widespread among graduate students. Clearly little if any attention is paid to these topics in the preparation of teaching assistants (Parrett, 1987). While the direct consequences of such omissions cannot be readily demonstrated, it is safe to assume that higher education ultimately pays a dear price—both in terms of internal functioning and of external relations—for the shortcomings that attend faculty preparation efforts.

Another essential element of the preparation process would be educating neophytes about *diversity* in American higher education—specifically, diversity among learners. (This is a topic that a good many current faculty members would do well to examine as well.) Consider for a moment the tidal shifts, in a remarkably short span of time, in the characteristics of postsecondary education students. The full-time eighteen-to-twenty-two-year-old white male student, in residence at a four-year institution, was the norm—or certainly he was the *modal* student—at a time when a large proportion of today's faculty members began their academic careers. Today, however, that norm, as is well known, has been rapidly disappearing. This "traditional" college student is swiftly receding into the pages of history. More specifically, among contemporary postsecondary students:

- Half attend on a part-time basis.
- More than half are women.
- Only two-fifths are twenty-one or under.
- About 14 percent are not white (which is about two and a half times their 6 percent proportion in 1960).

In all, no more than one in six contemporary college and university students actually fits the traditional mold so prominent only two decades ago.

With growing proportions of today's students being "nontraditional," a critical question arises: What is being done to accommodate these "new learners"? The answer appears to be "precious little" insofar as the preparation of future professors is concerned. Thus concentrated attention needs to be paid to these new learners—especially older students, minorities, and part-timers. There are crucially important lessons for would-be faculty members to learn about teaching strategies designed to engage these learners more effectively. And what better place to start than in graduate schools, which can encourage and facilitate at least *some* degree of orientation to the *next* generation of teacher-scholars? Moreover, we would do well to recall that at many universities the TAs are already engaged in teaching a significant proportion of undergraduate classes, especially at the lower-division level.

An important though largely underutilized resource for TA education exists on many of the campuses that prepare the largest numbers of future faculty members. These are the faculty members who teach in graduate programs in higher education. These programs, located at many of the leading public universities and some of the independent ones, have the potential for making a highly significant contribution. Many of the faculty members affiliated with such programs are well equipped to teach about topics that address the background and contextual elements of higher education—topics that are critical to a well-prepared future professoriate.

4. *"Certification."* Probably a certificate of some sort should be awarded to those who complete, say, a two-seminar sequence. The purpose would not be to certify that a graduate student is absolutely qualified to be a professor or even a competent teacher. No such sequence of seminars would, or should, suffice for those purposes. Rather, the purposes would be (1) to signal to the enrollees that the campus takes the preparation role seriously and (2) to provide some evidence to prospective employers that a graduate student has had at least some exposure to the topics of effective teaching and the culture and organization of higher education.

5. *Evaluation.* Whatever activities exist or are created to improve the pedagogical skills of future professors, a systematic effort to evaluate the effectiveness of those programs is critically important.

6. *Recruitment.* Such a development program might also attempt to encourage those students with considerable career mobility—perhaps especially outstanding undergraduates—to entertain seriously the prospect of an academic career. A series of faculty panels and talks on the joys and frustrations of academic life could be quite useful in influencing talented students to seriously consider an academic career.

The six areas outlined above are intended to illustrate the

kinds of activities that graduate schools might promote and facilitate—even take operational responsibility for—depending on local circumstances.

## Graduate Schools' Ability to Make a Difference

But *can* graduate schools really make a difference? Despite a number of obstacles, graduate schools almost surely can, in fact, make a substantial contribution in the preparation of the next generation of teacher-scholars.

Realism requires that we recognize that graduate deans and graduate schools (or graduate divisions) are in some respects anomalies. Like everything else in the sprawling, decentralized world of higher education, both the organization of the graduate education administrative units and their influence come in endless variations. Ordinarily, however, the graduate sector is seriously constrained in its ability to shape such fundamentals as curriculum and academic personnel matters, and its influence over campus research policies varies markedly from one campus to another. Accordingly, there should be no illusion that graduate schools possess magic wands that can be waved to generate fresh resources or to readily transform campus practices that bear on the preparation of future generations of professors. It is widely and wisely assumed that discipline-bounded preparation ought to be left in the hands of academic departments; thus decentralization and, in consequence, diffused influence are hallmarks of graduate education. This conviction is grounded in the powerful reality that the disciplines have different cultures, values, methods, and labor markets (Clark, 1987). Accordingly, strategies that rely too heavily on centralized, campuswide approaches to the preparation of professors would be ill-conceived and politically vulnerable. So there are obstacles aplenty to any graduate school having influence in these matters.

Conceding that barriers to a robust graduate school role abound, I nonetheless assert that graduate schools have the means to accomplish much more than they now do in redressing glaring shortcomings in the preparation of tomorrow's faculty members. Speaking to the role of graduate schools, LaPidus has noted, "TAs are part of the undergraduate teaching force, and department chairs as well as college deans may feel that graduate deans have no business interfering in what is basically an undergraduate instructional issue. But if the issue is defined in terms of the preparation of future faculty members, it becomes the business of all those to whom the continuing quality and vitality of the faculty is important" (1987, p. 10).

Graduate school leadership is well situated to address the problems at hand for at least five reasons:

- *Legitimacy.* The fragmented organization of universities means that few offices have a scope of responsibility that transcends the more parochial interests of the departments and colleges that the university comprises. On the other hand, the graduate school or division cuts across those boundaries. Its purview *is* graduate education. It necessarily shares in the responsibility for preparing future professors, from anthropology to zoology; the graduate school possesses inherent legitimacy for addressing graduate education writ large, including the issue of preparation. The only question is to what degree.
- *Familiarity.* While graduate schools have no monopoly on information about the problems and no special wisdom about effective countermeasures, they nevertheless are familiar with the nature and dimensions of the preparation problem. Their vantage point affords views across the many subcultures of the academy.
- *Variegated role.* Every graduate school setting is idiosyncratic; no single formula is conceivable to describe *an* appropriate graduate school role. On some campuses the graduate school can take operational responsibility for some programs designed to prepare professors more effectively; on others, the appropriate role—possibly the only acceptable role—would be that of a facilitator and catalyst—and advocate, of course. Thus the graduate school role will necessarily vary from campus to campus, but the *minimally* appropriate role surely is to encourage and facilitate significant activities.
- *Timeliness.* With report after report underscoring the shortcomings of undergraduate teaching, the time is ripe for graduate schools to become more creative in preparing more effectively

our future corps of college and university faculty members—a
corps that, not incidentally, is currently shouldering a significant fraction of undergraduate teaching.

• *Leadership vacuum.* Leadership to address issues of preparation
throughout the campus is commonly lacking. On most campuses a veritable vacuum exists, insofar as these issues are concerned, and the graduate school can act to fill the void. Graduate
schools are neither impotent to influence the complex environment in which they exist nor incapable of formulating and facilitating realistic programs to address pressing needs. They need
to become more involved—minimally as effective advocates, catalysts, and facilitators. Beyond that minimal role, and depending on the latitude afforded them, graduate schools may well be
positioned to take operational responsibility for key elements of
TA preparation as well. In such endeavors the prospects for
close collaboration with other units on campus will vary considerably from one setting to another. A successful approach may
depend upon graduate school initiatives to build a campus coa-
lition involving campus faculty development programs and academic departments interested in perspectives extending beyond
their immediate disciplines.

### Conclusion

In sum, as higher education moves toward a period of massive hiring, graduate schools must be open to supplementing the
academic departments' dominant role in transmitting the body of
knowledge and research methodologies crucial to the preparation of
new professors. Toward this end, graduate schools have a key role to
play in harnessing the capacities of the campus to teach *about*
higher education, to transmit the ethos of the academic workplace,
to pass on the culture and the ethics of the academic profession.
This role, though a supplemental one, should in no way be viewed
as incidental; it should *not* be seen as an optional add-on, included
only if ample resources somehow materialize.

Change will not come easily; the obstacles are manifest. As
Frederick Rudolph, a persistent critic of the present system, has
observed, "Professionalism among the professors, their narrow spe-

cialization, the complete neglect in their training of any concern with teaching or with any professional responsibility other than to scholarship, are conditions that inhibit optimism" (1984, p. 41). Addressing the threshold issue of graduate education's propensity to resist change, Paul Albrecht, a former board chair of the Council of Graduate Schools, has noted, "In the first place, some attitudinal changes on the part of faculty and administration would be very helpful. Principally, it is time . . . to embrace the future with its needs and opportunities. It would be desirable all around to move from a defensive static posture to a more aggressive, forward-looking one" (1984, p. 18).

Precisely how a particular graduate school might define and implement its role will vary considerably from one setting to another, of course. Much work lies just ahead in preparing the many thousands of new entrants into academic careers. Toward that end, the potential contribution of graduate schools, beyond the custom of near-total deference to academic departments, is enormous.

### References

Albrecht, P. A. "Opportunity and Impediment in Graduate Program Innovation." In M. J. Pelczar and L. C. Solmon (eds.), *Keeping Graduate Programs Responsive to National Needs.* New Directions for Higher Education, no. 46. San Francisco: Jossey-Bass, 1984.

Association of American Colleges. *Integrity in the College Curriculum: A Report to the Academic Community.* Washington, D.C.: Association of American Colleges, 1985.

Bayer, A. E. "Teaching Faculty in Academe: 1972–73." *ACE Research Reports,* 1973, *8* (entire issue 2).

Bowen, H. R., and Schuster, J. H. *American Professors: A National Resource Imperiled.* New York: Oxford University Press, 1986.

Bowen, W. G., and Sosa, J. A. *Prospects for Faculty in the Arts and Sciences: A Study of Factors Affecting Demand and Supply, 1987 to 2002.* Princeton, N.J.: Princeton University Press, 1989.

Burke, D. L. "The Academic Marketplace of the 1980s: Appointment and Termination of Assistant Professors." *Review of Higher Education,* 1987, *10* (3), 199–214.

California State Legislature. Assembly Concurrent Resolution 41, Chapter 103, Statutes of 1987.

Chism, N. V. (ed.). *Institutional Responsibilities and Responses in the Employment and Education of Teaching Assistants: Readings from a National Conference.* Columbus, Ohio: Center for Teaching Excellence, Ohio State University, 1987.

Clark, B. R. *The Academic Life: Small Worlds, Different Worlds.* Princeton, N.J.: Carnegie Foundation for the Advancement of Teaching, 1987.

Diamond, R. M., and Gray, P. *National Study on Teaching Assistants.* Syracuse, N.Y.: Center for Instructional Development, Syracuse University, 1987.

Drew, D. E. *Strengthening Academic Science.* New York: Praeger, 1985.

Jencks, C., and Riesman, D. *The Academic Revolution.* New York: Doubleday, 1968.

LaPidus, J. B. "Preparing Faculty: Graduate Education's Role." *AAHE Bulletin,* 1987, *39* (9 and 10), 3-6.

Lindquist, J. "Professional Development." In A. W. Chickering and Associates, *The Modern American College: Responding to the New Realities of Diverse Students and a Changing Society.* San Francisco: Jossey-Bass, 1981.

Oleson, A., and Voss, J. (eds.). *The Organization of Knowledge in Modern America, 1860-1920.* Baltimore, Md.: Johns Hopkins University Press, 1979. (Cited in Clark, 1987, p. 34.)

Parrett, J. L. "A Ten-Year Review of TA Training Programs: Trends, Patterns, and Common Practices." In N. V. Chism (ed.), *Institutional Responsibilities and Responses in the Employment and Education of Teaching Assistants.* Columbus, Ohio: Center for Teaching Excellence, Ohio State University, 1987.

Rudolph, F. "The Power of Professors: The Impact of Specialization and Professionalism on the Curriculum." *Change,* 1984, *16* (4), 12-17, 41.

Secter, B. "Foreign Teachers Create Language Gap in Colleges." *Los Angeles Times,* Sept. 27, 1987.

Sell, G. R. "Preparing Teaching Assistants as Future Faculty: Is This Really the University's Objective?" Paper presented at annual meeting of Association for the Study of Higher Education, Baltimore, Md., Nov. 1987.

Stokely, L. "Turning Specialists into Professors: The Preparation of Graduate Students for College Teaching." In *The Greening of the Future: Proceedings of the Seventh Annual Lilly Conference on College Teaching,* Miami University, Oxford, Ohio, Nov. 1987.

5

# Providing Career
# Consulting Services
# to Midcareer Faculty

*Daniel W. Wheeler*

Career consulting is probably as old as careers. And university
teaching is one of the oldest careers. Yet curiously, career consulting
for professors, on a systematic basis, is a very recent phenomenon—
one that is only now catching on. This chapter seeks to describe
faculty career consulting and to establish the expanding need for,
and opportunities presented by, the process. By no means is working with a faculty consultant a panacea; however, such consultation
can provide a more objective perspective on considering major career adjustments or fine-tuning an existing career.

Becoming a faculty member has a similarity to being called
to a religious order. There is a sense of performance of noble work
more prestigious than that of other occupations. The "one-life, one-
career imperative" described by Sarason (1977) dominates the profession. This imperative is intensified and reinforced through the
graduate school socialization process. This theme has been well
described: "The academic life is a good one for many: careers as
teacher-scholars in colleges and universities can be intellectually
stimulating and personally fulfilling. The independence, freedom,
and autonomy that characterize academic life are also highly valued
for career satisfaction" (Wyman and Risser, 1983, p. 2).

Truly the well-socialized academic sees the professional "calling" as a life's work—one that often totally consumes professional

84

and personal time and energy. And academics are willing to devote themselves to the good life, with its promised fruits of plenty.

### A New Context for Faculty

As described by Jack Schuster in Chapter One, much has been learned about the condition of the professoriate that indicates considerable concern about erosion of intellectual stimulation and autonomy in the collegiate environment. Certainly this is a mixed situation; some of the academic "stars" and better-off campuses are doing fine. But a range of factors—including limited mobility, an aging professoriate, changing student numbers and characteristics, and eroding compensation in a number of academic fields—has raised serious questions and concerns for faculty about the future. Many express the hope that circumstances will improve, but what they often describe for the present is increased expectations of them (particularly in terms of scholarly output and new demands in areas such as student recruitment and retention), diminishing resources (with the resultant press for outside research monies), deteriorating salaries, and little time for reflection.

Given this scenario, is it any wonder that a number of faculty are raising serious concerns and questions and looking for help? A number of the keen observers of the higher education scene, including Bowen and Schuster (1986), Eble and McKeachie (1985), Rice (1985), Corcoran and Clark (1984), Baldwin (1983), Furniss (1981), Barry (1980), Nelsen (1979), Centra (1978), Patton (1978), Gaff (1976), and Bergquist and Phillips (1975), have discussed the need for career counseling and life planning for faculty. The bugle was sounded more than a decade ago, and calls for help have become more strident in the intervening years. Yet faculty are in a bind, because the socialization process ordinarily has been so complete that to leave the "academy" is strongly frowned upon. So what often happens is that faculty take on bigger burdens, become more subject to doing a poor job on many activities because they are spread so thin, and eventually become vulnerable to burnout.

It is commonly assumed that "smart people"—in this case, faculty members—can take care of themselves. The expectation is that if a professor just thinks about the situation, he or she will come up with solutions. Certainly no one should intervene, for faculty are independent entrepreneurs who can figure things out for themselves!

In the last ten years, a number of researchers, particularly Brown and Speth (1988), Witt and Lovich (1988), Seldin (1987), Brown and others (1986), Gmelch (1982), and Melendez and deGuzman (1983), have studied the stress involved in academic life. Unfortunately, they do not cite earlier baseline studies to compare findings, but environmental factors related to working with colleagues and students, as well as budget constraints, the size of workload, and salary, are commonly identified as high sources of stress. Melendez and deGuzman (1983) speak of the person-environment (P-E) fit, a theory of stress that addresses the match or mismatch of people and their environment. Many faculty who are troubled by environmental stress simply go at it harder, not pausing to examine their lives and their circumstances. In these conflicting, intense circumstances, career consulting for faculty can play a crucial role. It is one means to help faculty do some sorting out of their lives—including the person-environment fit—and examine anew the appropriateness of their career decision in higher education.

## The Decision-Redecision Process of Faculty

As was mentioned previously, most faculty members now in professional roles made a career decision to enter the academic profession on the basis of assumptions and information available at a previous time. The sense of being trapped between two generations of scholars that many older faculty members feel has been well described by Volgyes: "Most of us do not even admit to ourselves that we are facing a major crisis. The admission of a fear of sameness, of there being nothing more in our profession to achieve except that which we have reached, the mere accumulative process—one more review, one more article, one more book—is frightening and psychologically so debilitating that its acceptance alone is enough to deny its probable existence. Coupled with it are concrete fears as well: fear for smaller raises in economically hard times, fear of being fired from our jobs when the academic market is closed, and the fear of being laughed at by colleagues on the up-side of the crisis years. These are all powerful inhibitors on getting the truth revealed" (1982, p. 10).

Many midcareer faculty (those whose decision to become an academic was made fifteen to twenty-five years ago)—responding to the strong socialization to the profession during their graduate school years and the continued reinforcement in the academy—find it threatening to reopen that fateful fundamental decision. Instead, they frequently use all kinds of denial and projection on others— including students, support staff, and colleagues—to maintain their idealized image of scholarly pursuits. This is not to argue that there are not a great many faculty members who are quite content, maybe even blissful, about their lot; for surely many, perhaps most, faculty members are satisfied with their circumstances. But unquestionably some are not—and it is especially for them that career consulting can be critically important.

Career consulting can provide the opportunity for all faculty, but particularly midcareer faculty, to examine this earlier decision so that they can either renew it or make new decisions. As one professor said after he had successfully navigated this stressful process, "I've broken the cast once, so I know I can do it again." Certainly "the cast was broken" with considerable pain and risk, yet this faculty member saw a new future and acquired a new sense of self. Best of all, he concluded to stay in academe and to recast the mold.

## History of Faculty Career Consulting

The professional literature contains a number of references to career consulting or counseling with faculty. Bland and Schmitz, in Chapter Three, report twenty-five citations for career counseling or life planning in the period 1965–1987. Only eight colleges or universities are identified in that review as offering such a service. Although the lack of citations could be due to the informality of such programs, only a handful of institutions—including Loyola of Chicago, the College of Charleston, and the University of Nebraska, Lincoln—are documented as having provided individual career consulting services for six or more years.

In addition, a number of colleges, universities, and higher education consortia have provided life-planning workshops for faculty. Two of the earliest workshops described were offered by the Associated Schools of the Pacific Northwest and the Council for the Advancement of Small Colleges. These activities were not planned as ongoing, on-campus career consulting programs (in contrast to the Fairleigh Dickinson, Loyola, and Nebraska programs), but rather as group experiences made available sporadically. It should also be noted that when career consulting services were perceived as "outplacement" (to encourage faculty to leave the college or university)—which was the case in the Associated Schools program and to some degree in the early phase of the Loyola program—faculty would have avoided the experience in order not to be stigmatized in the eyes of colleagues and administrators.

### Career Consulting and the Academy

In career consulting a professional consultant or peer aids the faculty member in assessing his or her career and examining factors that affect that career. Central features involve determining career direction, clarifying issues, identifying and facilitating the removal of barriers, determining what information is needed to make decisions, examining alternatives, finding necessary resources, and reinforcing new decisions.

There has to be a legitimacy to the process of examining careers in order for faculty to participate. One way to describe the consulting service is to compare it to automobile maintenance. With regular, preventive maintenance, autos usually perform well and avoid breakdowns that require major overhauls or unwelcome surprises in performance. If the message can be transmitted to and accepted by faculty that one need not have a "problem" or "crisis" to fruitfully use a career consultant, but that anyone can benefit from a "preventive checkup" by taking the time to talk through career plans, then career programs will be viewed as mainstream. Certainly they should not be identified as being just for people who need "major overhauls" or they will be perceived as "remedial"— and the unavoidable stigma will likely doom any such programs to death for lack of clients.

For the career consulting concept to have a positive reception requires understanding, commitment, and reinforcement by both faculty and administrators. One of the useful steps in establishing career consulting at Nebraska was a 1980 survey of faculty to determine the need for, and to assess whether faculty would use, such a service. About 25 percent of the faculty responded that they saw a need *and* would avail themselves of the service. A helpful association in this survey process was the depiction of career consulting as a parallel service to the instructional consulting service offered by the campus's respected Teaching and Learning Center. No doubt this association lent a credibility to the proposed service that would otherwise have been more difficult to establish (or at least would have taken time to achieve).

### Crucial Elements of Career Consulting

A comprehensive program needs to offer a full range of services, including personal, confidential consulting on a one-to-one basis; group activities, such as seminars, workshops, retreats, and support groups on various career-related topics, including but not limited to handling occupational stress, revitalizing a professional role, and consulting; and open dialogue on campus about the importance of career development (through newsletters, articles, and various meetings). Written materials on career issues and planning are also helpful, but judging from a 1984 evaluation of the Nebraska program and from scattered comments in the literature, few faculty seem to use these generic resources unless they are supplemented with individual consulting or group activities. (This lack of attention to career issues is understandable—even reasonable—given that faculty are so busy "juggling their various balls in the air." Many simply find little time to systematically reflect on and analyze their careers.)

A comprehensive program needs to meet a full range of client needs, including long-range career-life planning; discussion of such work-associated issues as poor relationships, overload, and loss of vitality (particularly among midcareer and older faculty); and counseling on major personnel actions, such as denial of tenure, job termination, or retirement. Providing this range underscores the essential message that *any* career issue is legitimate, and that career consulting is appropriate for more than the perceived negative personnel situations (denial of tenure, terminations, and moving out of the academy).

At this point, the skeptic may be musing, This kind of program *sounds* good, but how can we afford it? Higher education is one of the most labor-intensive enterprises, and faculty are by far the most critical resource to get an educational institution's creative work done. Thus one could just as easily ask how an institution can afford *not* to provide a service that can aid faculty in making sound career decisions and meeting individual and organizational needs. As Schuster pointed out in Chapter One, there is a joint responsibility for faculty growth and development, and this interface needs an advocate. Without such a consulting service, too many faculty will feel trapped in their negative images of the professoriate, and eventually they may become bitter about not finding a way out of their predicament. This bitterness—and we have all seen it—is sometimes projected onto students and often poisons the collegial environment. If you are one of those who say that this scenario can happen only to "bad" people, rest assured that circumstances can generate crises for anyone. Some faculty do a better job of monitoring and taking care of their needs, but they too can benefit from support— even though a crisis point has not been reached at which it becomes obvious to all that help is necessary. Other people end up doing (or redoing) the work of faculty in crisis; if for no other reason, faculty need to be cared for and nurtured in their careers, so that they can contribute meaningfully to the institution's workload.

*Types of Career Issues Addressed.* Those faculty who do address career issues tend to present them in two categories. First is a concern about overall career-life planning: What is my future? I don't want to do this anymore, but I don't know what else I might want or be able to do. I don't want to be teaching this same introductory class twenty years from now. What are my career options? Second are specific career-related issues: I feel overburdened and can't say no. I am considering a faculty sabbatical leave; how do I go about it? There is too much pressure for research (or teaching), and I came here to be a teacher (or a researcher), so where do I go from here? I didn't get tenure and I feel wronged, so what do I do now?

However, as noted in a previous treatment of career consulting (Wheeler, 1989), these two groupings are not mutually exclusive. Quite often a faculty member facing a specific issue will eventually explore larger issues, such as long-range career-life planning. For example, if a faculty member inquires about a faculty leave or sabbatical, the conversation may eventually include discussion of how the leave fits into long-range plans as well as short-term. Thus the emphasis is continually upon assessment of the status of a career, where one would like to be, and how to accomplish the career development desired.

*Obstacles Encountered in Career Consulting.* To consider a new path or to move in some new direction involves encountering "emotional stumbling blocks." Some of these, as often cited by faculty members and expanded from a list by Carol Payne-Smith (1980), include:

1. *Poor relationships* with students, colleagues, and/or administrators (including poor communication and a lack of respect). We find it difficult to function well when critical relationships are strained.
2. *Personal sense of powerlessness.* We find it particularly distressful to feel responsibility for whatever occurs but to perceive little control over the outcome.
3. *Role conflict.* Sometimes we feel pulled in different directions by the expectations of the community, clients/students, administrators, and our own personal philosophy, feelings, and thinking.
4. *Life changes external to the work situation.* Events such as the death of a loved one, divorce, moving, and so forth may diminish the energy and emotional strength we bring to our work.
5. *Life stages.* As adults we continue to experience predictable life stages (passages) that take precedence over the demands of our jobs.
6. *Internal sources of stress.* Our ideas, values, and attitudes may

cause us to experience stress in a situation that is not stressful to others.

7.  *Institutional practices and policies.* We sometimes find stressful policies that foster competition and evaluation.

8.  *Loss of purpose or meaning in life.* We may feel a lack of connection with others, a sense that the old assumptions do not work anymore.

9.  *Total socialization to the profession,* or the one-life, one-career imperative. We feel that to consider any alternatives would be a betrayal of commitment to the "chosen profession."

10. *Sense of being trapped.* We are fearful that there is nothing else we can do; our skills and abilities would not work anywhere else.

11. *Need for security.* We have a sense that to try something very different would entail considerable risk; it is better to hang on to what we have.

Although this is a list of the more common obstacles, individual faculty will state variations of these themes and may even view them as one global problem. In the latter situation, a career consultant needs to help the faculty member sort out the multiple factors involved and find ways to disaggregate and identify factors that can be changed or viewed in a different light.

From this list of obstacles, it should be apparent that the issues are quite varied and differently centered. Issues such as internal sources of stress, life stages, and loss of purpose are concentrated within the individual, while issues such as poor relationships with students or colleagues, role conflicts, and institutional practices and policies are more closely linked to the environment. Of course, multiple influences can affect personal factors—for example, loss of purpose may be a result of poor relationships in combination with institutional practices.

In confronting these obstacles through career consulting, faculty members may find a number of general observations applicable:

1.  Faculty members, by making appointments with the consultant, are forcing themselves to set aside time to address some-

thing important to their lives. Often discussion of the issue provides the clarification a person needs to make a decision, or at least reveals what further information is needed.

2. Faculty members know that when they come to a consulting session, the focus will be on them and their careers.

3. A consultant is an important "permission giver" as well as "coach" for the faculty member.

4. Questions and suggested alternatives will help to move the client past the either/or orientation so often expressed by faculty.

5. Various written materials can be suggested to provide perspective on life and career issues.

6. Various resource people can often be identified by the consultant—people who may be useful in helping clients to address their issues.

A word of caution about stumbling blocks is in order. Unless the faculty member addresses the barriers, he or she will be inhibited in moving to the next steps except in a perfunctory way. The "unfinished business" will continue to prevent the faculty member from examining options or moving in new directions. An illustration may be helpful.

A faculty member who was denied tenure had feelings of rejection, anger, and disappointment. No matter how logical it was that she was denied tenure (her record included lack of publications and an unambiguous warning two years prior to the tenure denial), she still had these feelings to handle. In short, she needed some sort of "closure" on this part of her life so that she could move to the next chapter. What can provide this closure will vary from person to person. For one, just discussing the situation fully is sufficient; for another, writing in a journal; for another, making an appointment to discuss the matter with the chief academic officer. For yet others, working through the faculty and/or legal grievance procedures may be the only satisfactory solution.

In the latter situation, faculty members may feel strongly that if they have their day in court and "lose," at least they will have had a fair chance for vindication. The aggrieved faculty members we should be most concerned about, even though the legal issues are often messy and costly, are those who deny their feelings and carry the unfinished business on into their next work situation.

In this avoidance situation, a faculty member unhappy about work and clinging to the one-life, one-career imperative will focus only on the supposed failure in his or her "calling." Until the "failure" is clarified and the underlying assumptions of the professoriate model have surfaced and been handled, the faculty member likely will be ineffective in moving on with career plans.

As noted, there are various paths to finding closure on a stage in one's life. Until some way is found to mark a troubling life segment, a consideration of alternatives will be at best a half-hearted effort. The goal of the career consultant is to help the faculty member find the way to close that chapter and get on with a new beginning.

Sometimes the time and effort spent in these pursuits seem halting and unfocused, but eventually the faculty member will usually see, behind the unpleasantness, the reasons to leave. We know that feelings and emotions can be a driving force in motivation, so we want them moving in a direction that enables rather than inhibits progress.

### Career Consulting Modes

Because so many faculty issues involve mid- or late-career faculty, I will focus on two situations common to those stages and describe the process a career consultant might use.

*Mode 1: Dealing with the Changing Rules.* Bowen and Schuster (1986) have identified the "press for research" in many collegiate institutions. Faculty who become associated with prestigious research universities expect this press and are attracted to it, because research is their primary university interest. However, a number of faculty who would describe themselves primarily as teachers are uncomfortable with changing expectations exerted by the research press. Quite often they describe their situation as one in which someone "changed the rules," thereby ordaining that merit raises and other resources go disproportionately to the research-oriented faculty (who often are the recent arrivals at their institutions). To the "abandoned" teachers, the research imperative appears to drive everything in the institution.

Many of these faculty will confide that they do not like to do research and even, in a number of cases, do not see themselves as adequately prepared to conduct it. In addition, they may resent the institutional power structure for bringing in outside "hot-shot" researchers, who often enter with higher salaries and who assuredly get the raises available. For many, theirs is the only institution they know, and they had expected to remain there throughout their whole academic career. But now they are raising some fundamental questions.

Aside from helping them deal with their feelings of betrayal and powerlessness, the career consultant will try to help them see what information they need to consider in making a new career decision. Specifically, they need some or all of the following information:

- How much is this situation like other places? In this regard, visits, job searches, and national conferences to "compare notes" can be helpful.
- Given the interests and skills I have, what roles could I fulfill in the university (or even outside a university setting)? Here a variety of techniques may be useful: talking to administrators, doing a skills assessment that might include some career testing, and talking with people who hold jobs that may be of interest outside the higher education environment.
- What would it take for me to become an adequate researcher? Am I interested? Who might work with me? In this case the faculty member might explore with "user-friendly" researchers how to become a part of a research team and try to determine what he or she might contribute.

If this process seems to be nearly a full-time job, note that unless this career redecision process is opened and settled, the faculty member is likely to become one who does just enough to get by and may well become a negative force in the department. Second, when faculty decide to tackle these projects so important to their lives, they seem to find the requisite energy and drive. In a period of only two weeks, some faculty have shown the capacity to collect all the necessary information, reach a fundamental decision, and move on with their lives.

What are the outcomes of such a process? After conducting some visitations and interviews, faculty sometimes will indicate that their situation is much better than they had thought; these may choose to remain. Others decide to move in a new career direction, either inside or outside of the institution. A number have begun to develop joint research projects, often with the goal of becoming more independent as they develop the needed skills and reputation. And yes, a few fail to get past or even through the exploration process; they become mired in negativity and isolated from the department. In summary, outcomes of the process will vary from one situation to another.

*Mode 2: Building Bridges.* Quite commonly, faculty members will have arrived at a particular idea of what they want in their career but not know how to get there. This situation is much less complicated than when faculty do not want to be doing what they are doing but have no idea what else they might do. This latter case may require a number of assessments, often including tests and inventories, such as the Strong-Campbell Interest Inventory and the Myers-Briggs Type Indicator.

If faculty members are sure of where they want to go, the major aid to be provided is to "build a bridge" from where they are to where they want to be. In some cases one major initial activity (for instance, returning to school) or a series of steps may be required before the bridge can be completed.

For example, one senior faculty member wanted to develop an independent consulting business. Rather than have him just leave the university and begin a consulting business, we looked at intermediate steps he could pursue with the long-term goal of becoming an independent consultant. These steps included doing what consulting he could as a faculty member, working during breaks on a particular certification that would strengthen his credentials, and planning a faculty leave that would involve a large dose of consulting.

In this phased change, the faculty member had the opportunity to sample some experiences and to develop some skills that were helpful in his various university roles. In particular, he was able to incorporate a number of these experiences into his teaching and research. This experimenting phase also allowed the faculty member to avoid taking too large a step without a sense of what was involved; he avoided severing ties with one position to catapult into something else for which he was not yet sure he was suited. (Flexibility is one of the useful benefits of the university, and we need to encourage faculty to use it fully, as they continue to fulfill their obligations.) This faculty member is now a successful consultant working all over the world. His leaving has allowed the university to recruit a young researcher, who is establishing a name for himself and the department.

This situation points out the various tradeoffs—giving up one benefit for another—involved in the movement of a faculty member out of the university. The faculty member in this illustration was perceived as wanting to do only consulting; he would have become a marginal, if not inept, member of the department had he been pushed down the traditional research-teaching path. In an important tradeoff, this faculty member made a successful transition to a new career, with the support of his colleagues, while his department gained a young, energetic faculty member committed to research and teaching.

Matching individual and organizational needs, an overriding goal in the employment relationship, was achieved in this particular example. Certainly career consulting is a useful process in facilitating that matching.

### Identifying and Understanding Alternatives

When faculty come to a career consultant, they often feel trapped by a perceived lack of choices. They see no alternatives. Their dominant feeling is that they do not want to be doing what they are doing; they just want to extricate themselves from their situation. This feeling is often expressed in terms of wanting to leave the university, but with little sense of what else to do.

If faculty do address crucial stumbling blocks and assumptions (as previously described), they will be able to move to the critical stage of generating alternatives. If not, they likely will respond with "yes, but . . ." to any suggestions, or reject them outright. For example, tenured faculty members who place a high value on security may not consider other options because of the safety of tenure and the stability of the economic situation. Until the security issue is effectively dealt with, there can be no movement. Resolution of this issue may require information about current financial circumstances (retirement options and funding, amount of funds available for faculty who leave), as well as financial possibilities outside the university.

When faculty do begin to generate alternatives, the "rule of three" seems to apply. That is, once they can suggest at least three alternatives, they are freed from a limiting either/or mindset and can usually generate many more possibilities. This development of alternatives liberates the client from the "stuckness" mindset so well described by Kanter (1977). For well-educated, often highly skilled people, many faculty have surprisingly little knowledge of any other career possibilities, and little confidence that they could perform in any other situation. Part of the consultant's role is to facilitate confidence building through discussion and through a plan of incremental experiences to test out clients' abilities in other situations. These might include, for example, attending nonacademic conferences or workshops, visiting with and informally interviewing nonacademics, and reading about examples of what former academics are now doing in nonacademic settings.

It is noteworthy that at the University of Nebraska most of the academics who have gone through the redecision process and scrutinized alternatives have in fact chosen to remain at the university. However, most have changed their roles, opting for much closer contact with nonscholarly pursuits. The crucial point is that these faculty used the flexibility within their professional roles and made a new decision—one that resulted in a new commitment to the university. They no longer felt trapped or merely reconciled to their work because there was nothing else they could do. Such revitalization and redirection is worth more than whatever conventional price tag might be attached to the process. Higher education institutions need to help faculty move in these constructive directions, as well as out of the institutional environment if their interests lead them there.

## Using the Existing Resource System

When more inherently personal issues arise, such as marriage concerns, depression, and other psychological situations that require counseling and possibly therapy, the client is referred to a professional psychologist. In these cases, the consultant's role is to be a good listener and to help the client sort out issues the consultant can address and identify other issues that require referral. Faculty are quite able to accept this more focused role from consultants; they do not expect the consultant to be a therapist for matters not directly linked to career planning. Linking to other resources is crucial.

As I mentioned previously, few institutions have offered career consulting or counseling on a systematic basis. You may conclude that your institution would not allocate the resources for this kind of service. If so, you might want to consider using some of the more general resources already available at your institution and in your community.

You may well ask how this kind of linkage and resource system could come about at your institution. In Chapter Seven Elizabeth Hosokawa describes the employee assistance programs (EAPs) that may already exist on your campus. EAPs are generally designed to provide initial and crisis counseling and then to refer people for further help. Some of these programs do provide career counseling as one aspect of their referrals. Counselors are not always available, however, and those who are available may have a limited understanding of the distinctive higher education setting.

Another resource can be the student counseling center. At Nebraska, for example, 65 percent of the counseling provided to students is career-related. The rest has to do with the developmental issues and personal crises one would expect. Before the career consulting option was available at Nebraska, the counseling center was a location to which some faculty went for help. A major problem in the use of such counseling centers is that their mandate, financial backing, and image is to work with students. Working with faculty falls way down the list of their priorities and is done only because of the goodwill of the center. If access to student counselors were to be a regular option, some financial arrangements within the university would need to be made, and counselors would need a better orientation to working with faculty.

One of the major problems with using an existing service such as the counseling center is that people already have images—many of them inaccurate—of what happens there or of the center's role in the university. Even the term *counseling*, for many faculty, connotes a negative or "remedial" image. Because many employee assistant programs began, and some have continued, with an emphasis on assisting people with alcohol- and substance-abuse problems, universities may have to launch an educational campaign before faculty see counseling centers as providing full-range, all-inclusive programs.

Unfortunately, another factor working against faculty use of existing structures is that many faculty see their issues as unique. They do not want to be included with students and staff. They desire a service that is tailored to *their* needs and that demonstrates an understanding of *their* issues. This may seem to be an elitist position—one not affordable in a time of constrained resources—but if we want faculty to participate, we cannot ignore these attitudinal aspects. Moreover, faculty members' training and jobs *do* distinguish them from other university constituencies.

No matter what structural design or arrangement is used to provide career consulting, it is imperative that the consultant bring a positive emphasis and be perceived as having legitimate qualifications to address career issues. However the service is presented, the most important factor will be faculty sharing their career consulting experiences with each other, and the assessments made. If the service is seen as an outplacement service or as dealing primarily with "remedial" cases, there will be a stigma associated with its use. If, as in the wellness movement—maintaining and nurturing a healthy career is the overriding focus, there will be a positive predisposition on the part of the faculty. No, all faculty will not use the service, but many of them will seriously consider it as a potentially useful resource. As one highly successful faculty member at Nebraska said, "Even though I have not used any of the services, I am glad to know they are there." For him and for his colleagues, who may never avail themselves of career consulting, the presence of such a service indicates that the institution cares; it provides an important symbol of that caring.

## Career Consulting Dissemination

Because the literature about career consulting is sparse, probably the best source of information is the Professional and Organizational Development Network conference. That conference, which occurs in mid to late October each year, brings together many of the faculty development practitioners, including those involved in career consulting or counseling. The conference is designed to include interactive, practical sessions and to facilitate networking among the participants. Accordingly, the conference is a good place to gain cutting-edge information and to exchange views with practitioners.

Another source of information is Richard Bolles's workshops, newsletters, and various books, including *What Color Is Your Parachute?* (1981) (a classic in career-life planning) and *The Three Boxes of Life and How to Get Out of Them* (1989). Bolles has done much to promote career-life planning, and these two books have been an important part of this thrust. In addition, Bolles edits a bimonthly newsletter, "About Life/Work Planning." He also offers two workshops a year—a four-day workshop oriented to professionals providing life/work planning, and a two-week workshop for individuals doing their own life/work planning. All of these materials and workshops are recommended as being well designed and practical.

At various times some of the professional associations have sponsored books and workshops addressing aspects of faculty careers. The American Association for Higher Education supported the writing of *Expanding Faculty Options* (Baldwin and others), a 1977 book about various career programs. In 1984 the New York State University system supported the preparation of *Teaching and Beyond: Nonacademic Programs for Ph.D.'s* (Reilly and Murdich), which describes and critiques programs offering career alternatives to Ph.D.'s in the humanities and social sciences. These and other publications from legitimate professional organizations have aided in breaking down the one-life, one-career imperative so strait-jacketing to faculty.

A recent telephone survey I did of various agencies that have been available to advise faculty on how to move out of academic careers revealed that most are no longer in business. When questioned as to why these programs were discontinued, people interviewed cited primarily lack of resources and diminishing needs. Overall, the cutbacks in this type of service may reflect an expanding academic labor market. Only time will tell if this is a reasonable interpretation.

Roger Baldwin (Chapter Two) has reviewed some of the adult development literature and its relevance to faculty development. Much of the literature he cites is useful in providing some of the framework for understanding changing interests and expectations over the faculty career span.

In short, there are some useful resources and networking possibilities in career consulting, but they are in general poorly organized and synthesized; they are based upon contributions from such diverse fields as adult education, psychology, sociology, business, and organizational studies. More to the point, few existing resources directly apply career consulting to faculty situations. That oversight, however, at long last appears to be changing.

### Parting Thoughts About Comprehensive Faculty Development

My view is that, ideally, each faculty development center, in many cases now restricted to an instructional development focus, should have a comprehensive faculty development orientation. It should include staff to provide career consulting or, at the least, be able to refer faculty clients elsewhere for career counseling. This would entail a commitment to addressing faculty members as professionals in their many roles—not just in their instructional or teaching role. The instructional improvement role is, of course, important, but given today's pressures and uncertainties, that limited role is not enough. A faculty development program must be more far-sighted if it is to serve the campus well. It should, in fact, make it easy for faculty members to address much more fundamental questions about their futures: Did I make the right professional choice? What information do I need to make a new decision about my professional future?

Without such a commitment in our institutions, we are destined to resort to programmatic band-aids or to concentrate on pressuring marginal faculty out the door. Neither approach is constructive or productive. If, however, higher education is about reflecting, learning, and making important decisions in one's own life, as well as expecting these behaviors in others (such as students), then we accept Socrates' wise advice: "The examined life is one worth living"—or, as it could be restated for careers, "The examined career is worth having." Faculty career consulting is one option to help faculty stay tuned to the developments that can enhance their careers.

### References

Baldwin, R. G. "Variety and Productivity in Faculty Careers." In J. W. Fuller (ed.), *Issues in Faculty Personnel Policies.* New Directions for Higher Education, no. 41. San Francisco: Jossey-Bass, 1983.

Baldwin, R. G., and others. *Expanding Faculty Options.* Washington, D.C.: American Association for Higher Education, 1981.

Barry, R. M. "Career Development Program at Loyola University of Chicago." Paper presented at annual meeting of Professional and Organizational Network, Berkeley, Calif.: Oct. 1980.

Bergquist, W. H., and Phillips, S. R. "Components of an Effective Faculty Development Program." *Journal of Higher Education,* 1975, *46,* 177–209.

Bolles, R. N. *The Three Boxes of Life and How to Get Out of Them: An Introduction to Life/Work Planning.* Berkeley, Calif.: Ten Speed Press, 1981.

Bolles, R. N. *What Color Is Your Parachute?* Berkeley, Calif.: Ten Speed Press, 1989.

Bowen, H. R., and Schuster, J. H. *American Professors: A National Resource Imperiled.* New York: Oxford University Press, 1986.

Bridges, W. *Making Sense of Life's Changes: Transitions.* Reading, Mass.: Addison-Wesley, 1980.

Brill, P. L., and Hayes, J. P. *Taming Your Turmoil: Managing the*

*Transitions of Adult Life.* Englewood Cliffs, N.J.: Prentice-Hall, 1981.

Brown, R., and Speth, C. "Professional Responses to Stress: A Self-Assessment Scale." *Review of Higher Education,* 1988, *11,* 285–296.

Brown, R., and others. "Stress on Campus: An Interactional Perspective." *Research in Higher Education,* 1986, *24,* 97–112.

Centra, J. A. "Types of Faculty Development Programs." *Journal of Higher Education,* 1978, *49,* 151–162.

Corcoran, M., and Clark, S. M. "Professional Socialization and Contemporary Career Attitudes of Three Faculty Generations." *Research in Higher Education,* 1984, *20,* 131–153.

Eble, K. E., and McKeachie, W. J. *Improving Undergraduate Education Through Faculty Development: An Analysis of Effective Programs and Practices.* San Francisco: Jossey-Bass, 1985.

Erikson, E. H. *Childhood and Society.* New York: Norton, 1969.

Furniss, W. T. *Reshaping Faculty Careers.* Washington, D.C.: American Council on Education, 1981.

Gaff, J. G. *Toward Faculty Renewal: Advances in Faculty, Instructional, and Organizational Development.* San Francisco: Jossey-Bass, 1976.

Gilligan, C. *In a Different Voice.* Cambridge, Mass.: Harvard University Press, 1982.

Gmelch, W. H. *Beyond Stress to Effective Management.* New York: Wiley, 1982.

Gould, R. L. *Transformations: Growth and Change in Adult Life.* New York: Simon & Schuster, 1978.

Kanter, R. M. *Men and Women of the Corporation.* New York: Basic Books, 1977.

Levinson, D., and others. *The Seasons of a Man's Life.* New York: Knopf, 1978.

Melendez, W. A., and deGuzman, R. M. *Burnout: A New Academic Disease.* ASHE-ERIC Higher Education Research Report, no. 9. Washington, D.C.: Association for the Study of Higher Education, 1983.

Nelsen, W. C. "Faculty Development: Prospects and Potential for the 1980s." *Liberal Education,* 1979, *95,* 141–149.

Patton, C. V. "Mid-Career Change and Early Retirement." In W. R.

Kirschling (ed.), *Evaluating Faculty Performance and Vitality.* New Directions for Institutional Research, no. 20. San Francisco: Jossey-Bass, 1978.

Payne-Smith, C. "Taking Care of Ourselves." Paper presented at annual meeting of Professional and Organizational Development Network, Asilomar, Calif., Oct. 1980.

Reilly, K. P., and Murdich, S. A. *Teaching and Beyond: Nonacademic Career Programs for Ph.D.'s.* Albany: State University of New York Press, 1984.

Rice, R. E. *Faculty Lives: Vitality and Change. A Study of the Foundation's Grants in Faculty Development, 1979–1984.* St. Paul, Minn.: Northwest Area Foundation, 1985.

Sarason, S. B. *Work, Aging, and Social Change.* New York: Free Press, 1977.

Seldin, P. (ed.). *Coping with Faculty Stress.* New Directions for Teaching and Learning, no. 29. San Francisco: Jossey-Bass, 1987.

Tough, A. *Intentional Change.* Chicago: Follett, 1982.

Volgyes, I. "Is There Life After Teaching? Reflections of a Middle-Aged Professor." *Change,* 1982, *14* (8), 9–11.

Wheeler, D. "Career Consulting: A Critical Segment of Comprehensive Faculty Development." In K. Lewis (ed.), *Individual Consultation Techniques for Faculty Development Personnel.* Stillwater, Okla.: New Forums Press, 1989.

Wheeler, D., and Bond, S. "Faculty Career Enrichment (1982–1985)." Final report to the Layman Foundation, Lincoln, Nebr., May 1985.

Witt, S. L., and Lovich, N. P. "Sources of Stress Among Faculty: Gender Differences." *Review of Higher Education,* 1988, *11,* 269–284.

Wyman, R., and Risser, N. *Humanities Ph.D.'s and Non-Academic Careers: A Guide for Faculty Advisors.* Evanston, Ill.: Committee on Institutional Cooperation, 1983.

6

# Promoting Faculty Health and Wellness

*Joan DeGuire North*
*John W. Munson*

Picture an entire faculty of happy, productive professionals and you will have captured the vision that wellness program managers have for today's campuses. Faced, however, with the reality of graying faculties and dwindling dollars, we as administrators and academics may tend to dismiss that vision as an impossible dream. But it need not be so. An increasing number of campuses are turning to the health promotion and wellness movement to improve faculty quality of life.

The wellness concept is broad, encompassing far more than prevention of illness. It is defined as "the process of adopting patterns of behavior that lead to improved health and heightened life satisfaction" (Opatz, 1985, p. 7). It recognizes that people are complex beings. Thus, while many programs in industry and higher education begin with the physical aspects of health, they should also address five additional wellness vectors: a person's intellectual, emotional, social, occupational, and spiritual aspects (O'Donnell, 1986). Worksite health promotion is defined as "systematic efforts by an organization to enhance the wellness of its members through education, behavior change, and cultural support" (Opatz, 1985, p. 7). Typical components of a wellness program include instruction for injury prevention, smoking cessation, stress management, physical fitness, weight loss and nutrition, and back care, as well as health risk assessment and employee assistance with emotional problems (Flinn and Kondrasuk, 1989).

In order to understand the usefulness and urgency of wellness programming, one can look back forty years, when such life-threatening diseases as pneumonia, flu, polio, and tuberculosis were brought under control. Since that time the major cause of death has been not infectious disease but disease induced by life-style (Berry, 1984). Heart disease, stroke, cancer, and untimely accidents (the so-called designer diseases) are the result of choices individuals make about their lives—choices involving seat-belt usage, stress levels, nutrition, and exercise. The notion that people have some control over their death has led to the belief that they also have great control over their lives and how fully those lives are led. The relationship between body, health, emotions, and performance undergirds the belief that living in wellness not only prevents illness and premature death but also heightens one's quality of life and one's performance at work.

As administrators, we know that loss of quality faculty members to premature death or disease, to early retirement, or, worst of all, to retirement on the job can wreak havoc on quality programs. Thus the question in the wellness context is not how to assist the faculty in *becoming* better professionals but how to assist them in *being* healthier persons.

### History of the Wellness Movement

Early in the 1970s the concept of wellness emerged with a pioneering report by the Canadian Ministry of Health and Welfare, *A New Perspective on the Health of Canadians* (LaLond, 1974), which strongly supported the notion that the only way to cure many diseases was to change individuals' behaviors. Added impetus to the wellness movement was provided by the recognition of the relationship between diet and disease. A select U.S. Senate Committee on Nutrition and Human Needs (Ardell, 1983, p. 8) illustrated in 1977 how drastically the health of people was being damaged by poor nutritional habits. We had become a society of sugar and fat consumers, especially in fast foods.

In 1979 the U.S. Department of Health, Education, and Welfare issued a decree calling for immediate action and strategies for prevention of disease (*Healthy People*, 1979). With the cost of medical care steadily rising in the 1970s (as it has continued to do to the present), the time had come to stress prevention rather than cure.

Throughout the 1970s and early 1980s, wellness programs were being implemented in industry, followed by school systems and more recently by universities. Corporate wellness programs provided the following for employees: information about health, facilities for exercising, health testing (blood pressure checks, cholesterol ratios, and the like), better food selections in the cafeteria, financial and other encouragements to change negative habits such as smoking, and counseling for substance abuse and emotional or family problems. Industry leaders believed that company-sponsored health promotion efforts aimed at improvement in diet and exercise patterns and reduction of smoking would bring financial payoffs to their companies by cutting the high cost of health care benefits and heightening employee satisfaction and productivity. Because there has been limited experience to date with wellness programs in higher education, the experience in business settings can be instructive. While the two settings differ in many respects, the experiences of the latter can surely help institutions of higher education to formulate appropriate programs.

The potential for savings through wellness programs is substantial, given that companies currently spend as much as $2,000 annually per employee for health care. It is no wonder that the percentage of worksites sponsoring wellness programs has increased; in 1985 32.4 percent of U.S. worksites employing over 250 employees had wellness programs, compared with 2.5 percent in 1979 (Karch, 1987).

New York Telephone, reporting results from its nine wellness projects (which concentrated on reduction of the risk factors of smoking, cholesterol, hypertension, and poor fitness), estimated their net savings at $2,700,000 annually (Opatz, 1985, p. 28). Health care savings attributable to industry wellness programs are high in part because employee participation is high: the staywell health promotion program at Control Data, carefully monitored since its inception in 1979, reported a participation rate of 70 percent of eligible employees.

Along with these encouraging results, however, is a general hesitancy among health promotion professionals to place too many eggs in the basket of health care savings. Bill Baun of Tenneco's wellness program cautioned others about the difficulty of proving cause-and-effect relationships in these settings and noted that improved health statistics may not show up for ten years (Baun, 1978). The future trend in industry may be toward noting the positive short-term effects of wellness programs on employee morale, recruitment, and retention, rather than documenting long-term health care cost reductions.

As the wellness movement grew, the need for trained professionals to implement programs increased. And higher education has responded: over 100 colleges and universities offer some type of academic program for health promotion professionals. Mostly on the undergraduate level (although there are master's and doctoral programs as well), these professional programs work closely with industry to educate the high-level professionals needed for health promotion settings. Among the oldest and most well-established academic programs are the those at American University, the University of Georgia, Loma Linda University (Calif.), Purdue University, Springfield College (Mass.), and the University of Wisconsin, Stevens Point.

## Wellness Programs in Higher Education

How widely has higher education implemented wellness programs to address faculty vitality or cost savings? To review current practices, the authors sent a survey in 1987 to all four-year campuses and conducted phone interviews with a sample of fifteen campuses that operate wellness programs.

Over 200 campuses, almost evenly divided between public and private institutions, reported that they offer faculty/staff wellness programs, although 70 percent of them were initiated only in the last several years. A full 80 percent expected to maintain or expand services. The survey also provided data on the kinds of activities sponsored, campus rationales for launching wellness programs, prime movers behind campus wellness, levels of funding, and varying administrative structures.

*Activities.* Although each campus presented a unique picture, there were activities common to many of the campuses, with the level of activity ranging from simple blood tests to comprehensive programs with extensive facilities. The types of activities can be categorized as follows: (1) interest survey, (2) personal health information, (3) general wellness information, (4) activities, and (5) environmental changes.

1.  Most programs begin with written and/or verbal questioning of potential participants as to their interest in such a program and their willingness to participate. Frequently, from these initial contacts members of a coordinating committee can be chosen.
2.  Providing individuals with information on their own health is usually a popular service: it requires little commitment on the part of those tested, and it appeals to their sense of curiosity. Types of assessments that are used include health risk appraisal questionnaires (which identify life-style and other factors that could lead to premature death for the individual), stress assessments (which identify the amounts and sources of stress in a person's life), nutrition analyses (which identify nutrients missing in a diet and highlight intake of potentially dangerous items, such as sodium, fat, and sugar), blood pressure checks, cholesterol tests, flexibility and endurance tests, lung-volume and grip-strength tests, values orientation, and financial security tests. Many of these are oriented toward the physical aspect of wellness, because many of these programs begin with that aspect and because that aspect seems to be most visible and most easily understood.

    Some of the more comprehensive programs (such as the University of Louisville's Total Wellness Program) offer "full-service" experiences for a limited number of people. After a variety of tests are administered and interpreted, participants are counseled and provided with an individualized "prescription" for health, covering suggested changes in exercise, nutrition, and life-style. Usually some periodic follow-up is also included. Some comprehensive programs are organized almost like health clubs, with a limited number of people who can participate at one time. The commitment level of participants is high, probably because of the limited access and because the experience tends to be more intense and personal than one-time-only seminars.

3. Information-giving activities are provided in the form of wellness newsletters and pamphlets, workshops and seminars on health topics, posters, videotapes, and "health fairs"—the latter designating a short-term (usually one-day) event during which health-oriented information, testing, and fun are presented (along the lines of the old county fair). The University of Georgia holds annual "renewal" conferences for faculty, during which a wide range of personal and professional wellness topics are addressed, including "enhancing self-esteem, positively single . . . , time management, burnout" (Simpson and Jackson, 1987, p. 90). Other topics covered through information-giving activities cover all six of the wellness vectors identified earlier: the extensive list includes smoking, substance abuse, nutrition, stress, depression, exercise and physical fitness, safety and first aid, the healthy back, family issues, eating disorders, career issues, and conflict management.

4. Our survey results reveal that most wellness activities are primarily in the physical wellness vector: aquatic exercise, aerobics, yoga, lower-back training, tennis/golf/swimming lessons, walking groups, Smokenders, weight-loss contests, fun runs, relaxation training, exercise paths, accessible gyms, and so forth. Another aspect of wellness—the social vector—is addressed by such activities as family volleyball evenings and canoeing outings for staff and families. Illinois State University's wellness program rents bowling or ice-skating facilities for staff and their families. Emotional wellness is often addressed through the campus employee assistance program.

5. Environmental changes that encourage healthiness as part of wellness programs were also reported, although far less often than the previous types of wellness activities. Some campuses reported initiating extensive smoking bans, painting stairs with

bright colors and symbols to encourage use of stairs, examining healthy levels of lighting, purchasing back-supporting chairs, and providing healthy choices and descriptive nutritional labeling on menus in campus cafeterias.

*Rationale.* A primary motivation for corporations' investment in employee wellness programs is the belief that health care costs to the company will be reduced and that healthy employees are more productive than sick ones. While there was some interest shown among higher education institutions in the cost-saving rationale (42 percent of survey respondents picked cost savings as one rationale), 95 percent of the campuses indicated that their rationale for starting wellness programs was to promote better health awareness. Other rationales identified were to increase productivity and decrease absenteeism (40 percent), to provide a practicum situation for health-related majors (27 percent), and other reasons (20 percent). Included in the "other" category were such rationales as improvement in faculty/staff retention, morale, perception of the workplace, sense of community, and personal-organizational transformation.

Recent research has centered on the connection between teaching excellence and personal wellness, with preliminary findings that "effective faculty members believe their teaching to be strongly affected by their personal wellness" (Jones, 1987). University of Georgia officials point out that faculty express gratitude that the university is doing something for them—something that acknowledges the whole person, not just the teaching-researching portion. At the University of Alberta (Canada), the extensive employee wellness program is considered a fringe benefit.

Some of the institutions we surveyed chose to invest in wellness programs as an extension of the campus's mission or reputation. This is the case, for example, at the University of Wisconsin, Stevens Point, which likes to think of itself as the "wellness capital of the world," and at John Brown University (Ark.), a college with a religious commitment to a healthy life-style. Regardless of the specific rationale, campuses indicated a hope for a higher quality of life for employees, which in turn should positively influence quality of work.

*Prime Movers.* The prime movers behind the adoption of wellness programs for staff/faculty varied considerably, with 44 percent of respondents identifying physical education faculty as the initiators, followed by 23 percent who identified student life staff, 20 percent who named the personnel office, 18 percent who named the president, and 24 percent who wrote in other responses, such as nursing faculty (six campuses), union (two campuses), other administrators (seventeen campuses), state government or university system (six campuses), grant or insurance company (four campuses). (Percentages total over 100 because of multiple responses.) The interest of faculty in physical education seems to stem in part from a professional interest in health and fitness and the need for practicum sites for students. Phone interviews revealed that individual presidents who took the lead in establishing wellness programs were frequently influenced by the death or illness of prominent faculty or staff. Interest on the part of faculty development staff and other administrators in faculty health promotion presumably stems from a perceived relationship between faculty vitality and healthiness. Student life personnel's influence on faculty wellness programs comes from extending wellness programs for students to the faculty and from the interest of health center personnel in health issues.

*Audience.* Only a handful of campuses reported that their wellness programs are oriented primarily to faculty (eight campuses) or primarily to staff (eight campuses). Campuses most often address both faculty and staff (seventy-six campuses) or faculty, staff, and students (fifty-five campuses). The questionnaire did not solicit actual attendance statistics, but phone interviews revealed certain patterns. At campuses where permission is given to use work time for wellness activities and there is strong representation of staff on the wellness steering committee, staff (especially classified staff) participation far outdistances that of the faculty. Illinois State University employees, for example, are allowed an hour and a half per week to participate in sponsored wellness activities; the staff-to-faculty participation ratio there is 3:2, with an overall 65 percent participation rate of employees. In its sixth year, this campus program also encourages families to participate and is hoping to extend its services to retirees. On the other hand, at the University of Georgia, where the fitness center is closely allied with the instructional development office (with which it often jointly sponsors activities, and which is perceived to operate for faculty members only), about nineteen out of each twenty participants are faculty members. Further, there is no provision for staff spending work time in wellness activities.

Some of the wellness centers also offer services for fees to community members and/or local companies.

*Funding.* There are vast differences in levels and sources of funding among wellness programs. Michigan State University and the University of New Mexico have received multiyear, multimillion-dollar foundation grants to infuse wellness concepts into their academic programs in medicine, nursing, psychology, health education, exercise science, counseling, and nutrition and at the same time to create wellness programming for faculty and staff. At the other extreme, Potsdam College of the State University of New York operates with no budget and no assigned personnel by using faculty volunteers and small profits from several aerobics classes.

The amount of funding the campus commits to wellness programming may be directly related to the extent to which the campus believes either that wellness and vitality go hand in hand or that wellness programming can produce financially beneficial effects through reduced medical costs, absenteeism, and so forth. Although any definitive statement is premature, it does appear that private colleges are in a better position to realize any savings created by wellness programs. Many public institutions of higher education are organized so that both the costs and the savings of medical care are absorbed at the state level, so campus financial incentives are lost. The time may be right for state university systems to take on the challenge of demonstrating cost savings with wellness programs by funding campus programs and determining return on investment. To date, only Montana has funded a statewide wellness program. As part of a change to state self-funding of health insurance, the Montana State Systems provided the six campuses with formula funding for wellness programming, beginning with $10 per employee three years ago. Because the state is keeping careful records of costs and savings, the higher education community could benefit from the Montana experience.

Almost 60 percent of the campuses we surveyed indicated that the campus funds all or part of the wellness program, while other sources of funding include participant fees, grants (including several grants from health insurance companies), contributions from departments that provide practicum students, and sale of campus wellness services and facilities to local agencies or companies. Most wellness programs charge participants for some of the services provided. For example, one university charges faculty and staff $60 for the first semester of Fitness Images Today, when extensive testing occurs, and $25 for subsequent semesters.

On those campuses with a strong commitment, fees are subsidized by the university. For example, the University of Louisville sponsors its Total Wellness Program, which includes exercise physiology testing, nutrition and weight-control counseling, stress management, and other services. This "Cadillac" program is limited to 200 employees and costs $200 per person. The employee pays $50, and the university pays the other $150. The University of California, San Diego, subsidizes $500 per participant for its wellness programming for upper-level administrators. Sharing or covering faculty fees for wellness activities becomes a way the campus can invest in the faculty.

Still another method of increasing resources is bartering with local agencies. A hospital staff may be given free aerobics classes or swim time in exchange for administering free cholesterol testing, for example.

*Administrative Structure.* Staffing of wellness programs frequently comes from full- or part-time release for faculty in health promotion fields, such as nursing, exercise science, physical education, and health promotion itself. Many programs utilize graduate and/or undergraduate practicum students in these fields. The number of professional staff is usually small (a portion of a person), although larger programs do exist. The University of New Mexico, with the help of a large grant, employs seventeen on its wellness staff. Montana State University's Employee Wellness Program (phone number: 99-IM-FIT!) employs seventeen part-time professionals "bought" from the health service, counseling center, and academic areas in nursing and nutrition.

Reporting channels include the personnel office, the president's office, the wellness steering committee, the benefits committee, the department of physical education, and the dean. Most programs are physically located in or near physical education facilities.

### Getting Started

If you look carefully, you will find health promotion and wellness personnel and facilities on almost every campus, so efforts to build programs do not have to start from scratch or wait until large foundation grants roll in. With that in mind, the following steps are offered to those hoping to initiate wellness programs.

*All-Campus Committee.* Campuses frequently create steering committees to plan and oversee the beginning stages of a wellness program. The membership should widely represent the various units to be covered—for example, classified employees, faculty senate, administrative staff. Usually the personnel office and wellness professionals are also represented. The size will vary with the size of the wellness group. The state of Nebraska utilizes a large committee of sixty government employees, called the WellTeam, whose members are subdivided not only by groups represented but also by the tasks the members have volunteered for. The task groups include the communication team (WellSaid), and the planning group (WellPlanned) (Kizer, 1987, pp. 56–58). A wealth of resource people reside on campuses. For example, religious studies faculty and philosophers can provide input for programs in values clarification, ethics, and moral development. Faculties in nursing, physical education, medical technology, psychology, counseling, family life, and business can all contribute to various components of wellness programs. Purdue University brought together constituencies from across the campus, who produced a noteworthy interdisciplinary proposal for a university wellness program.

*Top-Level Support.* The support of the top executive has been identified as perhaps the most important factor in predicting a successful wellness program. This person sets the tone, provides or allows the funding, encourages middle-level administrators to be supportive, and is instrumental in allowing work time for wellness activities. This is not to say that a wellness program cannot be initiated if the president is not an active participant. Passive support—even a wait-and-see attitude—will suffice.

*Budget.* The steering committee or wellness coordinator should spend some time considering probable costs, income potential, and any cost-benefit ratios that can be estimated. To economize, founders should look for faculty volunteers, free services in the community and on the campus (the American Heart Association or the nursing school, for example), and service providers who might barter with the university. They should also consider fee structures for participants. The variables are considerable.

*Visibility and Communication.* Immediate visibility is important in the implementation of a successful wellness program. Ideally, the campus should identify a coordinator of the program (at least a part-time appointment). Communication with employees will be a vital issue, especially in the beginning. Some programs use regular memos, specially designed brochures, attractive newsletters that announce services and also provide health information, stuffers in paycheck envelopes, and ads in the student newspapers. The more aware of activities the employees are, the more likely they are to attend.

Another factor identified in predicting employee attendance is the location of the service. Decentralized, building-by-building, or department-by-department services have much greater attendance. One university wellness administrator reported that if she offers a stress management seminar for the university, she gets a dozen participants; if she offers the same seminar for the history department, she gets a dozen participants.

*Assessing Individual and Organizational Health.* Several kinds of data can be useful in planning and evaluating a new program: demographic data, information on employee interest in wellness activities, direct and indirect information regarding health from personnel files, and individual health profiles (singly or aggregated into organizational health profiles).

From demographic data one can determine (by subpopulations) age levels and sex, both of which suggest different programming and/or timing for services. Most programs use an employee interest survey to determine the level of interest and the kinds of topics that should be pursued. Information regarding health may be gleaned from absenteeism records, data on sick leave, health care costs (broken out by types of problems), and so forth. If absenteeism is caused most frequently by health problems associated with lower-back pain, then lower-back programming would become an obvious programming choice.

Assessments that give health information to individuals occupy a major role in wellness programs. Because assessments are popular and are believed to have a motivational influence, they are frequently the cornerstone of wellness programs. Additionally, information generated from these assessments can be useful in selecting appropriate programs or followup—for example, programming for individuals with high blood pressure (Opatz, 1985, p. 43).

Health risk appraisals, a widely used method of individual assessment, identify individual risk factors likely to be related to a person's mortality. Such appraisals are far from exact, but they do provide individuals with health information specific to their own lives and can provide universities with aggregated results that determine overall organizational health and identify specific risk factors of employees. Because health risk appraisals concentrate on the physical aspects of wellness, some organizations also use wellness inventories that cover other aspects of wellness, such as social, occupational, spiritual, intellectual, and emotional inventories (Opatz, 1985, pp. 43-47).

## Dissemination

A number of professional resource organizations are emerging as the wellness movement expands. Many offer high-quality, standardized programs that can save effort in the beginning phases of program development. They often offer a variety of low-cost options to the beginning as well as the highly advanced program.

The National Wellness Institute, for example, is a nonprofit organization created by the University of Wisconsin's Stevens Point Foundation. Founded in 1977, the institute provides national and international leadership in the area of wellness, including the week-long National Wellness Conference held every July. This conference annually attracts 1,200 to 1,400 health promotion and wellness professionals and allows for dissemination of state-of-the-art wellness program ideas. The National Wellness Institute also serves as a resource center for the distribution and production of a wide range of program materials, including books, audiotapes, consulting services, and computer software. The institute can be reached at South Hall, University of Wisconsin at Stevens Point, Stevens Point, WI 54481 (715-346-2172).

The Association for Fitness in Business was established in 1974 to facilitate information exchange among fitness directors in industrial settings. Current membership attracts health educators, physicians, benefits and personnel managers, fitness directors, wellness program managers, and many others. The association, which sponsors a professional journal (*Fitness in Business*) and is a good source of information and direct networking with active professionals, can be reached at 965 Hope Street, Stamford, CT 06907 (203-359-2188).

Another professional journal is the *American Journal of Health Promotion,* which produces scholarly articles and reviews of books and products, and suggests networking possibilities. The journal can be ordered by writing to 746 Purdy Street, Birmingham, MI 48009.

One should not overlook the services offered by hospitals, public health agencies, and chapters of the American Lung Association, the American Heart Association, YMCAs, and local health and fitness organizations. A host of functional services and information can often be obtained at a relatively low cost. Hundreds of private groups are now offering assistance in the form of consulting services, software, and printed materials. While there are many reputable dealers, one should carefully evaluate the published outcomes of using such resources and contact others who have previously used these resources; some companies make unsubstantiated claims about product effectiveness.

## Conclusion

In July 1987 a group of twenty specialists representing collegiate curricula in health promotion and industry and hospital wellness convened in Stevens Point to discuss the creation of curriculum standards for the emerging major and graduate degrees in health promotion. One of the recurring themes that emerged was the certainty expressed by the group that the wellness movement is not a fad—especially given that it is still growing after fifteen years. Even Harvard University recently began a wellness center for students, staff, and faculty, and they have plans to insert more wellness concepts into their curriculum. The prospect for a wellness approach is bright: it has become a realistic and tested approach to helping people make responsible choices impacting their health and vitality. It has become for some a mainstay in a benefits package, a way to counter rising medical costs, a way for people to feel better about themselves, and a way for institutions to express concern for the whole person.

## References

Ardell, D. B. "The History and Future of the Wellness Movement." Paper presented at Stevens Point National Wellness Conference, Stevens Point, Wis., July 1983.

Ardell, D. B. *High Level Wellness: An Alternative to Doctors, Drugs, and Disease.* Berkeley, Calif.: Ten Speed Press, 1986.

Barbour, C. M. *Wellness at the School Worksite.* Washington, D.C.: Health Insurance Association of America and American Council of Life Insurance, 1985.

Baun, B. Unpublished comments at Health Promotion Curriculum Planning Committee, National Wellness Institute, Stevens Point, Wis., Aug. 3, 1987.

Berry, C. *Good Health for Employees and Reduced Health Care Costs for Industry.* Washington, D.C.: Health Insurance Association of America, 1981.

Berry, C. "Health Promotion in the Worksite." *Wellness Promotion Strategies.* Stevens Point, Wis.: Institute for Lifestyle Improvement, 1984.

Chapman, L. S. *Evaluating Your Employee Wellness Program: Strategies and Tools for Documenting Your Results.* Seattle: Corporate Health Designs, 1987a.

Chapman, L. S. *Planning Your Employee Wellness Program: A "How-To" Manual.* Seattle: Corporate Health Designs, 1987b.

Dignan, M., and Carr, P. *Program Planning for Health Education and Health Promotion.* Philadelphia: Lea & Febiger, 1987.

Flinn, C. M., and Kondrasuk, J. N. *Work and Health.* Greenvale, N.Y.: Panel Publishers, 1989.

Gendron, M. "Maricopa Community College's Wellness Program—Off to a Good Start." *Wellness Management,* 1986, *2* (4), 7-8.

*Healthy People: The Surgeon General's Report on Health Promotion and Disease Prevention.* Washington, D.C.: U.S. Department of Health, Education, and Welfare, 1979.

Jones, J. P. "An Investigation of Improving Teaching Effectiveness Through Improving Faculty Wellness." Pilot grant from the Undergraduate Teaching Improvement Grants, University of Wisconsin System, 1987.

Karch, R. C. "Monitoring Our Progress." *Fitness in Business,* 1987, *1,* 231.

Kizer, W. M. *The Healthy Workplace.* New York: Wiley, 1987.

LaLond, M. *A New Perspective on the Health of Canadians.* Ottawa: Government of Canada, 1974.

Leafgren, F. (ed.). *Developing Campus Recreation and Wellness Programs.* New Directions for Student Services, no. 34. San Francisco: Jossey-Bass, 1986.

O'Donnell, M. P. "Definitions of Health Promotion." *American Journal of Health Promotion,* 1986, *1* (1), 4-5.

O'Donnell, M. P., and Ainsworth, T. *Health Promotion in the Workplace.* New York: Wiley, 1984.

Opatz, J. P. *A Primer of Health Promotion: Creating Healthy Organizational Cultures.* Washington, D.C.: Oryn Publications, 1985.

Opatz, J. P. "Case Study: Stevens Point—A Long Standing Program for Students at a Midwestern University." *Journal of Health Promotion,* 1986, *1* (1), 60-67.

Opatz, J. P. *Health Promotion Evaluation.* Stevens Point, Wis.:

National Wellness Institute/National Wellness Association, 1987.

Pelletier, K. R. *Healthy People in Unhealthy Places: Stress and Fitness at Work.* New York: Doubleday, 1984.

Simpson, R. D., and Jackson, W. K. "The Faculty Renewal Program at the University of Georgia." In P. Seldin (ed.), *Coping with Faculty Stress.* New Directions for Teaching and Learning, no. 29. San Francisco: Jossey-Bass, 1987.

Wallace, J. P. "Administration and Organization of University-Based Health/Fitness Programs." *Fitness in Business,* 1988, *2* (6), 204-209.

7

# Adapting Employee
# Assistance Programs
# for Academic Settings

## Elizabeth P. Hosokawa

The first formal faculty assistance programs (FAPs) were established in the mid 1970s at Rutgers University and at the University of Missouri, Columbia. Several academic institutions had made efforts prior to that period to provide some form of access to treatment or an AA program for chemically dependent faculty, but these efforts usually developed as an expansion of the existing responsibilities of a faculty or staff member in recovery for alcohol abuse. The Rutgers and University of Missouri, Columbia, faculty assistant programs, with assigned full-time staff, were the first formal programs in academic settings designed to reach faculty with chemical abuse problems by offering services for a wide variety of personal problems. These programs, and the others that followed, also provided consultation and personnel management assistance to academic administrators. The programs chose to serve staff in addition to faculty, but each tailored outreach, consultation, and training activities to meet the differing institutional policies, job demands, and social culture within these two employee groups.

Faculty assistance programs have their philosophical roots in the employee assistance program (EAP) movement that emerged in the 1940s and 1950s. Pioneer programs, such as those at Eastman Kodak, Kemper Insurance, and Hughes Aircraft, initially focused on serving the long-term, skilled employee whose job performance had been impaired by abuse of alcohol. Due to the social stigma associated with the label "alcoholic," this single focus resulted in a reluctance on the part of supervisors, managers, and co-workers to make early referrals, for fear of making a diagnostic error.

In order to reach more employees and to intervene at an earlier stage of problem development, program philosophies and outreach efforts were broadened to include (1) any type of personal problem resulting in impaired job performance and (2) family members of employees as eligible clients, because of their ability to influence employee behavior. This broadened approach, often referred to as the "broad-brush" program model, is the one most applicable to faculty development needs and is the model on which this chapter focuses.

In the early 1970s Congress established the National Institute of Alcohol Abuse and Alcoholism (NIAAA). Within the institute an occupational branch was established, with the mandate to develop services that would reach and rehabilitate the employed alcoholic. Although various kinds of personal problems can affect job performance, chemical dependency is one of the patterns most resistant to change. Because alcohol dependency tends to take approximately seven years to develop, it often occurs among a particularly valued sector of the workforce: the experienced, skilled employee. The rationale for targeting the employed alcoholic was the discovery that, although many alcoholics would incur loss of marriage and family and acquire legal and health problems without changing drinking behaviors, they were often willing to seek help for their alcohol abuse when job loss was threatened. In one of its earliest actions, the occupational branch of the NIAAA trained and funded two Occupational Program Consultants for each of the fifty states, thus providing readily available technical assistance to organizations interested in developing programs for their own employees.

The concept spread rapidly among large companies, supported by the argument of cost-effectiveness, and more slowly among smaller ones. Some programs, poorly conceptualized or inadequately funded, existed solely on paper or soon sputtered into oblivion. Others flourished. By 1980 over half of the Fortune 500 companies had some type of employee assistance program in place (Wrich, 1980). In the college and university setting, employee assistance programming, along with other innovations in personnel management, has been more slowly adopted. Faced with shrinking financial resources, however, educational institutions have become increasingly interested in ways to improve their management of human resources. As a labor-intensive industry with slowed growth and a high percentage of tenured employees, the academy can no longer afford to neglect factors that adversely affect faculty productivity.

Colleges and universities are becoming increasingly stressful work environments for faculty. A faculty member of the 1980s in a higher education setting, as compared to one during the academic growth period of the 1950s, 1960s, and early 1970s, faces stress from an increasing number of different sources (Blackburn, Pellino, Boberg, and O'Connell, 1980; Cyert, 1980; Maslach, 1982; Ragland-Sullivan and Barglow, 1981; Roman, 1984; Shull, 1972). Although during this earlier period most campuses were characterized by stress related to growing pains, demands by students for participation in decision making, and political demonstrations, the overall circumstances in which faculty members found themselves were salutary: academic positions were plentiful, faculty income outperformed inflation, and faculty members generally had the satisfaction of believing that they had something to contribute to solving social issues and promoting technological growth (Furniss, 1981). It was largely a seller's market for those with skills. A "geographical cure" in the form of a new job or sabbatical leave was generally readily available to the academic experiencing job boredom, an unsatisfying marriage, a difficult midlife transition—or an increasing dependence on alcohol.

Now, in the late 1980s, unmet expectations constitute an important source of stress for academics. Like other professional groups requiring extended educational preparation, academics who trained during the period of expansion envisioned a single-track, single-work identity (Sarason, 1977). Career prestige and professional recognition, institutional monies for travel or conferences, opportunities to develop new course offerings or skills, salaries with stable purchasing power, and interinstitutional job mobility are all important elements that support the successful negotiation of typical academic career transitions. Unfortunately, these resources, which facilitate smooth passage through the developmental stages of a single-career cycle, are becoming increasingly limited in academe, accentuating for many faculty members feelings of boredom, anger, frustration, depression, and a sense of being trapped or "stuck" (Baldwin and Blackburn, 1981; Buspus, 1981; Carnegie Foundation for the Advancement of Teaching, 1985; Clark, 1985; Kanter, 1979; Schuster and Bowen, 1985).

According to Sarason (1977), universities choose, value, and promote their faculty members for individual performance. "The traditions, organizations, practices, and 'rewards and punishments' of . . . universities . . . define conditions guaranteeing a faculty who are unlikely to create or possess other than a superficial psychological sense of community" (p. 282). For many faculty, their sense of "membership in the community" is defined by their professional discipline or by affiliations based on shared research interests that extend far beyond the boundaries of an institution, state, or even country. While these affiliations may be stimulating alliances, they do not provide a readily accessible support system to a faculty member during periods of personal stress.

The rewards of an academic career are largely intrinsic. Successful academics tend to be self-motivated, be able to maintain an undistracted focus on a single research interest, and set exacting standards for their own level of expertise and performance in their chosen field. These qualities that facilitate creativity and productivity in an academic career also place the academic at risk for severe life disruption when an increasing number of work and personal life stressors go unaddressed.

Studies have shown that sustained stress, reduced self-esteem due to unmet vocational expectations, threat of job loss, and financial problems contribute to increased alcohol and drug, emotional, marital, and family problems among the population at large (Barling and Handal, 1980; Dooley and Catalano, 1979; Oliver and Pomicter, 1981; Kasl and French, 1962; Lieberman and Glidewell, 1978; Zander and Quinn, 1962). Although a faculty member may not experience a higher incidence of the stressors described above, he or she may be less willing to ask for support or professional help when needed, seeing such a request as a threat to his or her sense of self-competency. As one academic said, "If I'm recognized around the world as an expert in my field, I certainly should be able to solve this personal problem."

The implementation of a faculty assistance program is not the sole answer to faculty development needs on a campus. Its presence, utilizing a confidential, professionally staffed, individual service model, can greatly facilitate putting depressed, immobilized faculty in touch with the appropriate career or personal development resources at the time they need them. For some faculty, timely intervention that occurs in a face-saving manner may prevent the eventual development of more destructive, chronic, and intractable behavioral coping mechanisms.

### Program Design Considerations

In selecting a program model for a particular campus, program initiators need to take a number of factors into consideration. (The actual program model variations will be discussed in the following section.) Although it results in a more drawn-out decision-making process, there are important advantages to the use of a planning committee made up of the various constituencies that will use or be impacted by the presence of a program. "Perfect" programs implemented rapidly by administrators are often viewed with suspicion by faculty and may be interpreted by them as interference in their "academic freedom." Many of the decisions made in designing and implementing a faculty assistance program will be "best-fit" or compromise decisions. These choices are more readily accepted by groups who feel some degree of program ownership created by participation in the decision-making process. Faculty in large groups tend to be liberal when considering abstract ideas and conservative and critical when reacting to decisions that result in direct impact on themselves. For this reason, faculty senates generally do not make good program-planning groups. Constituencies whose participation in the planning process should be considered include academic administration, faculty unions, personnel, the institution's legal counsel, the campus health officer, the grievance officer, and faculty council or senate representatives.

Factors to be considered constitute a sizable checklist: the primary academic mission of the campus, size of the institution, institutional history and current issues, availability of social service resources on and off campus, degree of health insurance coverage for chemical abuse and mental health needs, degree of unionization, eligibility requirements for program services, administrative structure of the institution, physical campus layout, and policies and procedures that currently impede or facilitate personal problem identification or resolution.

The degree of campus heterogeneity also needs to be taken into account. This will be reflected in the number of separate divisions or colleges, diversity of academic degrees and specialization areas, number of academic programs offered, faculty demographics, and level of collegiality.

Geographical location and physical site factors can exercise influences relevant to program design in several ways. For example, concerns related to confidentiality may be more frequently voiced on the more closely knit campus in a small community, while the larger commuter campus will require considerably more attention to faculty outreach efforts.

Consideration also needs to be given to the social and moral values most prevalent within the targeted client group. Diversity of thought exists in these areas on any campus, but mores do vary. Help-seeking behavior for personal problems, for example, may be more socially acceptable in some regions than in others; such behavior may be viewed as a sign of moral weakness by some academics, regardless of level of academic preparation, and accordingly may inhibit help seeking.

In all, each institution has a unique campus ecology that reflects the influence of many factors. Thoughtful tailoring of a program to the social fabric of a campus will enhance the potential for program acceptance and effectiveness.

## Program Model Selection

Once relevant data regarding target population needs, history of the institution, and available resources have been collected and reviewed, decisions need to be made regarding the kinds of services to be offered and where and by whom these will be used.

Several models with different successful programming combinations are available for consideration.

*Internal Program Versus External Contract for Services.* A program can be contracted out to a community provider completely; partially contracted out for some of the program functions, such as management consultation, publicity development, supervisory training, and direct client services; or structured with all program functions provided by staff who are employees of the institution. Lack of appropriate community resources may dictate choosing an internally placed program. (This situation is more apt to occur for the campus situated in a rural setting or in a small community.)

One alternative under these circumstances, if a larger metropolitan area is nearby, is to contract for a satellite clinic to be made available locally on a limited basis. An institution with a history of perceived inappropriate use of personnel data or charges of interference with academic freedom may find completely external program placement more acceptable to potential faculty users. The smaller college also may find an outside contract more cost-effective, given the lower number of expected users. Studies have suggested that 8 to 12 percent of any employee group falls into the category of "troubled employees" who could benefit from some type of professional help. The number who will actually use a service during a year is much smaller, of course. This number varies widely, however, depending on previous availability and utilization of community resources and preexisting, established rapport with the designated FAP services provider. The ability of the externally contracted program to help faculty successfully negotiate stress related to job requirements or institutional change and politics may be less than that of an internal or partially internal program with access to the organizational grapevine.

*Types of Services to Be Provided.* If community resources for a variety of personal problems are available, a screening and referral mode may provide the most flexibility in meeting diverse and changing needs. If quality outpatient services in the community are inadequate for addressing priority problems, such as alcohol and drug abuse, an institution may prefer to expand FAP services by hiring a professionally trained counselor to offer short-term therapy.

It is difficult for a single individual to maintain in-depth treatment expertise in all of the areas of need that can be presented by clients to a FAP. However, it is quickly destructive to the credibility of a FAP if referrals are made to incompetent community providers. If competent referral resources do not exist locally, the internally placed full-scope program may be the only satisfactory solution. With either choice, credibility is maintained within an audience of potential users through clear statements regarding both range and limitations of resources.

*FAP Staffing Decisions.* The number of staff needed depends upon the types of services to be provided, the size of the institution, placement of the program (external versus internal), and whether or not the institution is spread over more than one site. FAP services are sometimes seen as a form of personnel services by administrators, to be placed under a human resources division and staffed by human resource personnel. Faculty rarely see themselves as "employees," however; they tend to contact personnel offices only when checking on the status of their benefits or requesting parking permits. Suggestions from faculty regarding administrative and physical placement of a program deserve serious consideration. A program established specifically to serve faculty needs to be made as readily accessible—both physically and psychologically—and as attractive to this group as possible.

### Critical Elements of Program Implementation

Some elements are critical to the successful implementation of a faculty assistance program, regardless of the model for delivering services that has been selected. While the development of programs in academe has been too recent to permit conclusive assessments, the available evidence suggests that some elements are prerequisites for a successful EAP in any setting. These elements would appear to be equally important for EAPs in higher education. They include:

*Endorsement by Upper-Level Administration.* Use of a FAP is both protected and sanctioned when the program is openly supported by the highest-level administrator on campus. It is important that this endorsement be given in writing as well as being orally communicated. Generally there are few written regulations governing expected work-related behaviors for faculty, while expectations for staff are usually explicit and detailed. This paucity of structure for academics allows for the exercise of creativity and independence in the selection of work style. This permits, for good or ill, considerable subjectivity to creep into an individual performance evaluation when salary, promotion, or tenure decisions are being made. Strong support of a campus FAP by a president or chancellor, plus clearly defined policy and procedures, helps to ensure that extraneous considerations do not unduly influence job performance evaluations. This approach explicitly deletes personal problem data from the process while establishing legitimacy for an appeals process if personal information appears to have been unfairly used.

*Clear Written Policy on Alcoholism and Personal Problems.* The institution needs to go on record, clearly and in writing, regarding its attitude about knowledge that an employee has or has had some type of personal life problem. A well-thought-out policy does not interfere with normal disciplinary or protective procedures, but it does prevent an employee from being penalized on the basis of subjective hearsay instead of current, documented performance deterioration. There are always a few human dilemmas that are viewed by some individuals as a sign of a character flaw, and people can become highly reactive to some problems and respond less objectively than they normally would. A policy that establishes that all job decisions should be based solely on performance creates a supportive work environment in which an employee can acknowledge having a problem and seek appropriate help. Such a policy also supports early intervention in problem development before negative impact is substantial and the problem behavior becomes resistant to change.

*Clear Written Procedures on Program Utilization.* Well-thought-out written procedures ensure that all employees have

equal access to program services. These guidelines should anticipate and answer questions such as the following: Can the faculty
member use the program on university time? If further services are
needed, based on the FAP assessment, are these on institutional or
personal time? Does the referring supervisor—ordinarily the department chair or dean—receive any information about use of the program by the person he or she referred? By keeping a faculty
member's use of a FAP separate from any progressive discipline
process, confidentiality will be better served, because less documentation is required and fewer people have a "need to know." Keeping
the two processes separate also protects the typically untrained academic manager from being manipulated by a faculty member who,
during the addictive process to alcohol or drugs, may become highly
skilled at denial, excuses, and blaming others.

*Guaranteed Protection of Confidentiality.* A FAP is either
completely confidential within the boundaries of its written policy
and procedures or it is not; word of *any* exceptions will be destructive to future self-referrals and likely will spread quickly through
the faculty grapevine. Regardless of design, no program will reach
and be used successfully by all troubled faculty. Bending the established guidelines to catch one elusive troubled faculty member is
not worth the ultimate damage to program credibility with the
larger faculty group.

*Cooperative Program Development by Constituency Groups
and Administrators.* Although there have been successful programs
developed by only one faction on a campus, in general a program
more rapidly develops acceptance by all groups on campus when
those groups have participated in the program design process.
Cooperative development requires a longer time period, but the
outcome of community ownership of the program is worth it.

*Use of an Advisory Committee.* Establishment and use of an
advisory committee helps to strengthen and expand program credibility and effectiveness on a campus. This is true regardless of the
actual service delivery model selected. The advisory committee for a
new or established program serves as an important information

conduit in two ways: it carries accurate information about the program and its services out into the campus community, and it conveys useful information back to the program about possible misconceptions, developing problems, and unmet needs. In times of stringent campus budgets, it can serve as an advocate group for continued program funding. This can be a critical function for program survival, given that a FAP, unlike most services, cannot ask satisfied clients to speak out without causing a break in anonymity. And the program direction cannot fill this advocacy role alone without appearing to be self-serving.

*Training of Academic Administrators in Referral Procedures.* "The buck stops here" is true for the academic administrator faced with the problem of a troubled faculty member. While academics may identify the functioning of a colleague as "impaired," they typically feel that intervention in such situations is the province and responsibility of the department chair or dean. Faculty rarely receive any training in personnel management when elevated to the role of an academic administrator, however. Faculty assistance programs vary in how they handle building identification and referral skills among those with supervisory responsibilities. Options range from extensive formal training to brief group orientations with later individual consultation as needed. Regardless of the strategy selected, a clearly described, systematic approach is required to ensure that confrontation with and referral of troubled faculty can be managed successfully.

*Publicity and Outreach.* The majority of clients using a FAP will be self-referrals. Like people in other professional occupations, faculty seek out individual service providers rather than organizations for care, based on the recommendation of a respected service provider or a trusted friend. While the referral advice of an authority figure, such as a supervisor, may be sought and followed by an hourly employee, that pattern is unlikely to occur with a faculty member who has decided that professional help is needed. Faculty may also seek out an individual provider on the basis of personal contact with that person under other circumstances, and both professional and hourly employees use social networks when seeking help. Increased emphasis on these networks by faculty, plus the fact that faculty are unlikely to confide in academic administrators, increases the importance of publicity and outreach efforts for a FAP.

Brochures and other printed materials need to be carefully tailored to the values and vocabulary of any targeted potential client population when self-referrals are sought. This is also true when a FAP is "stalking" the self-critical, perfectionistic faculty member. A faculty advisory group can be helpful in the development of printed materials by reviewing proposed publicity.

An academic has a tendency to feel that if he or she cannot resolve a problem, despite an advanced degree and expertise in some area, it will take an equally or more highly credentialed professional to help untangle the situation. This may be flawed thinking, but a program director with a Ph.D. usually will be able to build personal credibility with faculty more rapidly than one with another degree. In institutions where there is a sharp delineation between faculty and staff in areas of policies and perquisites (such as a faculty club), serious consideration should be given to a part-time or an adjunct academic appointment for the director, to facilitate informal outreach to faculty and to build credibility.

*Health Insurance Coverage for Chemical Abuse and Mental Health Problems.* Lack of health insurance coverage for chemical abuse problems can have a chilling effect on program utilization and effectiveness. Chemical abuse problems tend to drain the financial resources of an individual or a family unit before professional help is sought. Establishing some type of health insurance coverage, preferably both inpatient and outpatient, prior to initiating a FAP will help prevent the rejection of a program that can occur when expectations for help are raised and then not met. Some successful innovations in chemical dependency treatment have been developed over the past five years that are designed to be as cost-effective as possible. These include several program models that are carefully tailored to the treatment needs of the individual, while permitting the employed person to remain on the job as much as possible. In order to control costs for chemical abuse treatment while assuring an appropriate level of care, some organizations are requiring all employees seeking these services to be screened by their EAP providers prior to authorization of payment.

Many health insurance plans partially reimburse outpatient mental health care. This type of coverage facilitates the ability of the FAP to be helpful in meeting some client needs. If an institution's plan provides 100 percent coverage and the institution has decided to contract out FAP services, it needs to develop some type of referral review process with the contracting agency. When the clients are not paying a share of the cost of care, and the FAP contractor for screening and referral services is also providing ongoing mental health care, there are no brakes built into a potentially costly, possibly long-term process. Research evidence strongly suggests that health insurance coverage for treatment of chemical abuse and mental health problems can reduce costs incurred under other diagnoses. Ideally, these will be copayment plans covering a range of levels of care. A FAP can help control costs for chemical abuse and mental health treatment through a careful screening and referral process that matches level of need and level of care.

Most academic institutions, because they receive federal grants or contracts in excess of $25,000, must comply with the Federal Drug Free Workplace Act of 1988. A well-developed FAP that includes the elements described in this section can assist an institution in meeting most of the requirements of that Act.

## Conclusion

Faculty assistance programs can make a unique contribution to the enhancement of a faculty career. Their professionally staffed, confidential, personalized service approach fits well with the previously described tendency of academics to seek an individual service provider when feeling stuck, overwhelmed, and confused by a problem. The flexibility of a FAP to provide direct services for some needs while making referrals for others can increase utilization rates of other existing academic career renewal services. Conversely, a FAP can be used as a referral resource by faculty development professionals when they become aware that a client has additional problems outside their areas of expertise. This opportunity for cross-referral helps to ensure that the individual faculty member receives the services needed from the individuals most qualified to provide those particular services. Competent screening and referral skills require training, experience, an awareness of both individual and organizational issues and needs, and a willingness to spend time updating information about available services and maintaining good working referral relationships. Most FAP directors also seek to assist the campus in identifying and addressing unmet needs of the whole target group. These needs may be for additional services, increased accessibility to existing services, or changes in policies or procedures that inhibit self-help.

Academic institutions have a substantial financial investment in faculty; accordingly, it makes sound economic sense to provide at least the same level of maintenance services to faculty productivity as is provided to computers on campus. Faculty function well under a wide variety of environmental conditions, have prolonged periods of productivity before some become obsolete, and, unlike computers, can generate new ideas and solutions. A faculty assistance program will not be able to resolve all issues of faculty productivity, but its positive contribution will greatly exceed its cost. Beyond considerations of productivity and cost effectiveness, such programs, through their humane application, enhance faculty careers and the quality of life.

## References

Baldwin, R. G., and Blackburn, R. T. "The Academic Career as a Developmental Process: Implications for Higher Education." *Journal of Higher Education,* 1981, *52,* 598–614.

Barling, P. W., and Handal, P. J. "Incidence of Utilization of Public Mental Health Facilities as a Function of Short-Term Economic Decline." *American Journal of Community Psychology,* 1980, *8,* 31–39.

Blackburn, R. T., Pellino, G. R., Boberg, A., and O'Connell, C. "Are Instructional Improvement Programs Off-Target?" In *Current Issues in Higher Education.* Washington, D.C.: American Association for Higher Education, 1980.

Buspus, J. F. "Career Vitalization and Stress Among Professors: An

Attributional Model." Paper presented at annual meeting of American Psychological Association, Los Angeles, Aug. 1981. (ED 207 478)

Carnegie Foundation for the Advancement of Teaching. "The Faculty: Deeply Troubled." *Change,* Sept./Oct. 1985, pp. 31–34.

Clark, B. R. "Listening to the Professoriate." *Change,* Sept./Oct. 1985, pp. 36–43.

Cyert, R. M. "The Management of Universities of Constant or Decreasing Size." In *Current Issues in Higher Education.* Washington, D.C.: American Association for Higher Education, 1980.

Dooley, D., and Catalano, R. "Economic, Life, and Disorder Changes: Time-Series Analyses." *American Journal of Community Psychology,* 1979, *7,* 381–396.

Furniss, W. T. *Reshaping Faculty Careers.* Washington, D.C.: American Council on Education, 1981.

Kanter, R. M. "Changing the Shape of Work: Reform in Academe." In *Current Issues in Higher Education.* Washington, D.C.: American Association for Higher Education, 1979.

Kasl, S. V., and French, J.R.P., Jr. "The Effects of Occupational Status on Physical and Mental Health." *Journal of Social Issues,* 1962, *18* (3), 67–89.

Lieberman, M. A., and Glidewell, J. C. "Overview: Special Issue on the Helping Process." *American Journal of Community Psychology,* 1978, *6,* 405–411.

Maslach, C. *Burnout: The High Cost of Caring.* Englewood Cliffs, N.J.: Prentice-Hall, 1982.

Oliver, J. M., and Pomicter, C. "Depression in Automotive Assembly-Line Workers as a Function of Unemployment Variables." *American Journal of Community Psychology,* 1981, *9,* 507–512.

Ragland-Sullivan, E., and Barglow, P. "Job Loss: Psychological Response of University Faculty." *Journal of Higher Education,* 1981, *52,* 45–66.

Roman, P. M. "The Social and Organizational Precursors of EAP's: Assessing Their Role in Higher Education." In R. W. Thoreson and E. P. Hosokawa (eds.), *Employee Assistance Programs in Higher Education.* Springfield, Ill.: Thomas, 1984.

Sarason, S. B. *Work, Aging, and Social Change: Professionals and the One Life–One Career Imperative.* New York: Free Press, 1977.

Schuster, J. H., and Bowen, H. R. "The Faculty at Risk." *Change,* Sept./Oct. 1985, pp. 13–21.

Shull, F. A., Jr. "Professorial Stress as a Variable in Structuring Faculty Roles." *Educational Administration Quarterly,* 1972, *8* (3), 49–66.

Wrich, J. T. *The Employee Assistance Program: Updated for the 1980's.* Hazelton, Minn.: Hazelton, 1980.

Zander, A., and Quinn, R. "The Social Environment and Mental Health: A Review of Past Research at the Institute for Social Research." *Journal of Social Issues,* 1962, *17* (3), 48–65.

8

# Designing Options
# for Early Retirement

*Jay L. Chronister*

The early retirement of faculty members has become a topic of increased interest and discussion on college and university campuses and in the chambers of state legislative bodies over the past decade. The forces that have generated this interest are multiple but can generally be classified as falling into one of two broad categories: those forces that are endemic to the institutions themselves and those that are a function of the external environment.

### Factors Creating the Interest in Early Retirement Programs

The institutional factors that have contributed to the interest in early faculty retirement include the "graying" of the professoriate, high tenure ratios on many campuses, financial constraints, the perceived need to hire "new blood" (young scholars), a declining population of college-age students, and the need to respond to changing student curricular and career interests (Chronister and Kepple, 1987). These factors have converged to create a poor academic labor market for faculty—a condition that Fernandez has labeled an "academic depression" (1978). In this depressed market for faculty, institutions have also experienced a decline in graduate enrollment as potential Ph.D. students choose alternate careers that in many cases do not require the same graduate preparation that is required for the professoriate (Bowen and Schuster, 1986). Therefore, in addition to losing enrollment in graduate programs, institutions are faced with the loss of a significant proportion of the bright graduate students, who can serve both as a source of intellectual stimulation and scholarly growth for current faculty (Pelikan, 1983, p. 18) and as the candidate pool for the next generation of faculty. Within this institutional environment, "new scholars" serve as more than new faculty members; they also serve as a source of intellectual stimulation for senior colleagues.

At the same time that institutions began to face constraints created by these factors, policies promulgated by the federal government exacerbated the situation and provided impetus for the development of incentive early retirement programs for faculty. Two legislative measures enacted in the 1970s combined to create the initial flurry of activity surrounding early retirement programs: the Employees Retirement Income Security Act of 1974 (ERISA) restricted the ability of colleges and universities to make changes in pension plans in order to alter the retirement patterns of faculty members (Holden, 1985); the 1978 amendments to the Age Discrimination in Employment Act (ADEA) raised the allowable mandatory retirement age from sixty-five to seventy, with the potential effect of adding five years to the careers of tenured faculty members. (Tenured faculty members were exempted from coverage under these amendments for four years, delaying until July 1, 1982, the law's effect on them.) With passage of the 1986 amendments to the ADEA, mandatory retirement by reason of age has been abolished. This "uncapping" of the length of careers for tenured faculty provided for in the 1986 amendments takes effect for tenured faculty on January 1, 1994, unless states and institutions choose to abolish retirement based upon age prior to that time. Several states had already, before the amendments, uncapped mandatory retirement: Maine and Florida in the mid 1970s, with Utah and Wisconsin following suit in 1981 and 1984 respectively (American Council on Education, 1985). The Commonwealth of Virginia passed legislation in March of 1987 to abolish mandatory retirement, with an effective date retroactive to January 1, 1987.

For the majority of institutions, the reality of having no mandatory retirement age for faculty members has brought home the importance of creating a flexibility in faculty staffing that has not been available in recent years. Prior to the past fifteen or so years, flexibility was achieved through a natural attrition of faculty members created by death and retirement, by professorial mobility among institutions, and through the availability of adequate increased resources. But the environment has changed; natural attrition no longer provides adequate turnover in faculty positions, and additional resources are no longer available to create flexibility through an increase in the number of faculty positions.

The financial implications of the continued employment of faculty beyond a normal or mandatory retirement age cause a mounting concern in colleges and universities. Older faculty members are generally paid at a substantially higher rate than younger faculty. The turnover in faculty positions created by mandatory retirement has traditionally provided institutions with an important form of cost control. With the abolition of mandatory retirement, this relatively automatic control has been lost.

The mandatory retirement age also provided institutions with a mechanism for controlling tenure ratios and the age distribution of faculty through involuntary retirement. Now, however, colleges and universities can no longer count on an established age of sixty-five or seventy as an "end-of-contract" date for tenured faculty members. In the absence of such a retirement age, many institutions are concerned that they face an open-ended appointment for tenured faculty members in which the age of retirement is completely at the discretion of the individual faculty member. Compounding the situation is the fact that colleges and universities have been loath to implement systematic evaluation programs through which unproductive or incompetent faculty members can be removed "for cause."

The federal Omnibus Budget Reconciliation Act of 1986 included a provision that may exacerbate further the situation for many institutions. The provision, with an effective date of January 1, 1988, prohibits employers from discontinuing or reducing benefit accruals or contributions to pension plans for employees who continue to work beyond a pension plan's normal retirement age. This provision has two potential effects, both serving as disincentives to faculty members to opt for retirement: first, the institution's provision of benefits must be maintained as long as the faculty member remains employed (constituting thereby added institutional costs and a significant benefit to faculty members), and second, faculty members have the opportunity to increase their ultimate annuity benefit by continued employment, given the changed actuarial calculations that result from working to an older age.

From an institutional perspective, the combination of financial constraints, the conditions that underlie tenured appointments, and the requirements first imposed by the 1978 and subsequently expanded by the 1986 amendments to the ADEA can be viewed as a major motivation for the development of formal incentive early retirement programs.

Much of the recent interest in the early retirement of faculty is also a function of the conditions that underlie tenured employment. These conditions have been described as "an arrangement under which faculty appointments in an institution of higher education are continued until retirement for age or physical disability, subject to dismissal for adequate cause or unavoidable termination on account of financial exigency or change of institutional program" (American Association of University Professors and Association of American Colleges Commission on Academic Tenure, 1973, p. 256).

Operating within the requirements of the amended ADEA that set restrictions on their ability to force retirement by reason of age, their own lack of mechanisms for separating faculty members for reasons of incompetence and/or nonproductivity, and the other factors cited, colleges and universities have increasingly turned to early retirement plans as a means of manipulating the retirement patterns of faculty.

## Early Retirement: Concept and Definitions

Early retirement is conventionally viewed as retirement prior to a mandatory retirement age, or retirement prior to the normal retirement age as set forth in a formal pension plan. The normal retirement age in a pension plan is defined as that age at which a retiring employee is eligible for unreduced retirement annuity benefits. Another meaning of the term *early retirement* is retirement by an individual at an age earlier than the age at which retirement would have taken place in the absence of some inducement or incentive.

The purpose of incentive early retirement programs is to encourage and facilitate the voluntary retirement of personnel. Jenny (1974) has defined the formal incentive early retirement program as any arrangement between an employer and an employee designed to provide tangible inducements in the form of a monetary or an in-kind reward for early retirement (p. 8).

Incentive early retirement programs have been in existence in higher education for many years. Taylor and Coolidge (1974) conducted an analysis of such programs in the early 1970s, when institutions were utilizing them in an attempt to cope with the effects of what was then called "the new depression in higher education." They found that twenty-six of forty-eight members of the Association of American Universities had some type of early retirement plan for faculty in 1973.

Mounting fiscal problems, enrollment uncertainty, and passage of the amendments to the ADEA have created a growing interest in developing strategies to alter retirement patterns of faculty. Following passage of the 1978 amendments to the ADEA, an increasing number of colleges and universities developed formal incentive retirement programs, while other institutions expanded the number of options and incentives in their existing programs in order to make them more attractive to faculty (Chronister and Kepple, 1987). A report on incentive early retirement programs in existence at fifty-one public universities in 1984 indicates that the majority of the programs on those campuses were implemented between 1979 and 1984 (Chronister and Trainer, 1985). Significant development of such programs also took place in private colleges during the same period of time (Kepple, 1984).

Although it is difficult to acquire accurate information on the total number of institutions that currently offer incentive plans or on the number of faculty members who actually retire because of such plans, it appears that the number of such offerings is increasing. The 1987 *Campus Trends* report by the American Council on Education states that 42 percent of the 372 institutions in their study offered incentive early retirement programs for faculty. Within their weighted survey data the percentage of institutions, by type, offering the plans broke down as follows: doctoral universities, 74 percent; comprehensive universities, 61 percent; baccalaureate colleges,

37 percent; and two-year colleges, 35 percent. Public institutions were more likely (50 percent) to offer incentive retirement plans than were independent institutions (33 percent) (El-Khawas, 1987, p. 27).

It can be anticipated that institutions will place increased importance on the implementation of early retirement plans as a personnel management strategy in the coming years as the federal uncapping of mandatory retirement for tenured faculty becomes a reality with the phase-out of the seven-year exemption on January 1, 1994. The experience of institutions in states that have recently abolished mandatory retirement has provided fuel for this interest. As an example, when Wisconsin uncapped mandatory retirement in July of 1984, ten of twenty-three faculty members in the university system who would have retired at age seventy in 1985 chose to continue employment (American Council on Education, 1985, p. 7).

The objectives underlying the establishment of early retirement programs vary according to institutional need. The three most common objectives cited by a sample of public universities in 1984 were the following: to provide a faculty benefit, to provide for the reallocation of resources, and to create financial savings (Chronister and Trainer, 1985). In this same study a number of the institutions indicated that a need to provide for a renewal of the professoriate on their campus was a fundamental program objective. Increasing the quality of faculty during a buyer's market and providing an overall reduction in the average age of the institution's faculty were highly rated objectives provided by private liberal arts colleges that participated in a study of incentive early retirement programs conducted in 1983 (Kepple, 1984).

*Incentive Early Retirement Program Options.* Incentive early retirement programs offered by colleges and universities differ significantly in the types of benefits offered and in eligibility requirements of faculty. Inherent in the structure of the programs are the specific purposes for which they have been developed, the demographic and professional characteristics and needs of the faculty to whom they have been addressed, the type(s) of basic pension plan(s) in effect at the institutions, and the financial condition of the institutions.

In addition to these variables, incentive plans are also shaped by the ADEA requirements that cause such programs to be voluntary and by federal tax guidelines and requirements (most recently those included in the Tax Reform Act of 1986). The Omnibus Budget Reconciliation Act of 1986, which prohibits employers from discontinuing or reducing pension plan contributions for an employee while employment continues beyond the normal retirement age of a pension plan, will also have an impact in the coming years (National Association of College and University Business Officers, 1986).

Incentive early retirement programs may be either formal or ad hoc (Kepple, 1984). In formal plans specific incentives are established and apply to all faculty in a selected class. Faculty who meet the specified eligibility criteria (such as age and years of service) and who elect to participate in the program are eligible to receive the prescribed incentives. Ad hoc plans, on the other hand, provide for the individual negotiation of incentives with interested faculty members, and therefore the benefits and arrangements may vary significantly from one case to another.

The type of institutional pension plan in which faculty members participate sets a "normal" retirement age and also shapes to some degree the types of financial incentives that are included in early retirement programs. There are two basic types of pension plans: defined-benefit plans and defined-contribution plans.

*Defined-benefit pension plans* provide guaranteed retirement annuities based on a formula that generally includes the number of years of service in the system and a certain percentage of the final-year salary, an average of a number of years of highest salary, or a percentage of salary for each year of service. These plans usually have a minimum number of years of service and a minimum age the employee must achieve before he or she is eligible for an unreduced pension annuity. Retirement prior to the specified age and/or the required number of years of service creates a penalty situation for the employee and reduces the pension annuity. Such a penalty serves as a strong disincentive for early retirement. To offset this negative factor, a formal early retirement plan at an institution with a defined-benefit pension plan may credit the early retiree with a specified number of years of unearned service in order to reduce or remove the penalty. Many defined-benefit plans also include a cost-of-living index factor that is designed to make adjustments in annuity income to offset partially the impact of inflation on annuity purchasing power.

*Defined-contribution pension plans* provide a retirement annuity that is based on the amount of contributions that the employer and employee make to the employee's retirement annuity account, the earnings on the accumulated assets in the account, and the age at which the employee retires. In defined-contribution plans the employee assumes the risk on the performance of the investments and therefore on the eventual adequacy of the annuity (Commission on College Retirement, 1986). The retiree faces an actuarial reduction in benefits the earlier the age at which retirement takes place. A further disincentive for retiring early is that the longer one is employed, the greater the contributions to the pension fund and the longer earnings will accumulate in the fund. The Commission on College Retirement has indicated that by working an additional five years, a participant frequently can double the monthly annuity benefit, due to additional contributions and investment earnings and the actuarial adjustment to the retirement age (1986, p. 19).

*Types of Incentives Offered.* Recognizing these factors and the need for financial security during the years of retirement, colleges and universities have utilized a number of specific economic incentives to facilitate early retirement. Such plans usually contain one or more of the following incentives (Patton, 1979; Chronister and Kepple, 1987).

1. *Severance pay or lump-sum payments.* Under this type of option the early retiree receives a financial bonus that is normally some percentage (possibly more than 100 percent) of the salary of the last year of full-time employment. The payout may be in the form of a lump-sum payment, deferred payments over a period of years, or a tax-sheltered payment. This option, if not carefully structured, has the potential of creating significant tax liability for faculty members, in view of provisions enacted as part of the Tax Reform Act of 1986.

*Example:* Professor Smith, whose nine-month salary is $48,000, is offered a $48,000 one-time lump-sum payment or a deferred payment of the same amount spread over twenty-four months.

2. *Annuity enhancements.* The purpose of this option is to bring the early retiree's pension annuity up to a level that approximates the level that would have been received had employment continued until the normal retirement age. This goal is usually achieved by delaying the start of payout of the basic pension plan or by providing a supplemental annuity plan.

*Example:* Professor Green, whose retirement pension at age seventy would be $41,900, is offered the opportunity to retire at age sixty-seven. In order to bring the age-sixty-seven pension of $32,000 close to the age-seventy pension, the institution purchases a supplemental annuity for Professor Smith that will yield an annual sum to make up most of the difference.

3. *Liberalized actuarial reduction.* With this option the individual receives a pension annuity that is comparable to the annuity that would have been received had employment been continued until the normal retirement age. The awarding of a specified number of years of unearned-service credit in a defined-benefit plan is one strategy that has been utilized in support of this type of option.

*Example:* Professor Jones is employed at an institution with a defined-benefit pension plan. The incentive to retire early is the provision of two years of unearned-service credit, which will increase Professor Jones's pension annuity by about 4 percent of his final-year salary, thus offsetting the annuity penalty that would have been created by early retirement.

4. *Bridge benefits.* This approach to providing an incentive is a variation of annuity enhancement. The faculty member retires at the early retirement age and receives a cash supplement from the institution, paid out on a monthly basis for a specified number of years, but does not begin to draw on the retirement pension annuity until the end of the established bridging period. The early retiree may begin to draw a social security annuity during the bridging period if that period has been established to coincide with the availability of social security benefits. An advantage to the early retiree is that the institution may choose, as part of the incentives, to continue contributions to the retiree's pension fund.

*Example:* Professor Brown, whose nine-month salary is $35,000, retires at age sixty-two and does not begin to draw her basic pension annuity until age sixty-five. During the three years of early retirement, the college provides her with annual cash payments ranging from $13,750 to $14,600, which when added to her social security income provide her with an annual income equivalent to about 89 percent of what her net income would have been had she continued employment.

5. *Phased and partial retirement.* These options permit the early retiree to move gradually into full retirement by means of a reduced workload over a specified number of years. This gradual disengagement from full employment is attractive to many faculty members because it permits them to retain a tie with the institution and retain access to many institutional services, such as office space and secretarial assistance, while adjusting to retirement. It also provides a specified earned income during the years of phased or partial employment. An added benefit to the institution is that, in nearly all cases, the faculty members relinquish their tenured position when they sign the phased or partial retirement agreement.

One primary distinction between partial and phased options is that during the period of phased retirement the retiree often does not draw on the retirement annuity fund; the institution may, in fact, continue to contribute to that fund. However, most partial retirement plans make no such contribution.

*Example:* Professor White, with a nine-month salary of $44,000 at age sixty-two, enters a phased retirement plan for three years. During those three years she will receive half-pay for a half-time assignment, but the institution will continue to contribute to the pension plan and provide other benefits as though she were fully employed.

6. *Other incentives.* A number of other perquisites that have been found to be important to faculty members are the provision for continued participation in the institution's health insurance and life insurance programs and, in support of the career interests of faculty, continued access to office space, secretarial assistance, photocopying services, and library privileges. It has also been found that early retirees wish to retain access to social, cultural, and athletic activities and facilities of the institution.

Studies of incentive early retirement programs on college and university campuses provide evidence that faculty involvement in the development of an early retirement program can be important to the ultimate success of the program (Clevenger and Chronister, 1986; Chronister and Kepple, 1987). These same studies indicate that offering combinations of incentives or benefits also contributes to the success of the offerings.

*Success of Programs.* Although there are leaders in higher education who have expressed reservations about whether incentive early retirement programs are in fact an effective strategy for manipulating faculty retirement patterns, the majority of public institutions that were the focus of two recent studies indicated that their incentive programs had achieved the purposes for which they had been established (Chronister and Trainer, 1985; Clevenger and Chronister, 1986). In a similar fashion Kepple (1984) identified successful early retirement programs in private liberal arts colleges.

There are numerous examples of successful programs, but the three cases described below provide evidence of the success of plans that have been established to meet specific objectives.

• The implementation of a program with the expressed goal of facilitating a significant reduction in faculty positions was deemed successful at Michigan State University when about 100 faculty retired early (Kreinin, 1982).

• The University of Washington found their early retirement program to be a primary tool in achieving financial savings in 1982, in response to state reductions in funding. For a six-month period beginning in July 1982, 105 faculty members took advantage of the opportunity to retire at age fifty-five, permitting the institution to reduce staff, reallocate a number of tenured faculty to other units, and make selective new appointments (Olswang, 1987).

• A university in the northeast successfully utilized an incentive program to achieve the twin objectives of increasing staffing flexibility and providing for a phased reduction in staff (Clevenger and Chronister, 1986).

Statewide systems of higher education have also implemented incentive early retirement programs in the 1980s to encourage large-scale reductions in staffing. Offering a one-time,
three-month enrollment period in 1980, the California State University and College System achieved a significant reduction in
staffing when 416 faculty members retired under plan incentives
(Reinhard, 1981). Similar results were achieved in New York when
nearly 20 percent of the eligible staff, including 452 faculty members
in the State University (SUNY) and City University (CUNY) systems took advantage of the opportunity to retire early (Ingalls,
1985).

*Protection of Institutional Interests.* Although there are
many reports that incentive early retirement programs have been
successful in achieving the objectives for which they were established, there is a downside to this success: the loss of valued faculty
members is a potential negative consequence of an attractive incentive early retirement program (Clevenger and Chronister, 1986; Ingalls, 1985).

Some institutions have attempted to guard against a premature exodus of talented faculty members by including statements in
their program guidelines that reserve to the institution the right to
defer, for a specified period of time, a faculty member's early retirement through an incentive retirement program offering. Such statements are generally included to protect the integrity of academic
programs and usually contain a phrase such as "in the interest of
the institution" as the justification for such action. This type of
guideline reinforces the character of these incentive programs as
having been designed primarily to benefit the institution, as opposed to serving purely as a faculty benefit offering. When such a
deferment of retirement is invoked, the rights of the faculty member
are generally protected, so that when the deferred period is completed, the retiree achieves at least the same benefits that would have
been granted had early retirement been taken when initial eligibility
had been achieved.

The institutional benefit of such offerings is further reinforced when the plans are offered only for a limited period of time.

As an example, many programs are made available to a designated class of faculty (those who fall into a specified age range) for an enrollment period of one year or less. These offerings are generally referred to as "window offerings." The window may also be defined in terms of faculty of a specific age (such as sixty-two). The use of a window offering permits the institution to limit its financial commitments to the program and ensures that the offering responds to a specific institutional need. The Michigan State University (Kreinin, 1982) and University of Washington (Olswang, 1987) programs mentioned previously were time-delimited window offerings designed to meet specific institutional needs.

In the interest of meeting specific institutional objectives, incentive early retirement programs have been structured in some instances so that faculty members from selected academic disciplines are given higher priority in eligibility for program participation (Clevenger and Chronister, 1986). This approach is most often defensible when funding in support of a program is restricted and more faculty may apply for participation than funding will support. Such targeting of faculty cohorts has been applied to faculty from overstaffed departments (Clevenger and Chronister, 1986) or to faculty in units that were subject to elimination (Kreinin, 1982).

On the assumption that less productive faculty are paid less well and receive smaller merit salary increases than those faculty who are more productive, it is possible to structure incentive payments for early retirement so that such payments are more attractive to low-paid faculty than to higher-paid faculty in a department or school. The rationale behind a differentiated incentive structure that provides higher-level incentive payments to lower-salaried faculty is that a higher payment should be an encouragement for retirement for low-paid faculty members and a disincentive to the more productive, higher-paid faculty members whom the institution may desire to retain. The use of such a strategy that discriminates based on salary appears to underlie the plan in effect at Stanford. At that institution the incentive payment for early retirement is based on a formula that places primary emphasis on the relationship between the early retiree's salary and the median salary of faculty in the department (Stanford University, 1986).

## Factors That Shape the Retirement Decisions of Faculty

Against this background of institutional strategies for making incentive early retirement programs attractive for faculty, it is also necessary to give recognition to the factors that affect the decision of faculty members about when they will choose to retire. An understanding of these factors is central to the development of an effective incentive early retirement program and may assist the institution in retaining the services of faculty members it might choose *not* to have retire.

*Financial Factors.* First among these factors are the economic considerations. Of concern to most potential retirees is the financial condition they will experience, both short-term and long-term, based on the pension annuity they will receive and on other financial resources available to them during the retirement years. The relationship between financial concerns and the age at which voluntary early retirement will be considered is well documented (Patton, 1977; Palmer and Patton, 1978; Holden, 1985; Mitchell, 1981). In his study of the retirement plans of faculty at the University of California, Patton (1977) found that a large early retirement annuity was a major consideration for early retirement (p. 352). Mitchell's (1981) study of faculty aged forty-five and older in Oregon's public system of higher education in 1980 identified enhanced income at full retirement, continued health insurance coverage, and the possibility of part-time employment as key considerations in the decision to retire early (p. 8).

Related to the financial interests of faculty, but of enough significance to merit separate mention, are concerns dealing with personal health and health insurance. A 1986 Teachers Insurance and Annuity Association (TIAA) report provided data to indicate that per-capita spending on personal health care in 1984 for individuals aged sixty-five and older was nearly four times the amount spent on persons under age sixty-five (1986, p. 3). Health insurance during the employment years, whether paid for by the institution or cost-shared by the institution and the faculty member, involves a regular payment to cover the potential large expenses of a serious illness. The loss of health insurance at group rates after retirement is a concern of potential early retirees that should be recognized in early retirement programs. Retirement prior to age sixty-five may necessitate purchase of health insurance at a significant increase in cost unless the institution provides for such coverage at institutional cost as a plan incentive, or unless the retiree is permitted to purchase the coverage at a reduced cost within the institution's group plan. Retirement at age sixty-five creates eligibility for Medicare coverage under varying conditions, but even such coverage does not meet the majority of health care spending for persons aged sixty-five and older (Teachers Insurance and Annuity Association, 1986, p. 3).

*Professional Costs and Opportunities.* A major influence on the decision about retirement for faculty members relates directly to faculty careers and the "professional costs" of retirement. Holden (1985) found that those faculty members with a strong attachment to their professional work were less likely to consider retiring early than were those less attached. A relationship between the degree to which faculty are actively involved in research and publication and the desire not to retire early has also been identified by Palmer (1979). However, a preliminary report on a study of 188 early retirees undertaken by Kellams and Chronister (1987) shows that approximately 81 percent of the former faculty members continued to be academically and professionally active after retiring early under an incentive early retirement program.

These studies indicate that career involvement or satisfaction may weigh heavily on one's decision regarding retirement. The relationship between career satisfaction and the desire to remain professionally active may function as either a positive or negative influence on the voluntary decision about taking early retirement by faculty members. For some faculty members the opportunity to retire early is viewed positively, because it will provide the opportunity to continue the pursuit of scholarly activities without the encumbrances of scheduled classes and committee work (Kellams and Chronister, 1987). This perspective is countered by the research of Holden (1985) and Palmer (1979), who found that a strong attachment to professional work was a disincentive to retire.

Light, Marsden, and Corl (1972) have provided a paradigm

for studying academic careers that is useful in attempting to understand retirement decisions by faculty. The components of the paradigm are summarized as follows. "The framework of an academic career . . . consists of three analytically distinguished strands: the elements of each contribute at different times to the potential for success. These three strands are the 'disciplinary career,' the 'institutional career,' and the 'external career.' In actual careers, they are interwoven. Activities and positions analytically in one strand often have meaning and consequences in the other strands" (p. 8).

It is evident that the institutional career, which is contractual, is related to advancement in the disciplinary career, in that the institutional strand provides resources and rewards for advancement and recognition in the discipline. Light and his colleagues state that the institutional environment is the base for the development of recognition in the broader disciplinary context. Because there is evidence to suggest that many retirees continue their disciplinary career after retirement, institutions that offer programs to encourage faculty members to retire early should provide incentives that address the possible impact of such an action on the disciplinary career strand of the professionally active potential early retiree.

The external career strand generally begins later in the life of faculty and involves work outside the institution but related to the discipline (Light, Marsden, and Corl, 1972). Reports on the postretirement activities of early retirees support the significance of the external career strand to many former faculty members during retirement years (Kellams and Chronister, 1987).

Research has also shown that faculty choose to avail themselves of retirement for what can be classified as either positive or negative reasons (Chronister, 1987). These reasons can be further classified into those factors that are an outgrowth of conditions in the work environment (institutional strand) and those factors that are more a function of personal preferences and needs.

The relationship between conditions in the work environment and faculty vitality and productivity has been the object of increasing research in recent years (Clark and Lewis, 1985; Bowen and Schuster, 1986). In setting the tone for their evaluation of the changing work environment for faculty, Bowen and Schuster stated the premise that the rewards of the academic profession are to an unusual degree intrinsic (p. 113). Among the intrinsic rewards they cited as important was membership in a campus community where friendships exist, where colleagues provide intellectual stimulation, and where good work is recognized and rewarded. Results of the Bowen and Schuster research led them to conclude that the work environment had changed in recent years, creating among other things a sense of dissatisfaction among many senior faculty members. Many of those faculty members were embittered at changes in the compensation and reward systems that favored scholarship at the expense of teaching. Alienation from the institution by older faculty because of changes in these priorities and a perceived excessively high value placed on "privatized" junior faculty members by the institution at the expense of older faculty members was evident (Bowen and Schuster, 1986, pp. 149-150).

It appears from the Bowen and Schuster study that the institutional careers of some senior faculty members become a negative influence and therefore a potential incentive to leave the organization. How much influence do negative organizational factors have on faculty participation in formal incentive early retirement programs? A study of early retirees and eligible nonretirees at the University of Arizona, which had offered an early retirement program, addressed this question (Monahan, 1986). The study examined the relationship between faculty perceptions of selected characteristics of their academic departments and the decision to participate in the early retirement program. Results of the study indicate that the early retirees differed from the nonretirees on a number of variables that reflect an attitude of alienation from the organization. Among the differences were that a significantly larger proportion of the early retirees (1) felt that they did not "fit well" in the department (p. 13), (2) saw new faculty as less effective teachers (p. 14), and (3) were from departments with large student-faculty ratios (p. 15). This study indicates that individual faculty members' perceptions of their recognition and value to the organization are related to early retirement decisions.

Anecdotal information gathered as part of the 1986 study of early retirees by Kellams and Chronister (1987) lends support to the Monahan findings. The reasons that their respondents provided for retiring early can be viewed as falling into three main categories:

organizational concerns, professional interests and concerns, and personal reasons. About 30 percent cited organizational concerns, including such reasons as "leadership was negative," "there were no long-term goals in my department," "administrators' attitudes toward older faculty were negative," and external pressure because "the school needed to reduce staff." Changes in teaching duties, heavy loads, and excessive committee work were also expressed sources of dissatisfaction (Chronister, 1987).

Reasons for early retirement that were classified as professional were provided by about 22 percent of the respondents (Kellams and Chronister, 1987). Their comments, which reflected both positive and negative motivations in this category, centered more on individual than organizational factors. Several respondents noted, for example, that they were "tired of teaching, grading papers and exams," "felt [they were] marking time," and suffered from "cumulative academic fatigue." A number of the respondents included as a reason the "need to provide opportunities for positions for recent graduates"; they also "felt that recent graduates were better informed on concepts and techniques in the discipline." The desire for full-time writing and research without the encumbrances of teaching schedules and committee work was also expressed as a reason for early retirement by a small percentage of the retirees (Chronister, 1987).

*Additional Factors.* Beyond the preceding categories of reasons, many respondents also cited personal reasons and opportunities to be involved in ventures and activities outside of the discipline as strong motivations for retiring early. Not to be overlooked as a facilitating factor are the incentives and benefits offered by the institution. Nearly 53 percent of the respondents cited the attractiveness of the incentives as an important factor encouraging the decision to retire early (Kellams and Chronister, 1987).

Although continued reference is made to participants in early retirement programs as *voluntary* retirees, it can be assumed that some are less voluntary than others. There are examples of institutions that have provided early retirement options to faculty members in departments or schools that have been targeted for reduction in size or for elimination. Such appeared to be the case at

Michigan State University in 1981, when approximately 100 tenured faculty members retired early under an incentive plan in the face of a mandated reduction of that number of tenured positions in selected units (Kreinin, 1982, p. 37). In other instances the option to retire early under an early retirement plan is the "humane alternative" offered to marginal faculty who would otherwise be subject to dismissal proceedings.

### Faculty Reactions to Incentive Early Retirement Programs

As I indicated previously, the overall reaction at colleges and universities that have offered incentive early retirement programs has been that the programs have been successful in meeting the purposes for which they were established. However, it is important that those evaluating faculty reactions to these programs view them from the perspective of those who have taken advantage of the opportunity to retire early and those who have declined that opportunity. As might be expected, there is much more information on the reactions of participants than of nonparticipants.

The Kellams and Chronister study provided data indicating that about 94 percent of the 188 retirees were either satisfied or very satisfied with their decision to retire early (1987, p. 17). This response pattern mirrors almost precisely the findings of a study conducted by Kell and Patton (1978) nearly ten years earlier, when 93 percent of the interviewees from four institutions expressed satisfaction with the decision to retire early (p. 175).

Among the Kell and Patton respondents, 90 percent indicated that they would make the same decision again, and 88 percent stated that they were well off financially during their retirement years (p. 176). Among the early retirees of the 1986 study, 77 percent indicated that they would retire at the same age if they had the decision to make again, and 15 percent indicated that they would retire at an earlier age (Kellams and Chronister, 1987, p. 16). In regard to their financial situation after early retirement, slightly more than 72 percent stated that their standard of living was about the same as in the year before retirement, and (surprisingly) an additional 21 percent felt that their standard was higher (p. 16).

When these expressions of satisfaction with the early retirement decision and satisfaction with the postretirement standard of living are combined with the fact that both Kell and Patton (1978, p. 176) and Kellams and Chronister (1987, p. 6) found that a majority of their respondents remained professionally active, it becomes evident that separation from the institutional environment (the institutional career strand) does not mean a separation from the discipline or the profession.

Although the above results indicate a satisfaction with the early retirement decision by respondents, it is important to recognize that some of this satisfaction is related to the fact that some faculty members may be removing themselves from an institutional environment from which they feel alienated (Monahan, 1986; Kellams and Chronister, 1987). In addition, there is evidence that those faculty members who choose not to participate in an incentive early retirement program feel that the incentives are not adequate, or they do not want to lose the contact with students and colleagues (Palmer, 1984, pp. 23–24).

### Early Retirement Programs: Policy Considerations for the Future

The preceding sections of this chapter have provided a historical perspective on the forces that have shaped institutional interests in programs designed to encourage the early retirement of faculty members, the crucial elements of progams, and the relative success of those programs from both an institutional and a faculty perspective. In this final section it seems appropriate to look to the future and to present a perspective on incentive early retirement programs for the next two decades. Over the past decade these incentive programs have assisted institutions in achieving flexibility in faculty staffing by encouraging older faculty to retire, thereby creating positions for younger faculty, reducing compensation budgets, allowing the reallocation of positions to high-demand areas, and reducing tenure ratios. But such programs are not a panacea. If tenure ratios exceed a rate that institutions feel is appropriate, the tenure system should be reviewed and modified. If unproductive or incompetent faculty are the problem, the institution must take appropriate action to address that problem. However, studies of early retirement programs indicate that they fail in the whole to distinguish between highly productive, valued faculty members and those whom the institution may regard as marginal or incompetent performers. As a result, colleges and universities have lost senior faculty members who are productive and crucial to the fulfillment of institutional purposes.

With a commitment to vitality and productivity, colleges and universities have a responsibility to maintain and enhance the quality of their faculties through investment of institutional resources in activities appropriate to that end. Faculty renewal cannot be achieved solely through a process of faculty replacement, which is the contribution that early retirement programs can provide. The finding that large numbers of early retirees remain professionally active after retirement means that colleges and universities are losing faculty members who could have continued to make significant contributions to institutional vitality.

The need for retaining productive faculty members in the future has been succinctly stated by Bowen and Schuster, who indicate that by the year 2009 the number of faculty appointments that will need to be made will probably equal nearly two-thirds of the professoriate of 1985 (1986, p. 198). In view of such a projection, it appears that those institutions that have been using incentive early retirement programs to create vacancies in order to recruit "new blood" into their faculties may want to reassess this strategy.

In the years ahead, incentive early retirement programs may continue to play a significant role in institutional attempts to revitalize and renew their faculties, but the programs should be undertaken or continued in conjunction with other strategies described in this book. In view of the fact that age is not a valid determinant of faculty vitality and productivity, institutions will need to increase the intrinsic and financial rewards deemed necessary to retain the services of those senior faculty whom the institution desires to retain and who have the interest and capacity to continue to contribute to the vitality of the institution. Faculty renewal that is based solely on strategies that facilitate the turnover of faculty may be viewed as shortsighted and counterproductive in the long term.

## Sources of Information About Early Retirement Programs

Institutional interest in the development of early retirement programs has generated efforts by several professional associations to gather information about the characteristics of such programs, and two professional organizations have taken action to disseminate information on early retirement programs for faculty in recent years. The National Association of College and University Business Officers published brief listings of institutional programs in several 1984 issues of *The Business Officer.* The American Council on Education also presented information on early retirement programs for faculty in the "Focus on Faculty" section of *Higher Education and National Affairs* in 1985 and 1986. Pertinent information is also provided at times in the various publications of the Teachers Insurance and Annuity Association. (Examples of these publications are cited in the bibliography under the organization's name.)

Concerns about the possible impact on faculty retirement of the 1986 amendments to the ADEA and the tax reform legislation of the same year have resulted in the establishment of a Project on Faculty Retirement, which has been designed to gather data and assemble a set of studies that will help institutions understand the implications of the abolition of a mandatory retirement age. The studies for this research effort are to be completed during the 1989–90 academic year. The project, housed at Princeton University, is under the joint sponsorship of the American Association of University Professors (AAUP), the Association of American Universities (AAU), the National Association of State Universities and Land-Grant Colleges (NASULGC), and the Consortium on Financing Higher Education (COFHE); it is funded by the Andrew W. Mellon Foundation.

In addition to its involvement in the Project on Faculty Retirement, COFHE has issued a series of reports on the response of its member institutions to the potential impact of the 1986 ADEA and tax reform legislation on faculty retirement and benefit plans.

### References

American Association of University Professors and Association of American Colleges Commission on Academic Tenure. *Faculty*

*Tenure: A Report and Recommendations.* San Francisco: Jossey-Bass, 1973.

American Council on Education. "Focus on Faculty." *Higher Education and National Affairs,* 1985, *34* (17), 5-7.

Bowen, H. R., and Schuster, J. H. *American Professors: A National Resource Imperiled.* New York: Oxford University Press, 1986.

Chronister, J. L. "Managing Faculty Resources: The Faculty Perspective—Now That I Have Retired Early, I Find . . ." Unpublished colloquium paper presented at Claremont Graduate School, Claremont, Calif. Apr. 22, 1987.

Chronister, J. L., and Kepple, T. R., Jr. *Incentive Early Retirement Programs for Faculty: Innovative Responses to a Changing Environment.* ASHE-ERIC Higher Education Report, no. 1. Washington, D.C.: Association for the Study of Higher Education, 1987.

Chronister, J. L., and Trainer, A. "Early, Partial, and Phased Retirement Programs in Public Higher Education: A Report on Institutional Experiences." *Journal of the College and University Personnel Association,* 1985, *36* (4), 27-31.

Clark, S. M., and Lewis, D. R. (eds.). *Faculty Vitality and Institutional Productivity: Critical Perspectives for Higher Education.* New York: Teachers College Press, 1985.

Clevenger, B. M., and Chronister, J. L. *Early Retirement Programs for Faculty: Three Institutional Case Studies.* Occasional Paper, no. 11. Charlottesville: Center for the Study of Higher Education, University of Virginia, 1986.

Commission on College Retirement. *A Pension Program for College and University Personnel.* New York: Commission on College Retirement, 1986.

El-Khawas, E. *Campus Trends, 1987.* Higher Education Panel Report, no. 74. Washington, D.C.: American Council on Education, 1987.

Fernandez, L. *U.S. Faculty After the Boom.* Report for the Carnegie Council on Policy Studies in Higher Education. Project on Qualitative Policy Analysis Models of Supply and Demand in Higher Education. Technical Report, no. 4, 1978.

Holden, K. C. "Maintaining Faculty Vitality Through Early Retirement Options." In S. M. Clark and D. R. Lewis, (eds.), *Faculty*

*Vitality and Institutional Productivity: Critical Perspectives for Higher Education.* New York: Teachers College Press, 1985.

Ingalls, Z. "Early Retirement Option in New York State Attracts Hundreds of College Employees." *Chronicle of Higher Education,* Jan. 9, 1985, p. 27.

Jenny, H. H. *Early Retirement: A New Issue in Higher Education. The Financial Consequences of Early Retirement.* New York: Teachers Insurance and Annuity Association, 1974.

Kell, D., and Patton, C. V. "Reaction to Induced Early Retirement." *Gerontologist,* 1978, *18* (2), 173–178.

Kellams, S. E., and Chronister, J. L. "Life After Early Retirement: Faculty Activities and Perceptions." Paper presented at annual meeting of Association for the Study of Higher Education, Baltimore, Md., Nov. 1987.

Kepple, T. R., Jr. "Incentive Faculty Early Retirement Programs at Independent Liberal Arts Colleges." Unpublished doctoral dissertation, School of Education, Syracuse University, 1984.

Kreinin, M. E. "Preserving Tenure Commitments in Hard Times." *Academe,* 1982, *68* (2), 37–45.

Light, D. W., Jr., Marsden, L. R., and Corl, T. C. *The Impact of the Academic Revolution on Faculty Careers.* AAHE-ERIC Higher Education Report, no. 10. Washington, D.C.: American Association for Higher Education, 1972.

Mitchell, B. A. "Early Retirement in Higher Education." Paper presented at annual meeting of Association for the Study of Higher Education, Washington, D.C., Mar. 1981.

Monahan, D. J. "Departmental Characteristics and the Early Retirement Decisions Among University Faculty." Paper presented at annual meeting of American Educational Research Association, San Francisco, Calif., Apr. 1986.

National Association of College and University Business Officers. "Employers Must Continue Retirement Contributions for Older Workers." *Business Officer,* 1986, *20* (6), 9.

Olswang, S. G. "Facing Financial Distress: A Case Study of the University of Washington." *Higher Education,* 1987, *16* (2), 145–154.

Palmer, D. D. "Faculty Responses to the Higher Mandatory Retirement Age: Which Faculty Will Stay?" Paper presented at meeting of Midwest Economics Association, Chicago, Apr. 1979.

Palmer, D. D., and Patton, C. V. "Attitudes Toward Incentive Early Retirement Schemes." In *Current Issues in Higher Education.* Washington, D.C.: American Association for Higher Education, 1978.

Palmer, S. E. "Early Retirement: For Some Teachers, Financial Incentives Seem Inadequate." *Chronicle of Higher Education,* Feb. 1, 1984, pp. 23-24.

Patton, C. V. "Early Retirement in Academia: Making the Decision." *Gerontologist,* 1977, *17* (4), 347-353.

Patton, C. V. *Academia in Transition: Mid-Career Change or Early Retirement.* Cambridge, Mass.: Abt Books, 1979.

Pelikan, J. *Scholarship and Its Survival: A Carnegie Foundation Essay.* Lawrenceville, N.J.: Princeton University Press, 1983.

Reinhard, R. M. *An Analysis of the California State University and Colleges Early Retirement Incentive Program: A Report Pursuant to Chapter 656 of the Statutes of 1979.* Sacramento: California State Legislative Analyst's Office, 1981.

Stanford University. *The Faculty Early Retirement Program II.* Palo Alto, Calif.: Stanford University, 1986.

Taylor, A. L., and Coolidge, H. E. "Survey and Analysis of Early Retirement Policies." *Educational Record,* 1974, *55* (3), 183-187.

Teachers Insurance and Annuity Association. *Planning for Health Coverage in Retirement: Medicare and Health Insurance.* New York: Educational Research Unit, Teachers Insurance and Annuity Association, 1986.

Watkins, B. T. "Early-Retirement Options Gaining Popularity Among Colleges and Older Faculty Members." *Chronicle of Higher Education,* July 10, 1985, p. 19f.

 *PART THREE*

# Models of Successful Practice

Part Two illustrated five areas of developmental activity gaining currency in academic settings. Part Three now takes a step beyond that and presents five examples of campus-based implementation. The first four of these chapters demonstrate that individual campuses can mount faculty development programs that, extending beyond conventional modes, can be effective in enhancing faculty careers. The final chapter in Part Three depicts an intercampus program, showing that a consortium of small colleges, through collaborative efforts, can add important dimensions to faculty career development.

The multidimensional development strategy adopted at the University of Georgia is portrayed in Chapter Nine. Ronald Simpson and William Jackson describe a wide range of campus activities, encompassing personal, professional, and organizational components. Particularly notable is the integration of the so-called wellness vectors—social, occupational, spiritual, intellectual, and social—culminating in the university's annual campus renewal conference. The Georgia strategy goes a long way in taking into account the faculty career stages described in Chapter Two.

Chapter Ten presents a major organizational intervention—Project NUPROF at the University of Nebraska, Lincoln—which is directed particularly at midcareer faculty to encourage their renewal and redirection. Described by Joyce Povlacs Lunde and Ted Hartung, the program provides a structured change process by which faculty can break out of old patterns and allow new or suppressed interests to surface. The Nebraska strategy emphasizes the integration of individual and organizational needs.

Barbara Hill describes in Chapter Eleven a campus program at Loyola University of Chicago that embodies a distinctive strategy—one that underscores the importance of personal-professional development in a strong family- and community-oriented environment. The author describes Loyola's "person-centered program," which stresses "commitment to serving others . . . and the conviction that moral and humanistic questions lie at the heart of education." Within this strong value context, faculty have implemented many different professional and personal changes based on a systematic life-career planning process.

Chapter Twelve presents two organizational development strategies—faculty retraining and buyouts—developed at Fairleigh Dickinson University to respond to the realities of decreasing student enrollments. The author, Ann Lucas, demonstrates how FDU's strategies were effective in balancing organizational requirements and faculty interests and shows that drastic changes in the deployment of instructional staff require a number of different organizational development strategies in order to mesh the need for institutional flexibility with faculty members' individual preferences.

Chapter Thirteen shows how institutions can develop consortial arrangements by pooling resources to meet individual and institutional needs. Neil Wylie describes the Great Lakes Colleges Association, a consortium of thirteen small colleges that provides an array of faculty development opportunities. He demonstrates that shared arrangements can provide economies of scale for the member institutions and expanded opportunities for faculty members—arrangements that can enrich the professional experience in ways that single institutions (particularly smaller campuses) could not accomplish.

Together these five chapters provide models of successful approaches to enhanced faculty development. Every campus setting is idiosyncratic; a successful strategy at one campus will not fit perfectly at another. But each of these cases embodies elements that can be adapted to other campus settings.

9

# A Multidimensional Approach to Faculty Vitality:

## The University of Georgia

*Ronald D. Simpson*
*William K. Jackson*

Though the University of Georgia is the oldest state-chartered university in the United States, its emergence as a major research institution has been similar in nature to many other southern land-grant universities. Large numbers of World War II and Korean War veterans enrolled during the late forties and early fifties, doctoral programs were added rapidly during the fifties and sixties, and desegregation was experienced during the sixties. A dramatic shift from teaching to research as a perceived primary mission was witnessed by the dawn of the seventies. While this sequence of events was similar in universities throughout the South, the rapidity and magnitude of change was significantly more pronounced at the University of Georgia. It is this context that makes the following chronicle significant.

During the 1960s and 1970s the university made sporadic attempts to establish a unit that would deal with instructional and faculty development; but for philosophical and financial reasons the time was not right, and these attempts were unsuccessful. During the late 1970s separate recommendations from three different faculty committees were forwarded to the vice-president for academic affairs (VPAA), and in 1979 a decision was made to establish the Office of Instructional Development (OID). Two acting direc-

167

tors served until the appointment of the first permanent director, who arrived in the summer of 1981. The associate director joined the staff a year later, and it has been the philosophy of these two faculty members—along with the dedication of the OID staff, the enthusiastic response of the faculty, and the commitment of the central administration—that has led to the broad, multidimensional nature of this initiative (Jackson and Simpson, 1984).

## The Basic Philosophy

When the director and associate director began their work at the University of Georgia (UGA), no mandate or hidden agenda existed for how the Office of Instructional Development should function. The primary mission from the president and vice-president for academic affairs was to do whatever was needed to improve instruction at UGA. With this in mind, the director and associate director spent the first year talking to deans, department heads, and faculty members, listening carefully to their ideas and suggestions. At least five factors emerged as "guideposts" for the development of a successful multidimensional, holistic instructional and faculty development program.

The first factor, and one that still plays a key role in OID's operation, is that our work be closely tied to the office of the vice-president for academic affairs. It has always appeared to us that strong support from the top is essential to the success of any instructional development program. UGA's vice-president for academic affairs is the person ultimately responsible for the quality of the instructional programs on campus. Our approach, from the beginning, has been to make it clear that OID's efforts are an extension of this senior administrator's responsibility and that OID has the mandate to work on improving instruction campuswide. We also share our joys and accomplishments with this leader and give credit to that office when appropriate. As a result, it is clear throughout our campus that instructional development is a high priority of both the president and the academic vice-president.

A second and equally important guidepost has been to work diligently to establish credibility with and input from the faculty. To help facilitate this, the VPAA appointed a university-wide committee to advise the office. Today the committee members, each of whom serves a three-year term, continue to be a vital force on campus. This committee and how it functions will be discussed later in this chapter.

A third aspect important to our office has been the overall "model" we have chosen to follow. Rather than restricting our efforts to more narrowly conceived functions (such as curriculum development, instructional design, educational media, or faculty development), we have adopted an environmental or institutional approach. For example, we believe that effective teaching and learning occur best within an environment where there is a climate supportive of those activities. In other words, when it is perceived by faculty and students that teaching and learning are valued activities, members of the university community are increasingly motivated to engage in those processes. We have taken the position that it is our role to help the *institution* become an organization that encourages and rewards excellence in instruction; hence our efforts have been directed largely to that end.

Our fourth approach has been to do whatever we do with thoughtfulness and thoroughness, always expecting high-quality results. Initially we chose to focus on projects that were relatively "safe"—that is, that practically assured a win-win outcome. For instance, providing services for graduate teaching assistants (GTAs) was considered an excellent idea by administrators and faculty alike; GTA training therefore became one of the first services OID initiated. Later we worked on more difficult issues, such as facilities planning and substance dependence by staff and faculty. But regardless of what we have tried to accomplish, we have always said repeatedly to ourselves, "It has to be done *well*." We believe that if our clients—who are mainly the faculty—do not view what we do as valuable and of high quality, we are doomed to failure.

A holistic approach serves as our fifth guidepost. Our focus, although institutional in scope, does not lose sight of the individual faculty member as a human being—one with the same needs for support and recognition as any other human being. Bowen and Schuster (1986), in their alarming study of the condition of the American professoriate, stress the need for an institutional reponse to the personal needs of faculty as well as to their professional needs.

Cares and Blackburn (1978, p. 135) state that "an academic institution differs in important ways from product-oriented organizations. The full growth and development of human resources should be the major purpose of an educational institution as well as an integral part of its very process." Our holistic approach to faculty development pays special attention to faculty stress and burnout, while identifying environmental factors that influence faculty well-being in general. An institutional response to the individual needs of each faculty member, although a complex task, is crucial if a multidimensional, holistic approach to faculty renewal is to succeed.

The fifth guidepost also includes the concepts of breadth and flexibility. Our listening to faculty and administrators has revealed that there is a broad array of needs across our campus and that there is no "one best way" to meet those needs. We have therefore been dedicated to the notion that we should try numerous approaches, and the university's senior administrators have encouraged this strategy. We have also worked hard to be creative and to take risks. While not all of our ideas have been successful, many experiments have been pleasant surprises. It has been our experience that approaching problems from a multidimensional perspective can often lead to creative solutions.

### The Central Role of Faculty

One of the strengths of our office, as we previously indicated, has been the relationship we have maintained with the eighteen-member faculty committee that advises the office. The instructional advisory committee, appointed by the vice-president for academic affairs, consists of representatives from each of the university's thirteen schools and colleges as well as from the offices of student affairs, institutional planning, and continuing education. Great care is taken to select faculty members who are highly respected as scholars *and* who are committed to the instructional mission of the university. Members of the advisory committee serve staggered three-year terms, with the committee electing annually a chair from among the membership.

The advisory committee meets monthly; however, much of the work of this group is conducted through subcommittees that are assigned responsibilities for specific OID programs. These subcommittees typically include several advisory committee members, along with others from the university community who have special expertise that can be utilized in specific subcommittee activities. The areas of responsibility assigned to these subcommittees include faculty development, instructional facilities, teaching awards, instructional grants, publications and presentations, and graduate teaching assistant services. OID staff provide the support necessary to facilitate the work of the advisory committee and its subcommittees. When plans for an activity are generated by OID, the staff seeks advice from the advisory committee before the activity is begun. In cases where new activities are initiated by the advisory committee, OID staff provide the day-to-day administration of these activities. The presence of this working advisory group ensures that each program and activity of the OID has been endorsed, in many cases planned, and in all cases supported by a large group of respected faculty members. This approach ensures that OID-sponsored activities address needs of the faculty *as perceived by the faculty* rather than needs identified by a small group of administrators acting independently of faculty input.

## Focusing on Faculty Renewal

During the fall of 1982 two resource persons who had provided expert assistance to the advisory committee and its faculty development subcommittee met with the OID director and associate director to discuss ways of preventing burnout within the university faculty. These initial discussions led to the establishment of a special planning committee to formulate ways to address this concern. This fourteen-member committee consisted of the advisory committee's subcommittee on faculty development, expanded to include additional faculty and staff members from the helping professions. Designed to bring faculty expertise in human resource development together with other faculty and staff who were concerned about the continued vitality of the university faculty, the committee formulated strategies for promoting faculty vitality at UGA. Its discussions led to a multidimensional approach, focusing initially on a campuswide renewal conference to start the 1983 academic year.

*The Renewal Conference.* Although this renewal conference and its successors have been described in detail elsewhere (Simpson and Jackson, 1987), certain characteristics of this unique activity are important in our attempt to describe the university's approach to faculty renewal. The planning committee felt that the conference should focus on personal as well as professional concerns (see Gardner 1963). Sessions addressing the special needs of young, mid-career, and preretirement faculty and their spouses were included. The tone of the conference sessions was positive and action-oriented. Follow-up activities were planned for each session, and participants were urged to consider the conference as a starting point for continuing renewal. The following partial list of topics provides an indication of the breadth of this aspect of the conference (a more detailed listing is reported in Simpson and Jackson, 1984, 1987):

- Improving Your Physical Fitness
- Relaxation Through Hypnosis
- Managing Your Personal Finances
- Leisure—What's in It for You?
- Managing Your Time Wisely
- Managing Stress Effectively
- Dealing with Problems Faced by Minority Faculty
- Coping with Performance Pressure
- Strategies for Survival in a Dual-Career Family
- Creative Leave Opportunities
- Spicing Up Your Teaching
- Improving Interpersonal Relationships via Effective Communications

Most of these sessions were led by faculty who volunteered their time and expertise. Additional faculty participated in the program through the conference hobby fair, where faculty displayed and shared their hobbies with their colleagues. Another special feature of the conference was a health risk appraisal made available to all conference participants through the university's fitness center. This first two-day conference, held just before the beginning of the fall quarter, was attended by more than 250 people. Its success led to similar conferences, with only minor modifications, in 1984 and 1985.

In April 1986 the office of instructional development hosted the first National Conference on Professional and Personal Renewal for Faculty, and a second conference on the same topic was hosted in April 1989. These conferences provided opportunities for sharing institutional experiences similar to the University of Georgia's. Approximately 200 participants from forty states, Canada, and the Virgin Islands attended each conference. These three-day conferences featured a total of one hundred presentations on various faculty renewal topics. (Proceedings of these conferences are available for a small cost from the OID.)

*Ongoing Renewal Activities.* The renewal conferences held before the beginning of the academic year focused the attention of the university community on opportunities for renewal experiences available on campus throughout the year. Some of these opportunities were planned specifically as follow-ups to the annual conference, while others emanated from programs already in place.

Since its establishment, the office of instructional development has offered a variety of seminars, institutes, colloquia, and study groups addressing personal as well as professional dimensions of faculty development. Regularly scheduled seminars held during the noon hour during the academic year provide faculty with opportunities to interact with their colleagues on a wide range of issues. During the last five years OID has sponsored over 100 such seminars, at which faculty contribute their time as presenters. (In many instances the presentations are essentially those for which a faculty member has been or could be paid substantial fees in off-campus settings.) One of the beneficial aspects of the university's faculty renewal program has been that it provides a rare opportunity for faculty to share their expertise with colleagues in other disciplines. In this regard we have found our faculty to be generous with their time as experts, as well as appreciative of opportunities to be consumers of the expertise of others. The variety of topics addressed in these seminars is displayed in Figure 9.1.

Many topics do not lend themselves to a noontime seminar format. Three other formats that have been successful at UGA are

**Figure 9.1. Typical OID Noontime Seminar Topics.**

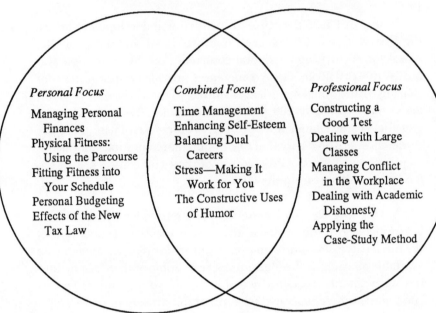

*Personal Focus*

Managing Personal
  Finances
Physical Fitness:
  Using the Parcourse
Fitting Fitness into
  Your Schedule
Personal Budgeting
Effects of the New
  Tax Law

*Combined Focus*

Time Management
Enhancing Self-Esteem
Balancing Dual
  Careers
Stress—Making It
  Work for You
The Constructive Uses
  of Humor

*Professional Focus*

Constructing a
  Good Test
Dealing with Large
  Classes
Managing Conflict
  in the Workplace
Dealing with Academic
  Dishonesty
Applying the
  Case-Study Method

one-day colloquia, one-week institutes, and extended study groups. An example of each is discussed in the paragraphs below. These formats allow for in-depth coverage of topics that require considerable time for understanding and skill development.

One way of achieving professional renewal is through the adoption of new teaching techniques. An introduction to a technique, such as teaching by the case-study method, requires more time for study and dialogue than is available in a one-hour seminar. For that reason OID regularly offers a day-long colloquium on the case-study method. The colloquium provides faculty with the opportunity to hear several of their colleagues discuss various aspects of this teaching methodology. The one-day format provides sufficient time for at least one session in which the method is demonstrated, thus allowing colloquium participants to serve as students in a simulated classroom. It works well to introduce teaching by the case-study method in this fashion, because the cases used in the simulations often deal with teaching issues rather than discipline-specific topics. Our faculty have been so receptive to these colloquia that waiting lists are often required for each offering (even though colloquia are scheduled before the beginning of the academic year or during breaks in the calendar in order to avoid conflicts with classes).

The impact of the microcomputer is pervasive in higher education, yet most of the faculty at an institution such as the University of Georgia received their formal training before the evolution of microchip technology. Although the new generation of faculty now entering our institution are usually skilled in this technology, a means to help others achieve similar skill levels is required. We have found a week-long Academic Computing Institute, which immerses participants in this technology, to be an effective approach. This format provides ample time for hands-on experience and allows faculty and staff to leave the institute with skills that can be applied immediately. We have offered seven such institutes, and each one has been filled to capacity. The first institute provided space for fifty participants; however, we have now reduced the size of the group to twenty-five in order to allow for more hands-on experience.

A number of renewal topics—particularly those dealing with personal dimensions—lend themselves to development in extended study groups. These study groups have usually been direct extensions of sessions held during the annual renewal conference. When a topic such as improving interpersonal communication skills, gaining control of life-style and work-style, or learning to relax through self-hypnosis is introduced in a renewal conference session, interested participants are given the opportunity to form a study group to examine the topic in greater depth. These groups typically meet once or twice each week for an extended period and are led by faculty members with expertise in facilitating group interactions.

## Extending Personal and Professional Renewal over the Life Span

Much has been learned from adult development theory about change over a lifetime. Erikson's (1963, 1968) theories of self-actualization, Levinson and others' (1978) *The Seasons of a Man's Life,* and even such popular books as *Passages* (Sheehy, 1976) have demonstrated that most people progress through predictable stages

of development. Cytrynbaum, Lee, and Wadner (1982) have summarized the views of current life-span theorists and have concluded
that adults who "manage" the transitions from one period to another are less vulnerable to stress and depression. Similar theories
have been rep' rted by career development researchers (Super, 1980;
Hall and Nougaim, 1968; Schein, 1971, 1978; and Baldwin, 1979).
Recent investigations into faculty career development (Baldwin,
1979, 1985; Furniss, 1981; Clark and Lewis, 1985) in general show
fairly significant differences among faculty at various career stages
in needs, expectations, and abilities. It would seem that by now we
would know enough about the major changes experienced by faculty over a career and lifetime that helpful interventions at the institutional level could be planned for and implemented.

     As we think about the needs of UGA's faculty over a lifetime,
at least three images come to mind. First, there is the twenty-eight-
year-old assistant professor, in her first faculty appointment, who is
told that she will have to be above average in research productivity if
tenure is expected. While she is enthusiastic and energetic, she
realizes that the next six years are crucial. She will have to manage
her time carefully, adjust to her new colleagues, serve effectively on
committees, deal with the needs of her students, and work toward
obtaining grants to fund her research. She knows that she will have
to be reasonably effective in all of these areas in order to survive.

     The second scenario involves the forty-five-year-old recently
promoted full professor who has done all the right things and is
now a recognized scholar in his field, in addition to being a popular
teacher. Though his path through life would appear to be lined
with roses, things are not that serene beneath the surface. He has
two children attending expensive colleges, his aging parents are
becoming a major concern, and he faces twenty or more years of a
job that in many ways will offer much the same challenges and
rewards as those he has experienced during the previous two
decades.

     The third image that comes vividly to mind is that of the
senior faculty member, now two years from retirement and suddenly
faced with several dramatic changes in his life. His wife of forty-five
years has recently died, and as a result he is experiencing acute
depression. Only a year ago he was enjoying his stature as a distin-

guished researcher and teacher in his field while being told by his wife and friends to slow down. Now he is withdrawn, increasingly inactive, and in need of help from friends, colleagues, and the university.

While fictitious, each of these scenarios may represent scores of faculty members under stress (Seldin, 1987). Each of the factors mentioned in the scenarios is potentially a reality for most of the men and women who constitute our faculty. Each of these situations can significantly alter the creativity, productivity, and happiness of a human being. Because the human resources embodied in our faculty represent the most valuable component of our university, and because most of the events we describe above are normal and predictable, it should be possible to plan interventions that will assist in meeting crucial personal and professional needs across the entire span of an academic career.

*Addressing Personal and Professional Needs of Young Faculty.* Most university faculty members begin their careers having recently completed highly specialized Ph.D. programs. For the most part these programs are designed to produce scholars with highly refined research skills (LaPidus, 1987); most graduate programs in academic areas do not include opportunities for skill development in teaching and other activities associated with instruction.

As new faculty enter the workplace, they are almost always met with instructional responsibilities. These young members of the profession are usually enthusiastic about this new role and want to be successful. It becomes critical, at this formative stage in their development, for them to receive assistance from their colleagues and their institution; for what happens during the first two or three years in this role may influence a lifetime of teaching and interaction with students.

The focus and leadership provided in this area by the Lilly Endowment appears not only refreshing but vital as we enter the 1990s. At a time when an aging faculty is being challenged to improve the academic preparation of young students, the nurturing of our younger faculty becomes increasingly critical (Mehrotra, 1984). It was within this context that OID first sought to implement a program designed to meet the specific needs of new faculty, particularly as these needs relate to instruction. In 1984 we were invited by the Lilly Endowment to submit a proposal for a teaching fellows program. We proposed the following six goals: (1) provide young faculty with an opportunity to further develop basic skills associated with effective teaching; (2) provide new faculty with information concerning instructional resources and services that exist at the University of Georgia; (3) demonstrate to young faculty that their university cares about good teaching and that this is reflected in the support systems available; (4) offer opportunities for dialogue and sharing of ideas with colleagues who have similar interests and backgrounds and who face similar problems; (5) develop instructional skills in young faculty through exposure to and interaction with role models who are master teachers; and (6) help to create an environment that will produce during this formative stage of development the best teaching scholar possible.

In writing the proposal, we reasoned that there are at least two major influences that shape the teaching behavior of most entering college professors. The first influence is any mentoring they may have received from their major professor; this determines for many the style of research, service, and teaching (Blackburn, Chapman, and Cameron, 1981). Recent research suggests, interestingly, that those who attain success in their discipline or profession are more likely to have had a mentor than those who are less successful (Torrance, 1984). Blackburn (1979) includes as one of the nine assertions about the academic career process that mentorship in the first years is critical in launching a productive career for the new faculty member. The second influence comes from multiple role models. As individuals are establishing themselves professionally, they are exposed to many teaching styles, with senior faculty members often serving as role models for junior faculty members. Our experience suggests that when incoming faculty sense that older faculty—particularly those who will be evaluating them for promotion and tenure—are dedicated, effective teachers, higher levels of expectation are established. This multiple-role-model phenomenon, no doubt operative in most academic settings, is most crucial within the first two or three years of most professional careers. Once instructional patterns are established, they become less malleable.

Upon OID's receipt of the initial $50,000 Lilly grant, eight faculty members at the end of their first, second, or third year at the University of Georgia were selected during the spring quarter of 1984 to participate as Lilly Teaching Fellows for the ensuing academic year. Candidates were required to be tenure-track assistant professors and recent recipients of a terminal degree in their field. Candidates were nominated by their department heads and deans, and applications were screened by a university-wide selection committee, with final approval coming from the vice-president for academic affairs.

OID received a total of $135,000 from the Lilly Endowment, spread over three years. The university has now assumed financial responsibility for the program's continuation—a condition encouraged by the grant. Proven effective, the program has remained essentially unchanged from the first year. It includes a two-day retreat held prior to the opening of the university in the fall; a teaching fellows resource room, where fellows can read, study, and work on projects; the selection of a mentor for the year for each fellow; bimonthly meetings featuring outside speakers or group discussions; development of an instructional improvement project; and an end-of-year retreat that includes mentors. During the years the project was funded by Lilly, all participants attended two national conferences and interacted with faculty from other funded institutions. This feature has now been replaced by an annual Lilly Day near campus, at which all present and past UGA fellows and mentors come together for a day of idea sharing and renewal of friendships. (We describe this program in greater detail than some others for what we think is a good reason: no other OID activity has addressed the concept of lifelong faculty development in such an integrative and thorough manner.)

In addition to our Lilly program, OID assists with a new-faculty orientation, holds additional seminars during the fall for new faculty, and sends written materials on instructional and faculty development activities to new faculty. Under the auspices of the office of the vice-president for services, a novel opportunity for new faculty is provided: they can participate in a week-long tour of many significant points of interest across our large and diverse state. OID is initiating a program called the Teaching Improvement Program (or TIPs), through which new, young faculty members will be matched with more senior faculty members, who will observe classes and exchange ideas about teaching.

Our work with young faculty grows out of our belief that it is important for them to know that the senior administration takes an interest in them personally as well as professionally. It is also important for them to make contact with faculty from other departments and colleges. From these interactions come the support and cooperation that may be lacking in the academic department. We also find that young faculty members, when nurtured carefully early in their careers, more rapidly come to appreciate their university, the new city in which they live, and the state and citizens from which they receive their ultimate support. The hypothetical twenty-eight-year-old assistant professor described earlier has a much better chance of being productive and happy in an environment where important resources and friendly support exist than in an environment perceived as cold and competitive. We know of several Lilly Teaching Fellows who have been pursued by other institutions but who declined to leave, at least in some measure because they appreciated the manner in which they were treated early in their careers.

***Targeting the Needs of Midcareer Faculty.*** Practically all of the programs offered by OID have potential for meeting the various needs of midcareer faculty. Even the Lilly and TIPs programs, designed for new faculty, call for more experienced faculty to serve as mentors and advisers. As we mentioned earlier, our regularly scheduled noon seminars, the colloquia on teaching by the case-study method, and the conferences on professional and personal renewal all contain features for coping with burnout and helping faculty with those things that are important to them at specific times in their lives. Two additional programs have been particularly helpful to midcareer faculty. Our annual Academic Computing Institute, referred to earlier, has helped hundreds of midcareer faculty to learn about important new technologies that are potentially valuable in both teaching and research. We have seen many examples of faculty who have "come alive" as a result of attending one of these week-long institutes. In addition, our assistance in providing small, internally funded instructional grants and in helping with proposal preparation for larger, external grants has been of particular value to midcareer faculty.

As we implied above, the needs of midcareer faculty are perhaps the most complex and varied. Many such faculty members face problems associated with their personal and family lives. At a stage when they may for the first time be questioning their direction and worth as professionals, they are also potentially facing personal challenges with adolescent children, dual-career concerns, diminishing health and physical stamina, and perhaps the crisis of dealing with aging or lost parents. These personal challenges tend to compound the professional challenges. For instance, some faculty at this time have to decide if they will accept administrative opportunities. Many are ready for change both in their approach to teaching and in their research efforts. Some consider changing departments, even institutions. At this juncture many have attained most of their professional goals and have begun looking at the remainder of their career in a new way; often their values change and their priorities in life undergo significant shifts (see Baldwin, 1985).

Our experience with midcareer faculty tells us that there is a need for mechanisms through which personal needs can be addressed. Indeed, our early work with the renewal conferences suggests that the personal needs are the ones that should be addressed first. Once personal needs are satisfied, we have noticed, it is easier to address professional needs. Learning about computers, changing approaches to teaching, and teaching new courses are examples of professional matters that midcareer faculty have addressed on our campus. Without an institutional climate to encourage such endeavors, many faculty do not feel free to reach beyond the status quo, in which they sometimes perceive themselves to be locked. It has been our goal to help open as many growth opportunities as possible. In those faculty who have taken advantage of some of the OID activities, we have seen numerous signs of revitalization. In fact, it has been surprising on many occasions just how little stimulus or intervention is needed to induce significant change. Consider, for example, several participants in the first OID colloquium on teaching by the case-study method: by the next quarter they told us that they had changed totally their approach to teaching. As one faculty member reported, "It had never occurred to me that students could learn just as much by asking questions and discussing ideas in class as by listening. I thought it was my job to tell them what they needed to know." By encouraging midcareer faculty to experiment and make changes, and by fostering a sense of community in the academic environment that makes all of this seem worthwhile, the institution can help rejuvenate many careers, and by so doing can benefit not only the individuals involved but the institution as well.

*Focusing on the Needs of Late-Career Faculty.* Many of the programs and activities at our institution that have benefited midcareer faculty have also been helpful to those late in their careers. While a different constellation of interests exists among preretirement faculty, the need for opportunities to meet personal as well as professional needs seems no less important to persons during this stage in life. We first realized how helpful faculty development programs can be to late-career faculty when we scheduled a session on financial planning at our first renewal conference five years ago. Later that fall and winter, OID sponsored two follow-up seminars, led by the same presenter, building on what had been taught in the first session. Over twenty people who attended these sessions contacted the seminar leader for additional information on how to obtain assistance in personal financial planning. Several of them emphasized how much better prepared they were financially to face the future—and eventually retirement—with the knowledge gained through the sessions. Faculty and spouses appear hungry for opportunities to learn about and discuss matters relating to investments, quality of life in later years, leisure activities, nutrition and health, strengthening family relationships, and many other topics when contemplation and reflection are possible.

We have also learned that teaching takes on added meaning for many late-career faculty. Many early- and midcareer faculty have been busy with administrative assignments or research projects that have competed for their classroom time. During the later years of their career, however, many—while savoring their other accomplishments—can return to the classroom with much more to give students than before. We find that seminars and workshops on the use of alternative teaching methods attract a large number of faculty from this group.

For many faculty the preretirement years represent a time when they can, in essence, start a new career. Many, we have discovered, become increasingly sensitive to the needs of undergraduate students and find energy in developing new interpersonal relationships that were not easily cultivated earlier in their careers. In addition, late-career faculty often better understand the importance of engaging in forums that address issues across departmental and college boundaries. Their experience enables them to understand more fully the concept of community, and they are often willing to share their expertise and otherwise help others obtain their goals. Both the Lilly and the TIPs programs have demonstrated that many older faculty are flattered to be asked to help younger faculty, and many are quick to volunteer to help students. As college faculty mature, they often become less selfish and more willing to work toward the common goals of the institution.

While late-career faculty have the potential we have just described, not always is it mobilized for the benefit of the academic community. On many campuses, including ours, experience tells us that some older faculty feel that they are of less value than they were earlier in their careers. Some perceive that the ability to obtain grants and be at the cutting edge of their field is the only ability valued in a research university. We sense that there are outstanding research universities in this country doing a good job of sharing their "elder statesmen" with students, particularly undergraduates. Harvard, for one, does this well. It is our conviction that retiring faculty should leave with dignity and know that they are valued. They should also know that they are not only welcome to return but that opportunities abound for them to volunteer elsewhere or give back to their institution their wealth of knowledge and experience.

In 1988, we received a three-year grant from the U.S. Department of Education's Fund for the Improvement of Postsecondary Education (FIPSE) to establish a senior teaching fellows program. This program, patterned after the Lilly program, is designed to facilitate "re-entry" into undergraduate education by outstanding senior faculty members. It is hoped that this program will be continued by the university when FIPSE funding ceases. We envision formal programs in which pre- and postretirement faculty can come together to share ideas, learn from each other, and offer their experience and help to others.

## Summary

During the initial years of OID we came to the conclusion—held more firmly now than ever—that great things happen when individuals are afforded a supportive environment in which to work. Underlying this kind of environment is the belief that human resources are precious and that both personal and professional needs of faculty at all stages in their careers should be planned for and addressed. Good teaching for effective learning is not just a function of technical skills and linear events; good teaching involves educational outcomes that make a difference in people's lives. This happens when committed, happy, productive faculty interact with motivated and enthusiastic students. And for this to happen there must be a system in place capable of supporting the kind of environment we are describing.

By understanding the unique needs of faculty at various times in their life span, and by planning for interventions in a multidimensional way, the institution can be transformed into one capable of supporting the kind of environment we know is necessary for continued personal and professional development. That is why we chose to adopt a holistic approach as opposed to a more narrow, technical approach. That is also why we have spent much of our time and energy focusing on ways in which we can facilitate renewal and help maintain the vitality that our institution is capable of. That is what we think our students and our sponsoring society deserve. We think that the multidimensional, holistic approach is capable of reaching most of our faculty who need help. We also think that this approach produces positive attitudes and upholds important values that should be embodied in today's college or university—values that *can* be made an integral part of the academic environment if the institution is prepared to make the modest, but essential, commitment to do so.

## References

Baldwin, R. G. "The Faculty Career Process—Continuity and Change: A Study of College Professors at Five Stages of the Academic Career." Unpublished doctoral dissertation, Center for the Study of Higher Education, University of Michigan, 1979.

Baldwin, R. G. (ed.). *Incentives for Faculty Vitality*. New Directions for Higher Education, no. 51. Jossey-Bass: San Francisco, 1985.

Baldwin, R. G., and Blackburn, R. T. "The Academic Career as a Developmental Process: Implications for Higher Education." *Journal of Higher Education*, 1981, *52* (6), 598–614.

Blackburn, R. T. "Academic Careers: Patterns and Possibilities." In *Current Issues in Higher Education*. Washington, D.C.: American Association for Higher Education, 1979.

Blackburn, R. T. "Career Phases and Their Influences on Faculty Motivation." In J. Bess (ed.), *Motivating Professors to Teach Effectively*. New Directions for Teaching and Learning, no. 10. San Francisco: Jossey-Bass, 1982.

Blackburn, R. T. "Faculty Career Development: Theory and Practice." In S. M. Clark and D. R. Lewis (eds.), *Faculty Vitality and Institutional Productivity: Critical Perspectives for Higher Education*. New York: Teachers College Press, 1985.

Blackburn, R. T., Chapman, D., and Cameron, S. "Cloning in Academe: Mentorship and Academic Careers." *Research in Higher Education*, 1981, *15* (4), 315–327.

Bowen, H. R., and Schuster, J. H. *American Professors: A National Resource Imperiled*. New York: Oxford University Press, 1986.

Brooks, M.C.T., and German, K. L. "Meeting the Challenges: Developing Faculty Careers." ASHE-ERIC Higher Education Research Report, no. 3. Washington, D.C.: Association for the Study of Higher Education, 1983.

Cares, R. C., and Blackburn, R. T. "Faculty Self-Actualization: Factors Affecting Career Success." *Research in Higher Education*, 1978, *9* (2), 123–136.

Clark, S. M., and Lewis, D. R. (eds.). *Faculty Vitality and Institutional Productivity: Critical Perspectives for Higher Education*. New York: Teachers College Press, 1985.

Cytrynbaum, S., Lee, S., and Wadner, D. "Faculty Development Through the Life Course." *Journal of Instructional Development,* 1982, *5* (3), 11-21.

Edgerton, R., and others. *Expanding Faculty Options: Career Development Projects at Colleges and Universities.* Washington, D.C.: American Association for Higher Education, 1981.

Erikson, E. H. *Childhood and Society.* (2nd ed.) New York: Norton, 1963.

Erikson, E. H. *Identity: Youth and Crisis.* New York: Norton, 1968.

Furniss, W. T. *Reshaping Faculty Careers.* Washington, D.C.: American Council on Education, 1981.

Gaff, J. G. *Toward Faculty Renewal: Advances in Faculty, Instructional, and Organizational Development.* San Francisco: Jossey-Bass, 1976.

Gardner, J. W. *Self-Renewal.* New York: Harper & Row, 1963.

Gould, R. L. *Transformations: Growth and Change in Adult Life.* New York: Simon & Schuster, 1978.

Hall, D. T., and Nougaim, K. "An Examination of Maslow's Need Hierarchy in an Organizational Setting." *Organizational Behavior and Human Performance,* 1968, *3,* 12-35.

Hodgkinson, H. L. "Adult Development: Implications for Faculty and Administrators." *Educational Record,* 1974, *55* (4), 263-274.

Jackson, W. K., and Chandler, J. B. (eds.). *Proceedings of the National Conference on Professional and Personal Renewal for Faculty.* Athens: Office of Instructional Development, University of Georgia, 1986.

Jackson, W. K., and Simpson, R. D. "The Office of Instructional Development as a Center for Personal, Professional, and Organizational Renewal." *Journal of Staff, Program, and Organization Development,* 1984, *2* (11), 12-15.

Ladd, E. C., and Lipset, S. M. "The Aging Professoriate." *Chronicle of Higher Education,* May 26, 1976, p. 16.

LaPidus, J. B. "Preparing Faculty: Graduate Education's Role." *AAHE Bulletin,* 1987, *39* (9), 3-6.

Levinson, D. J. "The Mid Life Transition: A Period in Adult Psychosocial Development." *Psychiatry,* 1977, *40* (2), 90-112.

Levinson, D. J., and others. *The Seasons of a Man's Life.* New York: Knopf, 1978.

Mehrotra, C.M.N. (ed.). *Teaching and Aging.* New Directions for Teaching and Learning, no. 19. San Francisco: Jossey-Bass, 1984.

Schein, E. H. "The Individual, the Organization, and the Career: A Conceptual Scheme." *Journal of Applied Behavioral Science,* 1971, *7* (4), 401-426.

Schein, E. H. *Career Dynamics: Matching Individual and Organizational Needs.* Reading, Mass.: Addison-Wesley, 1978.

Schuster, J. H., and Bowen, H. R. "The Faculty at Risk." *Change,* 1985, *17* (4), 13-21.

Seldin, P. (ed.). *Coping with Faculty Stress.* New Directions for Teaching and Learning, no. 29. San Francisco: Jossey-Bass, 1987.

Sheehy, G. M. *Passages: Predictable Crises of Adult Life.* New York: Dutton, 1976.

Simpson, R. D., and Jackson, W. K. "Promoting Professional and Personal Renewal." *Improving College and University Teaching,* 1984, *32* (4), 200-202.

Simpson, R. D., and Jackson, W. K. "The Faculty Renewal Program at the University of Georgia." In P. Seldin (ed.), *Coping with Faculty Stress.* New Directions for Teaching and Learning, no. 29. San Francisco: Jossey-Bass, 1987.

Super, D. E. "A Life-Span, Life-Space Approach to Career Development." *Journal of Vocational Behavior,* 1980, *16* (3), 282-298.

Torrance, E. P. *Mentor Relationships: How They Aid Creative Achievement, Endure, Change and Die.* Buffalo, N.Y.: Baerly, 1984.

10

# Integrating Individual and Organizational Needs:

## The University of Nebraska, Lincoln

*Joyce Povlacs Lunde*
*Ted E. Hartung*

Everyone in higher education would agree that our institutions should provide a positive climate for teaching and learning. On our campus, the University of Nebraska, Lincoln, we linked the need for a positive educational environment with a need for faculty development that would benefit both the individual and the institution. The awareness of our needs did not dawn instantly, however; the shape that our program eventually took developed over several years and involved a number of faculty members, administrators, and resource persons in the process.

The program in faculty development that we describe here was actually implemented in two different settings. The deans of the College of Agriculture at the University of Nebraska and the University of Minnesota, who had become acquainted through national and regional meetings in agriculture, arranged for joint visits and workshops between the two campuses that focused on faculty development and instructional improvement. These joint activities elicited common interests and concerns, which ultimately led to the joint venture in faculty development designated COPROF (Cooperative Program for the Professional Renewal of Faculty).

Leaders of COPROF included the associate dean of the College of Agriculture at the University of Minnesota, W. Keith Wharton; the specialist in professional development at Nebraska, Daniel Wheeler; and the two authors of this essay, the instructional consultant and the dean of the College of Agriculture at Nebraska, respectively. In addition, a group of faculty and department heads served as a steering committee on each campus.

Although the contact between our two campuses was fairly frequent, the program was different in each setting. Major program ingredients, however, were the same or similar. This chapter concentrates on a description of the program as it evolved at the University of Nebraska—the one we call NUPROF (Professional Renewal of Faculty at the University of Nebraska). In the following paragraphs we describe the setting, the genesis of our idea, its implementation, and its impact. We end with a set of recommendations that should be transferable to other campus sites.

### The Setting

The College of Agriculture at the University of Nebraska, Lincoln is a unit of the Institute of Agriculture and Natural Resources (IANR), which is headed by a vice-chancellor. The other major units in IANR are the Cooperative Extension Service and the Research Division; each of the three major units is headed by a dean. Faculty members who are engaged in teaching in the college usually have joint appointments in one of the other units as well, the most common arrangement being between teaching and research. These appointments are stated explicitly as percentages of a twelve-month appointment for each faculty member. Very few have 100 percent teaching assignments, which are nine-month appointments. At any given time approximately 175 faculty members hold a portion of their appointment in the College of Agriculture; this amounts to about 75 faculty FTE (full-time equivalent) engaged in teaching. Although the complex appointment structure in agricultural institutions may differ from that found in other colleges and universities, the attitudes, problems, and issues appear to be similar.

Prior to NUPROF, the general attitude toward faculty development in the College of Agriculture would best be described as passive. Events were staged in instructional improvement—for example, seminars, discussion groups, and workshops that contributed to faculty growth—but these did not carry visibility as faculty development. There was sufficient faculty participation, however, to provide a base from which to move ahead with a more visible program.

From an administrative point of view, one traditional resource in faculty development was not being well utilized: faculty leaves (the equivalent of sabbatical leaves) were not being actively pursued, and those proposals that were submitted in many instances had little consistency with departmental goals; rather, they tended to focus mainly on narrow interests and specializations. While there certainly was some evidence of change, it was not higher-level or second-order change, which includes change in perspective as well as direction (O'Neill and O'Neill, 1974).

As we looked at our situation, it was clear that we had to address major changes in the structure and economics of agriculture and in the explosion of knowledge and technology in our disciplines. The need for more interdisciplinary approaches to the issues faced by our institution was also clear. Further, we realized that significant growth in resources for our college was not realistic; indeed, resources were declining. We also knew that we were going to have to respond to the needs of faculty members, most of whom were at midcareer. Thus we felt the urgency of a proactive approach to faculty development.

## Antecedents

Models for our program came from a variety of sources, but no one program that we observed arranged the pieces in the sequence we wanted. We put together ideas from programs that stressed personal and career development, instructional improvement, and organizational development to benefit both the individual and the institution. Further, we wanted our program to provide a developmental sequence or structure that over time would lead the faculty member through steps of self-analysis, reflection, exploration, decision making, planning, implementation, and evaluation.

Our original program focused on improving teaching as its

main target; at the same time, we encouraged faculty members to examine the directions their lives were taking, and we included subject matter and interpersonal and administrative skill development, as well as instructional strategies, as appropriate areas to concentrate on.

Some ideas for NUPROF came from established programs in faculty development. Many institutions of higher education continue to have centers for faculty development (Erickson, 1986), but most of these focus on instructional services (Young, 1987), including the university-wide program at Nebraska. A cluster of programs in the late 1970s did focus on faculty career development (Baldwin and others, 1981). Some of these helped faculty with career evaluation (for example, the program at Loyola of Chicago), but institutional needs appeared to be peripheral. Other programs (California State University, Long Beach, and College of St. Scholastica) invited faculty members to retrain themselves in specified areas.

Another method to encourage faculty renewal is found in the concept of growth contracts (Carlberg, 1979). Gordon College (Wenham, Mass.) and other campuses use growth contracts (Simpson and Oggel, 1984) to encourage faculty development that meets institutional needs. The approach to growth plans we developed, however, was less formal—less of a "contract"—than that of those models.

One immediate model for our program came from the College of Agriculture at Michigan State University. A 1970s program that focused on training in creative problem solving, human relations, and industrial education, it was well received by faculty participants (Cooper, 1976). In an evaluation of this program, faculty reported gaining considerable self-understanding. This program, however, had neither an explicit sequence of activities nor institutional benefits as goals.

Whatever our antecedents and however much we owe to other faculty developers and other programs—and the debt is considerable—we did not find a program elsewhere that put everything together in the way we wanted it to go. As the first step in putting together our own program, we developed a set of assumptions, beliefs, and values, which through discussion and debate with a variety of faculty members and the steering committee became explicit guiding principles of our project.

### Assumptions and Roles

Our program reflects, in addition to the work of others in faculty development, the collective experience of its leaders. The resource persons and the administrators at Nebraska and Minnesota shared some assumptions. These assumptions, enumerated below, governed the roles we were to play on each campus.

1. *The program leaders at both Nebraska and Minnesota had a vision of human growth and development that rested on notions of personal autonomy.* As Freedman and others (1979) emphasized, faculty members must be free to grow, not ordered to develop. While we want the institution to benefit, each participant has to remain free to choose a course of action from alternatives that he or she establishes. The faculty member also controls the process of growth planning and implementation.

2. *The program leaders were also committed to taking the initiative.* While participation in NUPROF is voluntary, we encourage the involvement of those faculty members who we feel will benefit, and we also ask department heads to recommend members of their departments for participation. The instructional and faculty development resource persons are also proactive in seeing that arrangements are made for program events and that contact is maintained both formally and informally once participation gets under way.

3. *From the beginning, as we debated the terminology of our program, we determined that "faculty development" or "faculty renewal and redirection"—we use the terms almost interchangeabley—is for everyone.* While we direct younger faculty members to other resources and target midcareer, tenured faculty for NUPROF, we do not automatically keep any faculty member from participating. We have found, for example, that those faculty members close to retirement are valuable resources in themselves, as they serve as mentors for younger participants. The program, we have concluded, is for faculty at crossroads in their careers or disciplines—whatever their age—and for those affected by changes in department

structure, course offerings, and advances in the field. It is for those looking for new fields of endeavor, facing midcareer or midlife professional or personal issues, and just wanting time for reflection on where they are and where they want to go.

4. *We wanted our college to benefit from the individual's participation in NUPROF, but we knew that we had to take risks.* Instead of selecting participants for certain specified retraining, we help them explore alternatives. Most—but not all—of these individual-centered projects have had a direct payoff to the university. As NUPROF became established and participation grew, the program leaders and steering committee frequently debated the issue of personal development versus institutional benefit, and they always came down on the side of the individual. Paradoxically, in case after case, given the freedom to test the boundaries, we can point to institutional as well as personal benefits.

***Role of the Administration: Initiating Stage.*** In order for a systematic process of faculty development to move smoothly forward, there must be administrative commitment. A point of departure for our approach was that the administration had to be visible in the process but that the program had to be viewed as a collective creation of the college—as *our* program, not *their* program. During the initiating stage it was critical that this tone be set; and in retrospect, indeed it proved to be.

Given the passive attitude toward faculty development in our college, it was determined that the administration had to become actively involved. The following key messages needed to be communicated to the department heads and faculty:

1. Faculty growth was important to the administration and to the college.
2. The low level of faculty development activity in the college was not acceptable.
3. The college was going to address major changes in agriculture that had impact across the disciplines through an emphasis on faculty development and renewal.

These messages were conveyed by the dean to department heads and key standing committees of the college—the faculty advisory council, the instructional improvement committee (IIC), and the curriculum committee. While program leaders had some idea of what we wanted to do, the committees and groups of faculty from both Minnesota and Nebraska made contributions to program content. We began to search for seed money to implement our ideas. The IIC, by its nature, is an action-oriented committee; from its membership grew a team to prepare a proposal that would ultimately go to both campus and external agencies with a request for funds.

Several drafts of the proposed program were discussed with department heads and faculty groups on both campuses. The two deans played a major role in clarifying goals, directions, and activities, so that the final proposal embodied features that emerged as priorities for both campuses. (Obviously more coordination and communication were necessary with the two-campus design than would have been needed with a single-college proposal.)

Although no major funds had yet come into the program after over a year of discussion and planning, the deans on both campuses decided to initiate a program. It was felt that the situation was too urgent and that general endorsement was too strong to delay the implementation, even though only a shoestring budget was available. Accordingly, a pioneer group of twenty-seven participants from both colleges was assembled, and the first event—the jointly held Faculty Development Institute (described below)—was held at an off-campus site in Ames, Iowa. A second group followed in the spring of 1984. Fortunately, a few months after the second pioneer group was assembled, the proposed program was funded by a grant from the Fund for the Improvement of Postsecondary Education (FIPSE) of the U.S. Department of Education.

The willingness of the administration to keep the concept moving forward sent an important message to the departments and the faculty. This visible leadership should be recognized as essential in the initiation of any such program.

*Role of the Administration: Implementing Stage.* The visible administrative commitment exhibited at the initiating stage was continued into and during implementation. Program leaders agreed that the program had to have strong administrative endorsement, and yet it had to allow an openness in exploring options and addressing change; further, *it had to encourage risk taking.* The balance between strong administrative direction and faculty freedom was important. In light of the outcomes of the program over the next several years, this approach, which made it legitimate to look at and implement higher-level or second-order change, appears to have been a wise one.

Not only the dean but his associates and department heads had to send similar messages to the faculty. Early in the program these key figures had some mixed reactions, but as direct work with department heads continued, the process began to be better understood, and they encouraged their faculty members to consider participation. The best evidence to persuade department heads came out of the successes of the pioneer groups and the early participants under the FIPSE grant. The process clearly invites—indeed, necessitates—the involvement of department heads from the beginning.

The dean served as a leader and a facilitator, department heads were well informed and encouraging, and participants had freedom to explore; these three conditions led to early faculty acceptance and participation in the program. Because of the widespread understanding of the need for faculty development, the legitimizing of faculty development activities through administrative and faculty commitment, and the support available, faculty members of the college saw NUPROF as their own program and a useful resource for their professional development.

### Sequence of the Process

The components of our program are arranged in a sequence designed to assist faculty to look at change in their lives and in their careers in a fresh way. The sequence is this: (1) entering the program, (2) attending the Faculty Development Institute, (3) exploring options, (4) writing a growth plan, (5) implementing a growth plan, and (6) evaluating the process and the program.

The sequence of the program is intended to provide a backbone for the process of change. Even if no visible change occurs, we want participants to have a significant—not a superficial—experience. The process was deliberately designed to "unfreeze" behavior, create a measure of disequilibrium, and then (so important) give a support structure as new directions are undertaken. The six components of NUPROF activities as a change process for faculty development are further described in the following paragraphs.

*Entering the Program.* The program begins with an orientation and an early commitment on the part of both the participant and his or her department head. This stage is important in legitimizing involvement. All participation is voluntary; a faculty member can either indicate an interest in participating or be nominated by a department head. After the initial invitation letter goes out from the dean's office, faculty members indicate their interest— curiosity is sufficient—by choosing to attend an orientation session, which is held as a brown-bag lunch and includes a sharing of experiences by previous participants. (Provision is made for schedule conflicts.) After the luncheon meeting, participants are encouraged to indicate their interest within two weeks in joining the current "class" by filling out and returning a brief application form.

Since the program began, department heads and other administrators (who are also encouraged to participate) have been kept well informed. NUPROF mailings and word of mouth are important means of communication; in addition, information has been shared with department heads via workshops, brown-bag lunches, presentations at meetings of department heads, and one-to-one orientation of new heads. Participants are also encouraged to communicate with department heads. For example, each participant indicates on the application form that the department head knows about his or her intention to participate.

The selection process, guided by the steering committee and the program leaders, is infused by a desire to see that everyone's needs are met. We have been fortunate in that the flow of applications has matched the capacity to support individuals and that those who apply are appropriate for the program. Because NUPROF is described as being for midcareer faculty, the orientation program is sufficient to help faculty members decide whether they belong in the program. The main criterion we observe in the selection process is that the person and the institution must benefit in some way. Applicants who are worried that they do not have in mind a clear picture of what they want to do are assured that the desire to explore options is sufficient and that those who do enter with specific projects in mind usually become open to other alternatives too.

Throughout the entering process, the instructional and faculty development specialists remain active, sometimes encouraging individuals to apply, sometimes asking department heads for recommendations, and sometimes just answering questions and clearing up misconceptions.

*Attending the Faculty Development Institute.* One major requirement of NUPROF is attendance at the Faculty Development Institute (FDI). This retreat, held over a three-day period at an off-campus site, provides participants with the time to examine professional and personal issues in their lives and with the structure to clarify the steps they need to take.

Underlying the structure of the FDI is the theory and practice coming out of personal development and learning laboratories, as exemplified by the work of National Training Laboratories and other agencies and practitioners in applied behavioral science. One major approach to career planning and growth workshops we found useful is that described by Bergquist and Phillips in their handbooks (1975, 1977, 1981). Following their leads we planned the FDI in the form of a retreat because we wanted to allow enough time for a powerful intervention in the lives of the participants. It is time for reflection in a new setting, and usually with colleagues who are not the ones seen every day. Having participants from other colleges or universities also contributes to making the retreat a fresh experience.

The rationale for the structure of the retreat is provided in a simple formula for change (Edith Seashore, personal communication, 1983):

$$C = D + V + FS$$

Change = Dissatisfaction + Vision + First Step

(In our amended version, D + V + FS should also reflect the costs of change, because financial, personal, and emotional costs are inevitably entailed.) In the retreat setting participants engage in self-analysis, in locating the dissatisfaction or discord in their lives, in opening up to new goals or visions, and in planning the first steps in exploring alternatives. It became evident early on that it takes time and reflection beyond the scope of a retreat to give vision shape. Therefore, one might prescribe a *series* of first steps, the actual first step being a relatively easy thing to do. For example, telephoning a colleague is something that can be done within hours after the retreat is over. While the vision may still be a glimmer on the horizon—something that will develop as more information is absorbed—each person usually leaves the retreat with some notion of a concrete action that he or she can take and when it will be taken.

The format of the retreat is planned to initiate the change process. It starts with self-reflection, using the Myers-Briggs Type Indicator (MBTI) (Briggs and Briggs-Myers, 1984) as the major instrument of self-analysis. We then move on to career issues. We have used various tools, such as Schein's "career anchors" (1978) and motivational assessments that help participants examine what they find motivating and rewarding. We usually bring in a resource person external to our college or colleges who can address topics such as levels of change and career issues. We have also found that a free night midway through the retreat gives participants a variety of ways for dealing with the information overload, including both time alone and time for in-depth conversation with colleagues and consultants. On the last morning of the retreat, we ask participants to form groups of three, joining with persons not in their departments but from their campuses, to begin exploring options. In the trios each person is to have "air time" to discuss possibilities and problems. Further, the trio is to plan to meet at least once when they return to campus. The retreat finishes with the Deans' Lunch. Here the administrators who are present indicate their expectations and identify available resources, while participants begin to explore options and look toward writing growth plans.

*Exploring Options.* The program leaders are well aware of the danger of postretreat letdown. Without some proactive strategies participants would find it very easy to lose momentum at this critical point. Elements of the Faculty Development Institute are therefore designed to establish next steps. The clear structure of the sequence has been shared with participants, so they know that they will be invited to attend an on-campus Growth Plan Work Session a few months after the FDI. The formation of the trios is another deliberate strategy to see that the exploring stage moves forward.

The participants are encouraged to identify the resource and support persons in their lives. Those suggested are colleagues and peers, discipline experts, department heads, instructional and faculty development specialists, friends, family, and spouses. Participants have added to this list: support groups in their churches, ministers, their neighbors, the staff of the university counseling center, and a broad range of external experts.

During this phase of exploring options, a NUPROF dinner with a presentation, usually on the topic of personality types and change, is held for NUPROFers and their spouses (or significant others in their lives). For most participants this event, which has been well attended, falls into the exploring stage of their project and thus serves to broaden the base of support and direction.

On the whole, the program leaders do not hover over participants during the exploring phase. The instructional and faculty development specialists are frequently consulted, however, on topics ranging from external workshops and courses available to personal issues and private worries. The exploring stage is the time for participants to enter into negotiations, sometimes tough, with department heads and peers concerning current and future roles and responsibilities. The program leaders and steering committee are ready to assist in these negotiations and to suggest ways to break logjams, but the faculty member is responsible for making whatever arrangements can be made. Often these negotiations go much more smoothly than the faculty member anticipates. (Perhaps in the past faculty members have not asked clearly and directly for what they wanted. When they have done their homework, the myth of the impossible becomes the art of the probable.)

The program leaders also refrain from entering into the trio process. From time to time we hear about trios that continue to meet and bolster each other's resolve long after the FDI. If we hear that trios have faltered before having served their purpose, we make suggestions for restarting or rearranging groups. In the fourth year of NUPROF, for example, we gave everyone the opportunity to join a support group (led by a nonprogram leader); this intervention proved successful for about a half-dozen participants.

Without support, a goal, and a deadline, the exploring stage might mark the end of participation. Although participation in the program often stretches over several years, the program clearly has a next step. The benchmark that signals the end of the exploring stage is the invitation to attend the Growth Plan Work Session.

***Writing a Growth Plan.*** We offer assistance in writing growth plans at a work session held several months after the Faculty Development Institute. It starts in the late afternoon, includes a simple dinner, and finishes in the early evening. As the first step of the session, participants evaluate where they are in the exploring stage in a discussion in their trios or small groups. We then show them the flow chart in Figure 10.1 (prepared by Joyce Povlacs Lunde and Daniel W. Wheeler) which helps clarify structure and sequence once again. Usually participants are eager to put pencil to paper, whatever their stage, so that is what they do next—in a quiet corner, with colleagues and program leaders available for help. By the end of the evening most individuals have a good start on a rough draft. After the writing session the steering committee puts out a call for submission of growth plans, which are evaluated within a few weeks.

All persons who submit growth plans attend one or more work sessions. Over several years of program activity we have accumulated "stopouts" from earlier classes, who repeat attendance at growth plan work sessions. Because the faculty members control the process, we welcome their participation whenever they are ready. At the same time, our proactive stance allows for gentle encouragement along the way.

The format of the growth plan is dictated largely by the individual's needs and preferences. Instead of providing an application form, we suggest that growth planners follow a simple outline. (See Table 10.1.) Acceptable plans have ranged from a few pages to a dozen or more pages in length.

**Figure 10.1. Flow of Events in the Growth Plan Process.**

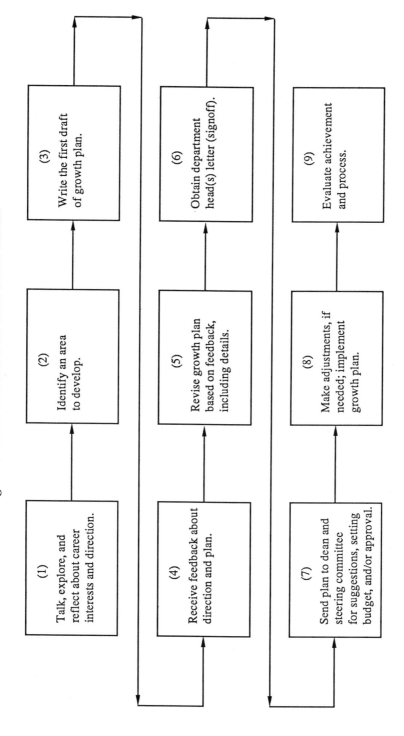

(1)

Talk, explore, and reflect about career interests and direction.

(2)

Identify an area to develop.

(3)

Write the first draft of growth plan.

(4)

Receive feedback about direction and plan.

(5)

Revise growth plan based on feedback, including details.

(6)

Obtain department head(s) letter (signoff).

(7)

Send plan to dean and steering committee for suggestions, setting budget, and/or approval.

(8)

Make adjustments, if needed; implement growth plan.

(9)

Evaluate achievement and process.

**Table 10.1. Growth Plan Outline.**

A.  Goals and objectives
    - How these relate to the individual's career
    - How these benefit the institution (students, teaching, curriculum, programs)
    - How these address renewal and growth
B.  Activities and time frame to realize the goals and objectives
C.  Support needed to realize the plan
    - Resource people, within and outside the institution
    - Peers
    - Administrative (particularly department heads)
    - Financial
D.  Evaluation of the plan
E.  Future directions after the plan

Once the growth plans are submitted, together with a statement of acknowledgment from the department head, the steering committee reviews each one and makes recommendations for funding and, in some cases, for activities to implement plans. The grants to fund growth plans are not competitive (in fact, we occasionally allow pregrant awards to applicants in a time pinch), and the approval process is flexible. The committee enters into dialogue with growth plan writers, offering many suggestions and (as the committee's experience grows) encouraging innovation and greater risk taking in place of the tried and true. Frequently, because of this dialogue between committee and participant, the final plan consists of several documents. In their growth plans faculty members have been able to describe themselves personally and professionally and indicate new goals, directions, and activities for themselves and for their families. In the program's early years participants tended to focus on teaching; more recently, plans typically have broadened to encompass other professional goals.

Experience has taught us to be explicit about the portion of the plan NUPROF is to fund. We have discovered that, because participants look at long-range goals as well as what they might undertake in the immediate future, their requests often exceed our resources. Nevertheless, we encourage development of long-range goals, and participants (either by themselves or with our help) often find other resources to support activities, including faculty development leaves (sabbaticals), beyond the scope of NUPROF funding.

As we have indicated, progress is at the faculty member's own pace. Initially we expected participants to complete their projects in anywhere from a year to eighteen months. However, it became apparent that some persons put their plans together only after much thought and exploration, not to mention trial and error and sidetracking. Two recently approved plans, for instance, were written by persons whose participation had begun two and four years previously. Another consideration of time is related to the question of formal faculty development leaves. Ten participants have taken faculty development leaves that began with or included NUPROF activities. Because applications for leave take at least six months to process, participants planning NUPROF projects in conjunction with leaves often take longer than the anticipated time period.

*Implementing a Growth Plan.* Close monitoring has not been needed to see that plans are carried out. Once funds are placed at the faculty member's disposal, events move under that person's direction. Sometimes a planned event is canceled or a better idea comes along. In such cases we ask the faculty member to submit a letter explaining the change. Usually the program leaders give informal approval to the change, with committee notification following. Of the thirty-seven growth plans that went through the approval process in the first four years of the program, only one— an early effort from a member of the pioneer group—was never activated.

The nature of the growth plan is complex, embracing personal and professional development in the context of institutional needs. The participant's total experience—from the Faculty Development Institute, to trios, to exploring with family and colleagues, to actually pursuing planned learning experiences—forms the growth process. Since 1983 we have had NUPROFers in various stages of implementing growth plans. Most plans are individualistic and highly specific. Faculty members have attended workshops in such topics as the case-history method and guided design; pursued new interdisciplinary areas in subject matter; integrated the use of the computer in teaching, research, or service; taken courses in management and educational psychology; continued work with personality types; or become involved in university-wide teaching, such as writing across the curriculum or freshman seminars. (For further examples, see descriptions of growth plan activities and their results, below.)

*Evaluating the Process and the Program.* Program evaluation rests largely on the faculty member's progress and experiences in the sequence of events in the program. However, we want each participant to treat the evaluation of his or her progress as something personal. The portion of the growth plan calling for evaluation has been the hardest part to write for many participants. After some experimentation, we are now recommending that the evaluation of the growth plan be handled in a series of questions that the participant answers to document that change in a positive direction has occurred. At the end of the implementation period, each faculty member submits a short written description of what happened, and the outcomes.

Those faculty members who have finished their growth plans have all given some evidence of renewal in their subject matter, teaching or other assignments, interpersonal communication, and attitudes. It is difficult to summarize the activity and growth of NUPROF participants, given the complexity and multidimensional nature of the change many of them pursued. Following are a few examples typical of the participants' reports, collected by the external evaluator in his visits to the Nebraska and Minnesota campuses (Fink, 1987).

- *Learning to work with students more effectively.* This faculty member investigated use of the systems approach in curriculum design, making a trip to Australia, and then used the Myers-Briggs Type Indicator and a learning-styles inventory in courses. Comment: "I . . . have much more enthusiasm for my work because I am learning how to implement some very exciting ideas."
- *Learning to take risks.* This faculty member wanted to make changes in research and teaching and found that the program came along at the right time. She developed a new research

interest and took a course in that area, redesigned a course, and attended a workshop on ethics. Comment: "I used to be a traditional full-hour lecturer. Now I rarely lecture for more than twenty minutes at a time. Instead, I have tried to make the students more active by using case studies, more outside readings, small groups, and writing activities. This past spring my student evaluations were the best I have ever had."

- *Discovering the role of feelings in the classroom.* This faculty member, who teaches in a quantitative discipline, was a traditional "chalk-and-talk" lecturer. Through the program he became acquainted with the Myers-Briggs Type Indicator and pursued further study in its use. Now he seeks out students who are not doing well and attempts to make the course a more satisfactory experience for them. Comment: "This all came to full fruition this semester. Last week, at the end of the final day of class, the students gave me a standing ovation! In my mind this occurred because of NUPROF. . . . My involvement in this project opened up a whole new and different dimension of teaching, and a new dimension of myself, to explore."

- *Developing new confidence.* This faculty member was at the crossroads in a career. After the Faculty Development Institute helped identify needs, she enrolled in an interpersonal communication course to learn to work with people better and also pursued work in artificial intelligence, expert systems, and creative problem solving, and developed self-confidence, research areas, and teaching skills. Comment: "More than anything else, NUPROF has given me new energy and excitement for my work."

Almost all participants have said in one way or another that the program made making change acceptable in their careers. As one told us, "It's really broken the cast. It made my role here experimenting and exploring and it will free it up [so] that I can change and experiment and [try] new approaches to teaching, new involvement in the classroom in the future." Viewing the program's overall record, the external evaluator wrote, "I was impressed with the long list of people who had undertaken activities that were imaginative, ambitious, and effective in terms of making fundamental improvements in their professional work" (Fink, 1987, p. 12).

The step of evaluating has given participants an opportunity to look into the future. Some are simply going on to the next step of their growth plan—for example, a faculty development leave. Others are pursuing new ideas and subject matters introduced in their NUPROF project, while still others are continuing on the track they had chosen years earlier, but with the knowledge that changing directions is still an option. (A videotape of six faculty members discussing their experiences in NUPROF is available on loan by contacting any of the Nebraska program leaders.)

### Institutional Impact

Since the beginning of NUPROF, with the visibility of the systematic process, a major strengthening of faculty development has occurred in the college. A variety of activities and events document the new awareness of the need for professional renewal, the resources available, and the active participation.

One piece of evidence of that new awareness is the increased frequency with which faculty development experiences are shared within and across departments. This sharing has prompted other faculty to become interested and involved. Most departments of the college have had at least one participant, and in several small departments almost all the members have been involved. The changes that faculty have made as a result of participation are viewed as significant.

Department heads over this four-year period of development have introduced the NUPROF concept into the annual performance evaluation. Either the department head recognizes and rewards participation, or the head encourages a likely candidate to become involved in opportunities in faculty development. Because the climate was set early in the process to encourage faculty members to discuss options openly and make their own choices, faculty members view such reviews with department heads as constructive and forward-looking.

*Participation.* Direct evidence of institutional impact is found in the NUPROF experiences of participants and of the three program leaders at Nebraska. As we noted above, in NUPROF's first four years at Nebraska (with fifty-seven participants), thirty-seven growth plans were written, submitted, and approved. Several faculty members who were members of the last class under the FIPSE project submitted growth plans that were supported institutionally after FIPSE funding no longer was available.

Something also needs to be said about the twenty faculty members from Nebraska who attended one of the Faculty Development Institutes in the early years but did not submit growth plans. Of these, six are no longer at the university. Of the remaining number, only one or two can be said to have exhibited no change. For others, the Faculty Development Institute was sufficiently powerful to give new direction to their lives. For instance, one faculty member came back from the Faculty Development Institute—newly energized, as he tells it—to plan a faculty development leave in a new research area. The external evaluator talked with several of the persons who did not submit growth plans (Fink, 1987). Several of these found the Faculty Development Institute to be helpful in providing the trio as a support group, in improving communications with spouses, and in facilitating plans for other academic work. One noted that the Faculty Development Institute had helped him establish personal and professional priorities; in the exploring stage he had discovered new friends and other university assignments that were extremely rewarding. Another was able to set research and other priorities more easily than he might have done otherwise. As the evaluator noted, the success or failure of the program should not rest on the number of growth plans submitted.

At the beginning of the program, it was expected that the systematic process would lead faculty to consider taking faculty development leaves. This impact did indeed occur, with approximately one-fourth of the participants submitting growth plans that included a faculty development leave and others planning leaves in the future. As a consequence, faculty development leaves in the college increased from three or four a year before NUPROF to about a dozen annually several years later.

*Continuation and Cost.* NUPROF is now being extended to all faculty members in the University of Nebraska's Institute of Agriculture and Natural Resources (IANR). That institute—composed of the Cooperative Extension Service and the Research Division, the College of Agriculture, and the College of Home Economics—is supporting a professional development program on the model already established. Since the termination of FIPSE funding, about fifteen faculty members—including those with research and extension service appointments—enroll in NUPROF annually. Faculty members from outside IANR and the university have also participated in recent Faculty Development Institutes.

The IANR program is supported near the levels available for individual growth plans as funded by FIPSE. The approximate cost per participant is $2,000, excluding staff time. This sum includes $1,500 for implementing the growth plan (typically for resource materials, for external conferences and workshops, and for travel) and $500 for the Faculty Development Institute and associated costs. While the sum may appear large, when averaged over time it is only a small percentage of a faculty member's annual salary (Fink, 1987).

Evidence of impact to date would suggest that a visible, systematic process of faculty development can lead to an acceptance of risk taking and to significant changes among faculty members. The process has further established the principle of encouraging faculty development in the context of the individual's professional and personal goals and the department's or unit's goals. The capability of the faculty members and the administration to negotiate individual goals, within. the institutional setting, has yielded immeasurable value to, and impact on, the college.

## Recommendations

The experience gained from NUPROF supports the idea that a visible, systematic process for faculty development—one that balances individual and institutional needs—will result in significantly greater development activity and increased benefits on a campus. As one participant exclaimed, "NUPROF *works!*" We also believe that although the design of any program in faculty development must be based on local needs, aspects of our program may be transferred to other campuses. Our recommendations, both general and specific, follow.

## General

1. During the initiating phase, it is essential that the philosophical basis of the program be developed, defined, and accepted (preferably embraced) jointly by faculty, unit administrators, and the college administration.
2. The faculty development program should be given an identity and carry with it a defined process that creates an open climate for looking at change and taking risks.
3. The administration must make a visible commitment to the program, both to facilitate its implementation and to provide the necessary resources (support staff and finances).
4. A key element in the success of the program is the role of the department head or unit administrator as an advocate and as a facilitator, especially during the exploration stage and in the preparation of growth plans.

## Specific

1. In the final analysis, participation in the program must be the decision of the faculty member.
2. In-house expertise in faculty development is extremely important to this systematic approach. (A person or persons with this expertise may already be available on your campus.)
3. A retreat of sufficient length (such as our Faculty Development Institute, which is more than two days long), held at the beginning of an individual's involvement, is essential to allow participants time for reflection, for self-examination, and for understanding the nature of change.
4. Including faculty participants from other colleges and universities in the retreat increases its impact.
5. Small peer support groups, growing out of the retreat, should be built into the program to facilitate individual change.
6. Seed money must be available for implementing the growth

plans. A minimum of $1,500 per participant (over a period of one or two years) should be considered.

7.  A growth plan work session serves as a stimulant to keep the process moving. However, not everyone will write a growth plan or be able to submit a final plan immediately.

8.  There should be a minimum of strings attached as growth plans are developed. Growth planning must be done in an atmosphere of mutual trust.

9.  The periodic staging of events for all participants, such as the dinner with spouses and significant others, keeps the process visible and intact.

10.  The program needs constant monitoring, with feedback gathered formally and informally from participants, administrators, committee members, resource persons, and outsiders. Adjustments should be made as needed.

11.  It should be made clear that a broad range of changes are acceptable, from major redirection (career, academic field, roles) to lesser shifts (new techniques and skills). Different kinds and degrees of change are appropriate for different individuals.

12.  Faculty members and administrators need to realize that while an extreme change (for instance, leaving the institution) may have its negative aspects (losing the individual), there are likely to be countervailing benefits (such as, for the individual, pursuing new goals, and for the institution, filling anew the vacated position).

13.  In sum, the program should be conceptualized broadly in order to encompass personal, professional, and institutional dimensions. Breaking out of worn patterns—on the part of both the institution and its faculty—should be a hallmark of a program in professional renewal and redirection.

## References

Baldwin, R., and others. *Expanding Faculty Options: Career Development Projects at Colleges and Universities.* Washington, D.C.: American Association for Higher Education, 1981.

Bergquist, W. H., and Phillips, S. R. *Handbook of Faculty Develop-*

*ment.* Vols. 1, 2, and 3. Washington, D.C.: Council for the Advancement of Small Colleges (now Council of Independent Colleges), 1975, 1977, 1981.

Briggs, K. C., and Briggs-Myers, I. *Myers-Briggs Type Indicator, Form G.* Palo Alto, Calif.: Consulting Psychologists Press, 1984.

Carlberg, R. J. *Professional Development Through Growth Contracts Handbook.* Wenham, Mass.: Gordon College, 1979.

Cooper, C. "Project PROF: A Professional Development Program for College Faculty." Unpublished paper, Agriculture and Natural Resources Education Institute, Michigan State University, 1976.

Erickson, G. "A Survey of Faculty Development Practices." In J. Kurfiss and J. Stone (eds.), *To Improve the Academy: Resources for Students, Faculty, and Institutional Development.* Lincoln: Professional and Organizational Development Network in Higher Education, Teaching and Learning Center, University of Nebraska, Lincoln, 1986.

Fink, L. D. "Revitalizing the Faculty: An Evaluation of the Professional Renewal Project in the College of Agriculture at the University of Nebraska [and] . . . at the University of Minnesota." Unpublished paper, Office of Instructional Services, University of Oklahoma, 1987.

Freedman, M., and others. *Academic Culture and Faculty Development.* Berkeley, Calif.: Montaine, 1979.

O'Neill, N., and O'Neill, G. *Shifting Gears: Finding Security in a Changing World.* New York: Evans, 1974.

Schein, E. *Career Dynamics: Matching Individual and Organizational Needs.* Reading, Mass.: Addison-Wesley, 1978.

Simpson, E., and Oggel, T. "Growth Contracting for Faculty Development." Idea Paper, no. 11. Manhattan: Center for Faculty Evaluation and Development, Kansas State University, 1984.

Young, R. E. "Faculty Development and the Concept of 'Profession.'" *Academe,* 1987, *73* (3), 12–14.

11

# Fostering Professional, Personal, and Family Growth:

## Loyola University of Chicago

### Barbara H. Hill

Trying times are times to try things. To meet the shifting social and academic demands of a changing world and to address the needs of the individual in that world, a unique and creative program was tried at Loyola University of Chicago in the late 1970s. Entitled the Career Development Program, it has thrived since 1978 and is viewed as a model of faculty development.

Faculty development, as defined by Jerry Gaff (1976, p. 14), "enhances the talents, expands the interests, improves the competence, and otherwise facilitates the professional and personal growth of faculty members." Gaff could have been describing the Loyola model, had it been around in 1976.

Traditionally, faculty development programs fall into three categories: those with emphasis on the faculty member as teacher (instructional development), as person (personal and professional development), or as member of an organization (organizational development). Most often the focus is on only one of the three, usually instructional development. What makes Loyola's program different is that it is *person*-centered, recognizing the various ways in which personal life contributes to professional life. As one faculty member

212

stated, "The Loyola Career Development Program is valuable because it is concerned with both professional and personal life. These categories are not separate in practice but are often treated as if they are mutually exclusive."

Ronald E. Walker, executive vice-president at Loyola, was dean of the college when the Career Development Program began. He describes the program as being "highly sensitive to faculty members as individuals—that is, the person behind the blackboard."

Loyola University of Chicago defines itself as an independent, private, urban, Jesuit, and Catholic institution of higher learning. This definition suggests that a certain core set of values— concern for the whole person, commitment to serving others, dedication to learning and intellectual inquiry, and the conviction that moral and humanistic questions lie at the heart of education— undergirds all the goals and activities of the university.

Because of Loyola's Catholic heritage and values, it also feels a strong commitment to family unity. The Jesuit philosophy of educating and developing the whole person is supported throughout the university by campus leadership that demonstrates this attitude of care and concern for the individual. This spirit is clearly captured in a letter from Richard A. Matre, senior vice-president and dean of faculties, announcing the new Career Development Program:

October 15, 1978

To the Faculty and Administrators of Loyola University:

There are many programs of faculty development in colleges and universities across the country. Most of these programs are structured on the basis of imposing themselves on the persons who teach in these organizations. This university has refused to enter into programs that would be inappropriate to the quality of the persons employed here.

The Career Development Program is an attempt to offer services to faculty and administrators so that they can involve themselves, freely and openly, in their own personal and career growth. The university is so committed to this program that it is sharing expenses with the Fund for the Improvement of Postsecondary Education, a division of the Department of Health, Education, and Welfare.

I am convinced that the Career Development Program will not only encourage the growth and development of our faculty and administrators, but will also result in improved classroom instruction, one of our continuing priorities.

The 1980s will be a crucial period in higher education. It is comforting to me, and I am sure to you as well, to know that Loyola University has sponsored a forward-looking, dynamic program. With programs of this type, the university can continue to improve the fine services of teaching and research required for the future.

I wish you all the best opportunities for the improvement of your professional careers.

This letter was significant not only as a formal endorsement from the administration but because it gave permission to faculty members to explore their careers freely and openly. Programs such as the Loyola model will continue to be relevant into the 1990s as they focus on the needs of the individual within the extended campus family in a time of change.

### History of the Loyola Program

The concept of the Career Development Program came from several individuals, in response to changes in higher education during the late seventies. Adult developmental theories were establishing that growth does not stop as we become older and that losing the chance to grow is something we all fear. Important literature—from Erik Erikson's (1975) work on stages of development for the adult years to Levinson and others' (1978) theory of adult career stages—was linking adult development to career development.

A handful of Loyola's faculty members were discussing a program that would go beyond the typical sabbatical and acknowledge that faculty members grow and develop as other adults do. At the same time, the administration was concerned about pressing issues confronting the campus: declining enrollments for the first time; a changing student market; and a graying faculty, with higher retirement ages. Robert M. Barry, professor of philosophy, had an idea about how to address the needs of the individual as he or she was affected by these problems. He took his concept for the Career Development Program to the faculty council and the administration to obtain the necessary support and then developed a successful grant proposal to the Fund for the Improvement of Postsecondary Education (FIPSE).

In 1978 the Career Development Program became a reality, opening its doors with a staff of two, Barry and the author of this chapter. The stated purpose of the program was and is the following: to offer professional and personal development services to all full- and part-time faculty, administrators, and professional staff (from the library, counseling center, and campus ministry), and their spouses. The program, now a part of the faculty development office under Barry, has procedures that support career expansion, exchanges within Loyola or with other universities, placement in business for a year, and other independent opportunities for growth and development. It also provides a personal support system and a series of workshops so that participants may explore their professional and personal lives for the purpose of career enrichment. Both internal and external consultants act as leaders of the workshops, with nominal fees charged for materials.

In its first nine years, over one-fourth of Loyola's faculty members have participated in various aspects of the program. Participants in the workshops, in small groups, or working one-to-one with program leaders have developed goals and plans to enrich themselves, their careers, their families, or their teaching.

## IPPG Workshop Program

At a faculty development meeting in 1977, Robert Barry had heard Elizabeth Wells discuss a new program, Integrating Professional and Personal Growth (IPPG), which she and Paul J. Munson had developed. As they worked with faculty on improving teaching with the administration on learning and improving management skills, they had discovered that the prime concern of both faculty and administrators was their own personal and professional lives.

Because Barry, too, had noted at Loyola that faculty members seemed to be consistently working to achieve a balance between these two areas of life, he felt that the IPPG workshop would fit in with his ideas for a faculty development program at Loyola.

Wells was hired to consult with the Career Development Program in its early years. She led two or three IPPG workshops each year, and trained Barbara Hill to lead them. In ten years 130 faculty members, 58 spouses, and 47 others have participated. Hill has also presented this program to faculty at other colleges and universities. Additionally, following the three-year grant period, a Dissemination Conference was held for 24 faculty members and administrators from around the country. Most participants have benefited significantly, according to their evaluations and two outside evaluators' impressions.

In 1980, several months after the workshops, Hill compared forty-four IPPG participants to forty-three randomly selected nonparticipants. All were full-time faculty. Her data showed that 30 percent (or thirteen out of forty-four) of the participants perceived their careers to be in transition and expected some important change within the next five years, while only one of the forty-three nonparticipants was contemplating a career change. While three-quarters (or thirty-two out of forty-three) of the nonparticipants expressed no significant concerns about their work, only one-quarter (or twelve out of forty-four) of the workshop participants reported no particular concerns about their work. Thus the degree of satisfaction with one's circumstances appears to be a prime motivating factor for participation in the IPPG workshop.

*Rationale for the IPPG Workshop.* It is well known that the human organism possesses tremendous potential to change, grow, develop, and adapt. Central to the IPPG program is the belief that people grow, desire to be useful, and want to live meaningful, productive lives. Given an opportunity to grow, personally and within their existing organizations, individuals (and consequently their organizations) prosper. This Loyola premise makes the Career Development Program different from faculty development programs that have their roots in the idea that people need to be changed to meet organizational demands. The following assumptions illustrate the philosophy upon which IPPG and the Loyola program are based:

1.  Individuals are rich in ideas and information that deserve to get into the mainstream of higher education.
2.  Internal motivation is a powerful source of individual and organizational development.
3.  Individuals grow when they feel strong and supported.
4.  Individuals and organizations are most effective when they deliberately plan to express their values, use their strengths, and fulfill their purposes.
5.  New teaching technology is used more effectively when it relates to one's own professional and personal goals.

*Method and Structure of the IPPG Workshop.* The IPPG workshop has three parts: planning, implementation, and evaluation. The planning phase takes place during a two-and-one-half-day workshop, typically held over a weekend and in an off-campus setting. Usual group size is between twelve and sixteen, with one to two trained staff members to lead the group. Participants pay between $95 and $195—about half the actual cost—depending upon what site is selected and how much the program's budget is able to subsidize.

During the planning phase participants first clarify their values, strengths, operating styles, and purposes in a structured, supportive environment. Organizational values, resources, and purposes are also identified. In light of this self- and organizational assessment, a "life analysis" is undertaken to answer the question, "To what extent are you currently expressing your values, utilizing your strengths, developing your operating styles, and fulfilling your purpose?" Participants then use the information gathered about themselves and their personal and professional organizations to select one goal on which to concentrate for the rest of the workshop. They alone create measurement criteria for themselves and develop numerous strategies, resulting in a detailed management plan to accomplish their goals.

Three primary possibilities exist: (1) one's current situation is satisfactory, (2) one's current situation is unsatisfactory but can be enriched by the setting of new goals or by the letting go of old habits or outgrown activities, or (3) one's current situation is unacceptable, and there is a need for change in job or career direction. After the intensive self- and organizational assessment, few participants reach the third conclusion.

The variety of participant goals—some of them having little to do directly with career development—demonstrates the freedom of choice that workshop participants enjoy. Leaders do not impose their own expectations. The ruling assumption is that the individual knows what he or she wants to accomplish and can make choices appropriately. Based upon participants' evaluations, this respect for the individual has been valued.

Some examples of goals that participants have identified are completing an academic degree, writing papers or articles, conducting a research project, learning a new technology, or taking a course. One faculty member in the school of education decided to pursue a law degree. Today he is using it in his classroom and in his community as he consults with local school boards on legal matters. One professor decided to adopt a child; she found her family supportive and willing to share in the child's care.

Many participants selected travel goals for themselves: a trip to Europe, an archeological dig, an international conference. Others wanted to learn to fly, to ski, to play the piano. One administrator decided to clean her closets, perhaps symbolically clearing away the clutter so that she could move to other projects or her next goal.

The implementation phase takes place after the weekend workshop, as plans for accomplishing individual goals are put into action. Workshop leaders are available to assist group members— for example, to help with barriers or resistances. Time management is often the identified barrier; thus leader and participants work out some additional strategies to set priorities or delegate some current responsibilities. Occasionally a few group members meet informally on their own during this time.

During the evaluation phase participants meet again in a follow-up session six to eight weeks after their planning weekend, to assess their own progress toward their goals. More than 90 percent of the participants attend these follow-up sessions, showing a definite enthusiasm for meeting again. This is not surprising; close bonds develop during the initial weekend. In fact, some groups are still meeting on their own after six years. One group went to Iowa for a weekend to visit a couple who had moved there.

Evaluations of the workshop show high levels of satisfaction. Rated in terms of usefulness on a scale of 1 (low) to 5 (high), the average rating from 184 participants across fifteen criteria was 3.99. (Included in this group were faculty, administrators, spouses, and some persons from outside Loyola.) Eighty-six percent reported that the program had a positive effect on them personally. They were "more self-confident," "more willing to take risks," "less uptight."

Participants have identified four major outcomes of the workshop:

1. *Improved self-management skills.* The greatest workshop benefit has been in helping faculty and administrators to acquire self-management skills. One participant noted, "IPPG helped me realize the importance of maintaining my own personal time and space, and gave me some tools for reconciling those needs with my need to do well in my job." From a couple who attended together: "We have realized our goals as a couple more clearly and have been able to articulate what we want and need from each other." Others mentioned "becoming more organized and having a plan," and "having a system for reaching my goals."

2. *Increased self-awareness.* Faculty members have reported a variety of insights gained from the workshop experience, including greater awareness of themselves, of other family members, and of members of their department. "I have been able to see myself, my strengths, and my weaknesses from a more realistic point of view. This has helped me relate to my peers and chairperson better and on a more in-depth level."

3. *Increased sense of personal growth.* One faculty member expressed personal growth as "being more in tune with setting personal goals." Another said, "After attending the workshop, my family and I established priorities relative to our family life. I know what is important to me."

4. *Improved life-planning process.* The process of setting and reaching one's goals proved to be a helpful tool not just initially but also over time. "IPPG gave me more control over and the capacity to influence my career," said one participant. A spouse

reported, "I now have a process to use whenever I want something for myself—even those wild and crazy ideas like my first goal of flying a plane." (He now has his pilot's license.)

Another outcome has been to bring together faculty and administrators from throughout Loyola's three disparate and distant campuses and ten schools. They have learned from each other and now understand one another in a more personal way. One English professor got to know a department colleague much better at the workshop—someone he said he had barely known or talked to before, even though he occupied the office next door. Now they are supporting each other's goals and discovering that they have much in common outside of their discipline.

*Spouse Participation: A Broader Dimension.* About 25 percent of the IPPG workshop participants have been spouses; in some cases spouses have attended by themselves. The reasons given for participating include the following: to spend an unencumbered weekend with husband or wife away from the children and responsibilities at home; to find ways to balance multiple roles; to obtain help in transition; to find career direction; and to gain greater awareness of self. One spouse said that she came to have fun and not cook all weekend, while another confessed that he had come to escape the weekend chores.

One couple emphasized the benefit each felt from better understanding the importance of certain matters to the other person. As one of them observed, "In spite of thirty years of happy marriage, I think these new insights strengthened our marriage even further." A female administrator stated, "I attended with my husband, who is struggling through a career change. The workshop was very helpful in raising both his confidence in his abilities and his self-esteem as a professional."

One of the benefits of a spouse's participation is that the workshop provides opportunities for couples to understand and support each other in what is often a transitional period. Some participants noted that they had never previously explored such crucial matters as values, purpose in life, and how they might improve the quality of their life with their mate.

In summary, it seems clear that the Integrating Professional and Personal Growth workshop program can make a specific and distinctive contribution to a comprehensive faculty development program. It combines elements of the three essential components (personal and professional development, instructional development, and organizational development) in a structured and applied way that participants have found useful. The process itself fosters considerable fellowship, resulting in feelings of increased effectiveness, support, and productivity.

### Other Program Workshops

In addition to the IPPG workshop, the Career Development Program offers between ten and twenty other workshops each year, serving from 125 to 350 different people. Most of the topics are suggested by faculty members and are implemented by program staff, although both internal and external consultants are used. Outside consultants are selected after the program director or assistant has heard them present their workshop to another group. Most programs have worked well; a few have not, and those have been discontinued.

Workshop topics have included the following: financial management (the most popular year after year), income tax, time management, working/living with aging parents, career assessment, teaching/learning effectiveness, writing a *curriculum vitae*, intimacy, and the dual-career couple. The latter two workshops, as they relate to spouses and family, will be discussed below.

*Workshop on Intimacy.* This workshop, with topics ranging from identifying different kinds of intimacy to anger education, attracted both couples and singles. Anger was described as a barrier to intimacy, a normal emotion with a bad name in our culture. A segment on sexual intimacy included an explicit sex-education film. Domeena Renshaw, director of the Sexual Dysfunction Clinic at Loyola's Medical School and a well-known psychiatrist, author, and lecturer, led the workshop. Evaluations and participants' comments following the program showed that the workshop provided a much-needed forum for topics not often openly discussed, especially in a faculty development program. The program had high attendance at first, then did not draw well and was discontinued. It may be presented again when there is more interest.

*Workshop on the Dual-Career Couple.* Offered three times with four or five couples attending each weekend, this workshop, like the IPPG, used an off-campus setting so that couples would not be distracted by routine responsibilities. Areas of focus included ways in which a couple and family can support each other, appreciation of individual differences, and ways for both partners to get what they want within the family or relationship. Also discussed was the importance of purposeful living, in contrast to working merely for the sake of working.

One man came to this workshop thinking that *dual-career* meant one person with two careers; he came to learn how to juggle his teaching career in academic medicine with his practice. Another couple came to find a way to work together in the theater. They had encountered many barriers, but five years after the workshop they have now achieved their goal. Responses to the question, "How has this workshop helped your personal/family development?" have been varied. "I am able to relax more and do more with my family. We are more aware of disagreement and we discuss it." One faculty member, not ordinarily assertive prior to his participation in the workshop, reported that his family had constantly intruded on him at home when he was trying to do his research. With hard work he was able to learn to set limits so that his children could respect his time to work. This was not an easy task; it took almost a year before any progress was noted. The workshop, he said, had "helped only indirectly, but I am able to more clearly state my needs about my work."

It's important to mention that follow-up sessions were also a part of this program. One comment, heard repeatedly, emphasized that "the most helpful part of the workshop was learning there are other couples like ourselves—struggling, with problems and challenges." The we-are-not-in-this-alone feeling proved to be a cohesive factor for these groups.

### Illustrative Cases

A sharper sense of workshop efficacy can be conveyed through the actual experiences of three faculty members. Alan (the names are not real, of course) was chair of his department. This job, which he enjoyed but found demanding, complicated his already overextended life. His wife was in a career transition; she had just finished her Ph.D. but was still unemployed. They enrolled in both the IPPG and the dual-career couple weekend workshops. The initial IPPG workshop brought about several changes: Alan made a plan to reorganize his department; he set a goal of getting back to his research; with a consultant's help and some time-management techniques, he was able to adhere to a schedule and begin to publish again; he also dropped some activities that he labeled as "not as important to me anymore." The reorganization was appreciated by others in the department, and Alan felt they respected him more for making and acting on his decisions. He delegated to others more comfortably and let go of the idea that "if it's going to get done, I've got to do it myself."

His wife continued to work with the Career Development Program until she found a teaching position. She attended weekly career discussion groups, made contacts with other universities in the area, and expanded her "network." She appreciated the valuable self-assessment and the confidence she felt as a result of concentrating on her strengths.

Betty has attended practically every workshop offered during the past nine years. She says that she learns new things that help in her everyday life and in her department. She complained at one time that so many workshops emphasized couples and families that singles were largely overlooked. One response to her observation was a financial management workshop for singles, which attracted thirty faculty members and administrators. The program was complemented by a chili supper, making the evening into a social event. Betty reports that she has made remarkable progress with her own finances since the workshop: she has set goals for saving and been able to buy a condominium and new furniture as well as set money aside for her retirement. She has also taken some trips, learned to ride a bicycle, and joined a singles biking group. All this at age sixty!

Charles appeared one day at the office of the Career Development Program, saying that he was "miserable," tired of working with little or no recognition. He wanted to explore his options and had heard that this was one of the specialties of the program. After several consultations with a staff member he decided to talk to academics who were in the business world doing various things. He also began to look back over his past worklife to see what "threads" he could find. A love of writing surfaced, which put him on a public relations track for a while. Then he remembered that the stock market had interested him as a child and young adult. That led him into a new area of exploration, and he was referred to a former professional staff person who had taken a job in securities and was "just the right person to talk to."

Now a financial consultant, Charles says that he is "reaching new peaks and shedding garments as I go," feeling as if he is shifting into another gear. "I'm having fun doing what I'm doing, and I'm very happy with it," he notes. He is learning not to take himself too seriously; he can poke fun and feel fun. (Incidentally, he was a professor of theology.)

### Features Contributing to the Program's Success

One of the reasons for the Loyola program's success has been its place on the organizational chart. The director of the program reports directly to the senior vice-president and dean of faculties. Because top leadership is supportive, this reporting relationship has facilitated a flexible, ongoing program.

Another strong feature is the physical location of the program office: just across the street from the campus, with a rather obscured side entrance. This may seem to be a small matter, but the distance is just enough to assure confidentiality for those who appreciate it. There is also an outside telephone line so that calls do not come through the university switchboard.

The modest cost for all services and workshops is another

positive feature. The FIPSE grant provided financial support on a declining scale, from 75 percent the first year to 25 percent the third. When the grant ended, Loyola had gotten into the habit of paying. The program's cost has varied between $10,000 and $15,000 per year—not including the salaries of the assistant and the director—with all money coming from the budget of the senior vice-president and dean of faculties and administered by the director. That is quite a moderate amount for the number of services offered. Some of the ways that budget dollars have been stretched include the following: using internal and local resources, available in every college and university; advertising several programs in one flyer; inviting persons from other universities or from the business community to attend some of the workshops at full cost; holding follow-ups in faculty members' homes; and finding low-cost accommodations for off-campus workshops.

Another characteristic contributing to the program's success has been its continual consultation with and commitment to faculty. When professors are listened to, when programs are planned to address their needs, and when spouses are included, faculty say that they feel recognized and supported. Indeed, many who have not participated in any of the program activities say that just knowing they exist is a reassuring sign that the university cares about them.

Another successful feature of the Loyola model is the option to take a leave of absence without pay to spend a year in business, thereby gaining an alternate experience in the corporate world for the purpose of increasing vitality and renewal, personally and in the classroom. Loyola supports this career enrichment leave with the belief that faculty members who work in the business world for a year will have an expanded view of their possibilities and skills and that they will gain an inside perspective of the corporate world. The assumption is that faculty members who return will do so with a renewed energy and interest that will liven their teaching, and that those who choose not to return would have left anyway. By granting a leave and helping faculty throughout the career shift, the "extended campus family" is helping its members to grow. In the last nine years, six full-time faculty have taken part in this leave program; three have stayed in business and three have returned. The program leaders have assisted faculty members with their career planning techniques, but finding a position during the leave has been the responsibility of the jobseeker (except in two cases, when placements were arranged).

The business leave program, at low cost to the institution, provides benefits to both the individual and the organization. It is not for everyone, of course. Sometimes the arrangements seem too complicated and the year away seems too risky; faculty members may fear that they will not be able to remain state-of-the-art in their field or that their job will not be there when they return. Changing environments for a year is also inherently difficult, not only for faculty but for spouses and children.

## Recommendations Based on the Loyola Experience

1.  Begin with faculty. The best way for a program to get started is from the ground up.
2.  Cultivate the support necessary from the top administration and show them why it is important to have a program.
3.  Be faculty-responsive. Provide an array of workshops to meet faculty needs; schedule continual needs assessments, interviews, evaluations, consciousness-raising programs, and group meetings.
4.  Involve spouses and families. Invite and expect spouses to participate.
5.  Increase awareness of the many ways an individual's personal life contributes to his or her professional life, and vice versa.
6.  Take stock of resources within the university and surrounding community. Do not overlook the obvious and less expensive consultants.
7.  Be visible in your institution. Offer to speak at department meetings so that you can personally invite colleagues to your workshops and let them know about development opportunities. Continually "market" program services, informally and formally.
8.  Find program leaders who are knowledgeable about the institution and the organization's structure.
9.  Have follow-up components for your workshops. The leader's

commitment to continue working with participants after the seminar ends is essential.

10. Persevere in spite of negative reactions. Be flexible and learn from failure. You can always make a U-turn or build on criticism and disappointment.

### Summary of Program

The Career Development Program of Loyola University of Chicago is a faculty development program that emphasizes personal, professional, and family growth for the purpose of career enrichment. This is stated in the program brochure. Most members of the Loyola community are familiar with the program and the array of services it offers: workshops, discussion groups, individual consultations, and a leave of absence option to work in the business world.

Our outside evaluators have been generous to us, giving us confidence that the Loyola model is effective. Seymour Sarason, a professor of psychology at Yale University, reported the following in a 1979 evaluation: "I have heard about many college and university career development programs. I have had firsthand contact with several of them. Without question Loyola's program is the most balanced and creative of them all." He noted that the faculty who participated in the program were bright, mature people, on the young side and tenured. They were not frustrated, stagnated persons. They were trying to learn about themselves and "extract as much meaning as possible from their personal and working lives."

Joseph Katz, then director of research for human development and educational policy at State University of New York at Stony Brook, wrote in his 1980 evaluation, "The availability of a continuing person, office, and program is crucial. It institutionalizes the support, renewal, and re-direction functions. Moreover, as the effects of workshops and similar interventions are continuing, an agency to whom one can turn for information, clarification, and advice is needed." The involvement of spouses, he observed, further contributes to program effectiveness. He also noted that even a modest investment could bring about major changes in the professional and personal activities of those who participated, as the Loyola model has demonstrated.

"The need for faculty growth is overwhelming," Katz stated in his evaluation. "When this need is not met, faculty can become stagnant in their professional and personal ways." As Blackburn (1979, p. 53) observed, "A genuine loss—personal and societal— occurs when an academic person stops growing and developing, learning new things, exploring new interconnections."

The Loyola model addresses crucial faculty needs for growth and development. By emphasizing the person and his or her family, the program strives to increase awareness of the ways personal life contributes to and interacts with professional life. Perhaps the best conclusion is these words of one faculty member: "By supporting the Career Development Program, the university is telling its faculty that they want them to be whole human beings and they want them to bring their wholeness into the classroom."

## References

Baldwin, R. G. "Adult and Career Development: What Are the Implications for Faculty?" In *Current Issues in Higher Education.* Washington, D.C.: American Association for Higher Education, 1979.

Baruch, G. K., Barnett, R. C., and Rivers, C. *Lifeprints: New Patterns of Love and Work for Today's Women.* New York: McGraw-Hill, 1983.

Blackburn, R. T. "Academic Careers: Patterns and Possibilities." In *Current Issues in Higher Education.* Washington, D.C.: American Association for Higher Education, 1979.

Blackburn, R. T., and Baldwin, R. G. "Faculty as Human Resources: Reality and Potential." In R. G. Baldwin and R. T. Blackburn (eds.), *College Faculty: Versatile Human Resources in a Period of Constraint.* New Directions for Institutional Research, no. 40. San Francisco: Jossey-Bass, 1983.

Bumagin, V. E., and Hirn, K. F. *Aging Is a Family Affair.* New York: Crowell, 1979.

Erikson, E. H. *Life History and the Historical Moment.* New York: Norton, 1975.

Gaff, J. G. *Toward Faculty Renewal: Advances in Faculty, Instructional, and Organizational Development.* San Francisco: Jossey-Bass, 1976.

Gardner, J. W. *Self-Renewal: The Individual and the Innovative Society.* New York: Harper & Row, 1963.

Gould, R. L. *Transformations: Growth and Change in Adult Life.* New York: Simon & Schuster, 1978.

Holland, J. L. *Making Vocational Choices: A Theory of Careers.* Englewood Cliffs, N.J.: Prentice-Hall, 1973.

Levinson, D. J., and others. *The Seasons of a Man's Life.* New York: Knopf, 1978.

Naftzger, B. H. "A Comparative Study of Loyola University Faculty Members: Career Development Workshop Participants and Non-Participants." Unpublished master's thesis, Department of Guidance and Counseling, Northeastern Illinois University, 1980.

Sheehy, G. *Passages: Predictable Crises of Adult Life.* New York: Dutton, 1974.

# ✵ 12

# Redirecting Faculty Through Organizational Development:

## *Fairleigh Dickinson University*

*Ann F. Lucas*

Colleges and universities sometimes must respond to new realities that necessitate major interventions to enable faculty members to adjust. In this chapter two organizational development interventions are described that helped Fairleigh Dickinson University (FDU) cope with difficult academic personnel issues. The administrative unit responsible for formulating and implementing these interventions was the office of professional and organizational development (OPOD).

Founded in 1982 with external funding, OPOD was responsible for revitalizing 58 faculty members through retraining and transfer to other responsibilities within the university. It also administered a career transition program, which arranged buyouts for 102 faculty members who had left FDU. Since OPOD was originally founded for the specific purpose of dealing with faculty overstaffing and reducing faculty dislocation (thereby effecting a better match between human resources and university needs), the office was intended to operate for a limited time, unlike most faculty development offices whose primary goal is instructional development. During its six-year existence, OPOD's accomplishments (in addition to that of achieving its main goals) included: leadership training for deans and academic chairs (Lucas, 1986a, 1986b), team building and conflict resolution in some academic departments when two colleges within FDU were merged (Lucas, 1988), and a career transition program for 40 professional and administrative staff. This chapter, however, focuses only on the faculty retraining and the career transition activities.

In the late 1970s FDU, a private institution located on three campuses in northern New Jersey, began to face a problem familiar to many institutions of higher education. Student enrollment was dropping, and increasing numbers of freshmen began to choose majors in business, engineering, and computer science over liberal arts and education. These conditions resulted in the dual problems of faculty overstaffing and dislocation.

Faculty in the humanities and education, who had spent their entire careers in an expanding university, responded initially with disbelief and denial to two widely publicized projections: that numbers of students available for entrance into college were decreasing, and that students would more frequently be taking majors that were clearly job-related. Gradually, however, faculty in a number of disciplines found themselves no longer able to teach advanced courses in their specialties; they were forced to teach introductory and "service" courses instead. Faced with the reality of a steadily declining enrollment, faculty grew discouraged and morale plummeted.

At the national level, Kanter (1979) has argued for a fundamental rethinking of our assumptions about academic careers and the nature of academic work. Furniss (1981), who described the radical changes in faculty working conditions that began in higher education in the late 1970s, presented a variety of institutional approaches to resolving some of the difficulties faculty members face. His book rests on the premise that "faculty members individually and as representative[s] of a profession are almost by definition bright and competent. This statement is ensured by the processes of training and selection. If at some point in their careers they do not seem to show the ability and talent they had when they entered the profession, it is worth looking at the environment to see where it might be altered so as again to give them the chance to shine"

(p. ix). That same year Baldwin and others (1981), in response to the question of what colleges were doing to facilitate the development of new career options, published a survey of the first college faculty career development projects. Surprisingly, Baldwin stated, "Most of the programs we uncovered serve primarily a population of advanced graduate students and recent Ph.D.'s" (p. 6).

The work at FDU described in this chapter differs from those programs that Baldwin and his associates described and from other programs geared primarily to retraining academics for business (see Clark and Lewis, 1985, pp. 163-164). The FDU faculty—both those who retrained for positions within the university and those who made use of career transition services before leaving the University—were all tenured, with a median of fifteen years of service. (Those who left academe are now functioning in a variety of fields.)

Although overstaffed in the humanities and education, FDU began the 1980s facing shortages of faculty with academic qualifications for teaching business, engineering, and computer science courses. Because of this, retraining of faculty who were willing and motivated to make a successful transition to another part of the university became a high priority. FDU had an organizational development problem—one of human resource allocation and retraining.

Organizational development (OD) has been defined as "a process by which behavioral science knowledge and practices are used to help organizations achieve greater effectiveness, including improved quality of work life and increased productivity. Organization development differs from other planned change efforts . . . because the focus is upon human resources and their motivation, utilization, and integration within the organization" (Huse and Cummings, 1985, p. 1). French and Bell (1984, p. 1) describe an additional factor: "The orientation is on action—achieving desired results as a result of planned activities." Establishing an office to deal with such organizational problems in an institution that had not previously focused on systemwide changes, however, required funding at a time when financial resources were already strained. The university had traditionally depended heavily upon tuition income, and now enrollment was dropping.

### Founding the Office of Professional and Organizational Development

As part of a capital campaign effort, two FDU deans wrote a proposal to several foundations, requesting funding to establish an office of professional development for faculty. (Fully two years later, as it became clearer that we were engaged in interventions in which the *institution* was the client, the word *organizational* was added to the name of the office.) The proposal stressed (1) the university's twin problems of faculty overstaffing and dislocation, which resulted in an organizational need for faculty retraining; and (2) the fact that when faculty are at the cutting edge of their fields, the benefits of this updated knowledge base are shared with industry, whose employees FDU educates in large numbers as part-time students and in continuing education programs.

The sum of $290,000 was raised for a six-year period. A search-and-screen committee, having decided to select an internal candidate as founder and director of the office, chose for this three-quarter-time position a clinical psychologist with industrial organizational experience (who had already served for a year as chair of a faculty opportunity committee).

The search-and-screen committee, which included the two deans who had secured the funding, specified both that the director of the new office should report to the office of the vice-president for academic affairs (VPAA), and that there be an advisory committee to the director made up of five members: one faculty member from each of FDU's three campuses, one administrator, and one faculty member at large.

At the first meeting with the VPAA, the director and advisory committee were given a charge: the VPAA defined the office as serving a human resource planning function and told members, "You are to take the role of 'matchmaker.'" The task was to evaluate university and faculty needs, to select candidates who were interested in and capable of retraining, and to coordinate the retraining and transfer of faculty from overstaffed to understaffed departments. A budget was drawn up, with about $17,000 allocated specifically for career retraining projects during the first year. One-half of the director's three-quarter-time salary (the other half was picked up by the university) and a full-time secretary's salary were charged against the grant. A photocopier, office supplies, funds for one overnight faculty career development conference, some travel funds, and money for a formative evaluation at the end of the first year were the only other items in the budget.

The new staff spent much of the first semester doing a needs analysis and developing ownership in the office by faculty and administrators. In order to be effective, a professional development office must be accepted by faculty and all levels of administration. This grass-roots part of the project was time-consuming, but any new professional development office that fails to provide opportunity for input is doomed to function on the sidelines, in splendid isolation—underutilized and having little impact on the organization. All of the formal and informal leaders among the faculty, including members of all standing faculty committees and members of the administration, from deans up to the president, were interviewed. We chose not to conduct a written survey; we feared that such a procedure might raise unrealistic expectations about what the office could do.

## Faculty Career Development Conferences

One of the important beginning steps in faculty retraining is getting faculty thinking about other careers within and outside the university. This enables them to stop defining their worth in terms only of how much value others place on their particular academic discipline, and to transcend the mindset that their discipline is the only one in which they can function.

To change attitudes and develop ownership in the project, two separate overnight Career Development Conferences were sponsored about six months apart. A total of about 70 faculty members attended. An outside guest speaker talked about faculty careers, the stages of professional academic life, the short career ladders for faculty members, and some of the causes of low faculty morale. Another speaker focused on the transferable skills faculty have developed, such as "platform" skills, writing skills, problem-solving skills, skills in learning complex issues quickly, and the ability to explain concepts so that others can readily understand them. These skills, which faculty often take for granted, are highly valued and often in short supply in industrial organizations.

Part of each conference was devoted to small-group discussions. In the first conference some original academic case studies of relevant faculty problems were used to trigger discussion; in the other conference small groups talked about career-related problems they were experiencing within the university. These conferences helped faculty reevaluate their own careers, made it acceptable to talk about career transitions to others, and brought faculty attention to OPOD as a helpful resource.

This brings us to a description of career retraining activities, faculty buyout agreements, and career transition services at FDU.

### Career Retraining for Internal Positions

A basic principle of professional development is this: devote the most time to faculty who are "winners"—in other words, those who are hardy, flexible survivors. It is such faculty who will be most effective in changing and who will derive the greatest benefit for themselves and for the university. It can be seductive to fantasize about offering services to a depressed faculty member who writes widely circulated memos about being an ill-used scholar, reduced to teaching introductory courses; such an enterprise, however, would be overly time-consuming and offer little chance of success. It would create an association in the minds of faculty between the office of professional development and faculty "in need of serious help," which can prevent other faculty from contacting the office.

Therefore, during OPOD's first year we were actively working toward our first "success story"—one that would establish our credibility with both faculty and administration. It began in the spring, after a college faculty meeting at which the OPOD director had chaired a discussion on faculty development. A member of the foreign-language department approached the director. Very much aware that there were now fewer language majors, and no longer having any opportunity to teach Italian (her recent teaching assignments had been limited to sections of introductory and intermediate Spanish), this faculty member felt discouraged and demoralized. Moreover, the woman was highly regarded by other faculty, had a reputation as an excellent teacher, and could always be counted on when there was work to be done.

Thinking that she might enjoy using part of her teaching load to work in one of the university's several learning centers, the faculty member requested that OPOD provide her with tuition so that she could take six credits in remedial reading at a nearby university. Her goal seemed realistic. However, to enable her to make a well-informed decision, she made an appointment to discuss her objective and its implementation with the director of one of the learning centers.

At that meeting, which was also attended by the director of OPOD, the faculty member seemed to grow three feet taller right before our eyes. The learning center director, a supportive and highly reinforcing individual, was very impressed with several modules of English as a second language that the faculty member had already created. The director offered her an internship at the learning center, which would enable her to earn six graduate credits. It was also arranged for her to take an additional· twelve graduate credits in developmental education through an excellent program supported by a grant from the state's Department of Higher Education, which was to be offered on campus during the summer.

In one year all of this work was completed. The faculty member was appointed acting director of one of the learning centers, replacing someone who wanted to leave this temporary assignment and return to his own discipline. Under the leadership of the new acting director, more than 240 students used the learning center during her first year. Student test scores were boosted by 12 percent; and in strong testimony to the center's effect on retention, 74 percent of these students returned to the university the next year. All of this cost a mere $395 (spent on books and tuition for the summer program), as well as six credits of released time for the faculty member while she completed her internship.

Since this first success story, fifty-eight people have been retrained to perform different functions within the university. The initial steps in the retraining process have usually been as follows:

1. A faculty member voluntarily approaches OPOD for assistance in clarifying a career goal and discovering whether there is a university need in the area identified.

2. For many faculty, the next step involves some career counseling. This process may be brief (if, for example, the faculty member appears to have a rational basis for a clear-cut goal) or it may take considerable time (if the individual seems to be making an impulsive decision or is not sure what a career change will accomplish). In a situation in which a hasty decision has been made—perhaps out of anxiety, because an individual's department seems overstaffed—the task of the career counselor is to help the faculty member reevaluate the decision. Counseling usually includes some self-assessment as a means of helping an individual look realistically at the current situation in the university and at his or her life in general. Tests and questionnaires can be used to identify skills, interests, and achievements, as well as satisfactions and frustrations in the present job. Useful practical guides to this process of assessment for both a faculty member and the career counselor may be found in Storey's (1986a, 1986b, 1986c) classic *Career Dimensions* books.

3. Once a specific goal is agreed upon, implementation steps need to be developed. A new career goal might (a) involve retraining for transfer to another department, college, or campus in the university; (b) focus on the acquisition of knowledge or skills that can be incorporated into a course (for example, word processing skills to be used in teaching English composition courses); or (c) include the development of a new course or program, if a market for such a course can be demonstrated.

4. If retraining is required, several options are available. (a) A member of the OPOD staff, working with one of the deans, might help a faculty member obtain a retraining sabbatical. Having had a recent sabbatical for research purposes is not considered a deterrent to being awarded a paid retraining leave. (b) Faculty members who do not need a sabbatical for full-time retraining may be given released time and a grant to cover retraining costs at another institution of higher learning. (c) Full-time faculty may take graduate or undergraduate courses at any of fourteen other institutions in New Jersey, on a space-available basis, as part of an enrichment program. No credit is recorded, and no tuition is charged. (d) Faculty may also take individual courses for credit at our own institution without paying tuition. (e) A faculty member may serve an internship as a

professional staff member in another part of the university. (f) A faculty member may also serve an internship in an industrial organization for any period up to one year. Whether or not industry provides a stipend, the university provides the faculty member with a wage no less than the individual's current salary, as long as it can be shown that the university will also benefit from the learning experience. Some successful retraining projects completed at FDU are shown in Table 12.1.

A change in assignment, a new course to teach, a new area to explore—all these can be revitalizing for faculty. When these changes also satisfy a university need, an effective allocation of human resources has been accomplished. Moreover, faculty motivation is highest when the achievement of a university goal is congruent with the realization of a faculty member's goals. For example, a faculty member's status is enhanced when a program the individual has developed is praised by an accreditation group.

Directed toward goals of effective human resource reallocation and faculty revitalization as well as personal satisfaction, a number of faculty members have transferred to temporary or permanent assignments on a full- or part-time basis. Their tenured status in the university is protected, and if they have become administrators or professional staff, they are free to move back to faculty positions as openings come up. A psychologist has worked full-time as a senior staff member in the development office for several years; a sociologist is now employed as executive assistant to the president; a biologist had a one-quarter-time assignment as counselor to members of an athletic team. A number of arts and sciences faculty have each taught one or two courses in the College of Business; three philosophers teach courses in business ethics; a historian teaches a course in the history of industrial organizations; a psychologist teaches a course in consumer behavior; two other psychologists teach courses in management and organizational development. Such assignments are negotiated annually, when schedules are set up for the following year.

## Faculty Buyout Agreements

Although fifty-eight faculty members had been retrained by 1984, and many had transferred to other departments, colleges, cam-

Table 12.1. Successful Retraining Projects.

| Discipline | Cost and Intervention | Results of Intervention |
|---|---|---|
| Biology (1) | $500; 25 percent released time to contact authorities in the field, assess needs of nearby industries, and develop materials. | Developed course in environmental ethics and interdisciplinary course with College of Business. |
| Chemistry (1) | $1,000 for books, supplies, and commutation; N.J. faculty tuition grant. | Earned M.S. in computer science; now teaching courses in computer science. |
| Dentistry (1) | $500 (partial funding) for summer preceptorship as training for fellowship exam in radiology. | Published three papers on use of high-speed film to reduce radiation on patients. |
| Education (2) | FDU courses in telecommunications and microcomputers in education. | Now teaching new courses to update curriculum. |
| English (3) | $1,000 in tuition at another university for one person; course work taken at FDU by two other faculty. | Now teaching ESL courses as part of load. Much cross-fertilization of ideas among the three faculty. |
| English (2) | $1,090 for two faculty members to attend workshop on computer applications to the teaching of writing. | Wrote proposal funded by N.J. Department of Higher Education for $75,000 for purchase of computers and software for faculty training. As a result, more students using word processing and data bases in writing research. |
| Fine arts (3) | $400 for workshops on computer graphics. | Artist incorporated new knowledge into his teaching; had proposal for $47,000 funded by N.J. Department of Higher Education. |
| | $400 for workshops on computer-assisted composition and computer pitch recognition. | Musician now using interactive video approach to music theory and ear training in class. |
| | $400 for course in photojournalism. | Musician, also a photographer, taught photography course to complete teaching schedule. |
| Foreign language (1) | Internship at FDU. | Now teaching one course in ESL. |

Table 12.1. Successful Retraining Projects, Cont'd.

| Discipline | Cost and Intervention | Results of Intervention |
|---|---|---|
| History (1) | $500 for conference on technological aids to medieval studies. | Incorporated new teaching strategies into his classes. |
| Leadership Ed.D. (2) (Program eliminated.) | $6,000 tuition (shared by OPOD and the College of Business). | Completed 22 graduate credits in management and marketing; transferred to College of Business. |
| | $1,000 as partial support for Peace Studies Program at Ben Gurion University, Israel. | Served as mediator for black and Jewish groups in city of Newark; now developing curriculum in peace studies for philosophy department and teaching in our new interdisciplinary core. |
| Mathematics (3) | $1,500 for books, supplies; tuition grants. | All three are now teaching computer science courses. |

puses, and positions within the university, there was still a serious problem of faculty overstaffing. (We had an excess of about 20 percent, or 400 faculty members.)

As I mentioned previously, until the late 1970s FDU had been a steadily expanding university. Student enrollment, including both full- and part-time students, had peaked in the mid seventies at about 20,000. Between 1980 and 1985 the number dropped by 25 percent to 15,000 students. Faculty cutbacks seemed mandatory if the university were to continue as a vital institution. In order to forestall potential large-scale faculty terminations, the administration and the American Association of University Professors agreed to a buyout program that was developed in conjunction with career transition services.

For several years FDU had been projecting student credit hours per semester and the number of full-time equivalent faculty (FTEF) needed to teach these credit hours. As an associate VPAA at FDU at the time indicated, "The data on FTEF clearly identified the overstaffed disciplines: biology, fine arts (speech, theatre, art, and music), foreign languages, health/physical education, sociology/ anthropology, social work, and education. A general notice was sent to faculty in these disciplines, noting the overstaffing and inviting them to consider a buyout. Every faculty member in the affected disciplines who requested a buyout received one. Faculty from other disciplines, such as accounting, also applied and were bought out if they did not need to be replaced" (Paul, 1985, p. 114).

Moreover, at this time a decision was made to phase out, over a three-year period, three separate programs: a doctoral program (Ed.D.) in leadership studies, a master's program in human development, and a bachelor's program in social work. When the collective bargaining agreement between administration and faculty was settled late in 1984, a detailed buyout plan was established. "Features of the buyout agreement are: 1) availability to tenured faculty in overstaffed disciplines; 2) completely voluntary; 3) tenure rights relinquished; 4) available January 25 or August 15 (of) each year; 5) entitlement is to twice the participant's current base, distributed at his or her option over a period not to exceed five years; 6) tuition grants available to participant and family (enrolled at FDU) until programs are completed; 7) entitled to health insurance for the two years following resignation; and 8) part-time teaching at FDU available" (Paul, 1985, p. 115).

The buyout package reduced the size of the faculty by 20 percent, from 507 to 405. The overall cost to the university was over $6.4 million, which would be recovered over several years of lower salary costs.

Approximately 75 of the 102 faculty who signed the buyout agreement came from the seven disciplines that had been identified as overstaffed and the three programs designated to be phased out. These faculty would not otherwise have left the university and consequently had done little planning either for an alternative career or for retirement.

Recognizing this, the director of OPOD, working closely with the associate VPAA, planned the following steps for setting up career transition services: (1) interview faculty to determine needs, (2) provide support and immediate counseling, (3) select an outplacement firm to do workshops on job-search skills, (4) work directly with representatives of the outplacement firm to ensure that the program would be sensitive to the needs of academics, (5) monitor and evaluate the program, (6) set up a retirement-planning program, and (7) provide follow-up services for faculty.

When a sizable number of faculty members leave a university, career transition services must be provided. Many academicians have never been employed outside of higher education, yet few academic positions in the humanities are currently available in other colleges. Thus faculty require considerable assistance in identifying and making a transition to a nonacademic career.

Since 1980 many industrial organizations have terminated as many as 25 percent of their employees, either to increase productivity or to raise their profit margin. When someone in industry is terminated, however, he or she usually has a job title for which a parallel position exists in another organization. An executive recruiter, an investment analyst, a corporate attorney, or a training coordinator can move to a similar position in another company, because it is believed that each possesses recognizable skills that are easily transferable.

Consider the academic: the comparative biologist, the specialist in nineteenth-century English literature, the musician who teaches composition. Though the faculty member may feel relieved that a generous buyout package has provided financial assistance and medical benefits to reduce immediate anxiety about survival and to allow time to make a career change, he or she may have no idea what skills can be transferred to another job.

Moreover, there is a psychological adjustment that must be made. Someone leaving academe is no longer a university professor but is simply unemployed—or, to use the term currently popular in England, "redundant." Subtle changes begin to develop in the way such an individual is treated by family and friends. Even before the actual time of leaving the university, a loss of prestige and identity is experienced that triggers feelings of anxiety and depression. This loss of self-esteem is based partly on a belief that one's value as an individual is diminished because talents and skills that took years to develop seem not to be valued either in academe or in industry.

And if these adjustments are not enough, a new set of skills and attitudes must be learned to secure alternative employment. Former faculty must face the bitter facts that employability might be enhanced if the résumé includes no mention of the Ph.D. and that scholarly publications may be perceived as further corroboration that the individual has lived in an ivory tower out of touch with the real world.

It is clear, therefore, that career transition services for faculty must be based on a strong sensitivity to faculty feelings and concerns and on an awareness that those leaving academe have a different set of problems than do employees who leave or are terminated by industry.

## A Career Transition Program for Academics

There were 102 faculty buyouts at FDU. Of the faculty who used our career transition services, within three months more than 60 percent were successfully employed in careers that they indicated they liked as much as or better than their faculty positions. After six months the success rate topped 90 percent.

*Determining Responsibility for Program Components.* One of the first issues that needs to be addressed in setting up a career transition program is which services can be provided in-house and which must be handled by external organizations. Three important criteria in making this decision are competence, credibility, and cost. Which parts of the career transition program can be handled competently by internal resources? Do these internal professionals have credibility with the faculty who will use their services? Will the high cost of external services be worth the money?

When the FDU administration developed a buyout package to encourage faculty in overstaffed departments to leave, it first decided to hire an external outplacement service to work with faculty; however, the OPOD staff felt that our faculty—as faculty and colleagues—had some needs that were different from those who took buyouts in industry. *(Outplacement* is defined as teaching people the skills needed to secure their own employment as opposed to getting jobs for people. That distinction is an important one—and one that frequently gives rise to misunderstandings.)

The OPOD director, after consulting with her staff, wrote a proposal to the administration requesting that we be permitted to coordinate the career transition services internally. The proposal

included the following: (1) our plans for the program and its implementation, (2) a listing of services to be handled internally and
externally, (3) a breakdown of additional financial resources required, and (4) the résumés of the OPOD staff, highlighting specific
experience and skills relevant to this project.

After our proposal was discussed with top administration,
the associate VPAA advised us that the plan was acceptable and that
resources would be made available. The OPOD staff—at that time a
full-time director and two faculty members, each with one-quarter-
time responsibility to the office—coordinated the entire program.
OPOD handled all of the services except for a three-day outplacement program, which was administered by a multinational outplacement organization.

The university decided to have a screening committee (made
up of three high-level administrators and the director of OPOD)
choose the external outplacement firm, so that faculty could be
assured that they were working with an experienced organization
with a proven track record. Once the outplacement firm was selected, the director of OPOD coordinated the entire program, keeping the associate VPAA informed of progress.

*Initiating the Outplacement Program.* The OPOD staff met
with a representative of the outplacement firm during the planning
stage to decide who would do what. Outplacement firms typically
offer two sets of services. The less expensive arrangement includes
teaching job-search skills to groups of twelve to fifteen people. In
1984 this cost between $1,500 and $2,200 a day, for a minimum of
four days. (The fourth day is left unscheduled to allow between
thirty and forty-five minutes of individual counseling for group
participants.) The more expensive service—the so-called executive
package—costs the organization between 12 and 15 percent of the
annual salary for each terminated individual. This higher-priced
contract provides the basic three-day program that teaches job-
search skills; in addition, it provides office space, someone to take
telephone messages and type letters of application, and ongoing
availability of a career counselor until the individual is successfully
employed elsewhere.

We felt that our colleagues were entitled to the best services possible while they were undergoing the trauma of a career transition, yet the cost of the executive package was prohibitive. OPOD's director had been trained and formerly employed in career counseling; moreover, we felt that our intimate knowledge of our faculty and of the university helped us to be more "tuned in" and caring than any outside agency, which would necessarily be more concerned about cost and profit factors. Therefore, FDU selected the basic arrangement and OPOD handled all additional services.

In order to provide a well-integrated program, the OPOD staff participated in mini-sessions of what individuals would later experience in the three-day outplacement program. Our feedback and recommendations to the external psychologist were useful in determining program content.

We decided that the OPOD staff would handle all of the interviews with faculty buyouts to determine individual career transition needs. All 102 faculty were contacted. Of these, 85 were interviewed; 17 did not respond to telephone calls or memos. Because work in groups would be more supportive for faculty and be more efficient, we then identified those needs that could be addressed in groups; the remainder would require individual attention.

*Workshops and Other Group Work.* Because a sizable number of people were interested in particular services, several workshops were planned to facilitate the outplacement. Three TIAA-CREF financial-planning conferences were held, one on each of our three campuses. In the retirement-planning conference that OPOD sponsored, the segment most enthusiastically received was that in which retired colleagues returned to talk about their experiences after leaving the university. The most popular conference, attended by seventy-five faculty members, was one on developing consulting skills. Many faculty felt that part-time consulting was an area they wanted to explore.

Interviews with faculty buyouts revealed that a number of them were depressed about leaving the university. Others, concerned about new employment or retirement, were experiencing anxiety related to making a major life transition. Some requested immediate career counseling. However, because faculty made up their minds to take a buyout at different times of the year, and because the most efficient and least expensive way to set up the three-day outplacement groups was to wait until there were from twelve to fifteen people who could take the program at the same time, some problems in logistics were created: there were always some people waiting for a group to begin. Interim career counseling groups, conducted by an OPOD staff member to help faculty who had made early buyout decisions, offered strong support for faculty who experienced anxiety, loss of identity, and alienation from colleagues.

Some self-assessment and a focus on how career choices had been made in the past were helpful, both in these groups and with individuals. With these tools faculty could evaluate how well matched they were with their faculty positions. At this point, in a supportive counseling relationship or group, people sometimes became aware that their work had not been very satisfying for a long time. It then became easier to look at career options, to recognize that there were other professions that might provide greater challenge and fulfillment.

At this stage workbooks (De Roche and McDougall, 1984) and other reading materials (Bolles, 1988; Morin and Cabrera, 1982; Krannich and Banis, 1981) were helpful in focusing attention on significant topics, such as personal financial planning, résumé writing, developing self-marketing strategies, networking, making relocation decisions, and early retirement. For coping with the stress of impending unemployment, usually accompanied by a lowered self-esteem, Burns (1980) offers some innovative and effective strategies from the field of cognitive therapy.

Some faculty who felt uncomfortable about joining a group came to OPOD for different kinds of assistance: sometimes counseling, most frequently help in writing a résumé. Some of the most time-consuming requests for counseling came from faculty who were agonizing about whether or not to take a buyout.

*A Closer Look at the Outplacement Program.* The three-day outplacement sessions conducted by the external organization dealt with core concepts of the job search. Follow-up work with faculty as they attempted to put their new skills into practice, including reinforcement of their efforts when they felt discouraged, was an important and time-consuming activity that was handled by the OPOD staff. Faculty found that using the skills they had learned was often difficult, and successful experiences increased when they had someone to talk to who was encouraging and supportive. This support, provided individually and in groups, was one of the most important aspects of the program and contributed significantly to its success.

Because outplacement groups teach the skills necessary to secure employment but do not get jobs for people, it is important that goals be clarified for participants so that their expectations are reasonable. The three-day program covered (1) an assessment of individual interests, accomplishments, and values; (2) setting up a job-search network; (3) developing self-marketing skills, including turning a *curriculum vitae* into a job résumé; (4) self-presentation skills (developed through the videotaping of simulated employment interviews); and (5) negotiating a salary.

All those who engage in outplacement work share a common core of information. It may be packaged somewhat differently from firm to firm, but it is all basically the same. Because outplacement firms are often big businesses, it is important that prospective clients be able to separate out what are essentially marketing strategies—ones that give the company a marketing edge but do little else—from those services that are genuinely useful to the participants. Moreover, it is difficult to persuade outplacement personnel not to include a part of their usual packaged program if it is something that distinguishes their program from the others. For example, the group leader at FDU was asked in advance not to show a particular videotape. (In the judgment of OPOD staff, who had previewed the rather simplistic sixty-minute tape, it was based on highly controversial assumptions presented as scientific facts and was packed with more information than could be absorbed.) During work with two different groups, however, the film was shown. When asked about it afterwards, the group leader explained, "Well, it's company policy to show this videotape."

Despite the fact that external outplacement firms may be experienced and knowledgeable about the world of industrial employment, none of them has had much experience in working with groups of academics. They seem to know little beyond the obvious about how the skills of an academic might transfer to industry and often lack sensitivity regarding a faculty member's feelings about leaving the only world that most academics know. These are factors to keep in mind in deciding who will handle career transition services for faculty and in preparing an agreement on exactly what content and process will be used.

*Results.* The director of OPOD monitored all outplacement sessions, served as a liaison with the outplacement firm, and had each group of participants do a written evaluation afterwards. Evaluations indicated that one of the most useful segments of the outplacement portion of the program was that dealing with the topic of self-presentation skills. Faculty valued the opportunity to practice employment interviews on videotape. Receiving feedback from the facilitator and from other participants on what they had handled well and how they could be more effective made them feel better prepared to handle employment interviews.

Outplacement facilitators also worked with faculty on responding to hard questions without being negative. Many faculty were angry because a drop in enrollment in their disciplines had created an overstaffing problem instrumental in their leaving the university. This anger, if expressed to a prospective employer, could create problems in an employment interview. How to handle questions about why they left the university in a matter-of-fact fashion, without coming across negatively, was perceived as extremely useful by faculty buyouts.

Another area in which faculty valued assistance from the outplacement firm was in résumé writing. Turning the usual lengthy *curriculum vitae* (the one that lists every committee on which the individual has ever served) into a résumé is a difficult task for many faculty. There seems to be agreement in industry that a good résumé is no longer and no shorter than two pages. Bulleted accomplishment statements are much more appropriate than lists of committee memberships. However, convincing a faculty member to eliminate mention of activities that are valued in academe but will never be appreciated by an employment interviewer in other fields can be difficult.

Our decision to hire an external firm to handle the three-day outplacement program was made to assure faculty that they would be in the hands of experienced professionals who knew the industrial marketplace and who had a good track record. The OPOD director and staff had been full-time academics for many years; therefore, they would not have been perceived as knowledgeable about the job market. Personnel in our student career counseling service are competent, yet because this group has worked almost entirely with undergraduates, the faculty would probably have had a negative perception about using their services. In the first year of our buyout program, we used an outside organization with an excellent reputation. After that first year, when credibility for our work had been established, we handled the entire program ourselves; and faculty reactions were positive.

The comprehensive services provided by OPOD for faculty buyouts have had a positive impact on the morale of the rest of the university community. When an attractive buyout package and high-quality professional services are provided to help respected colleagues make a career transition, the rest of us can feel assured that the university is following its humanistic traditions.

We have used our OPOD newsletter to inform the rest of the university community about our career transition services. The outplacement portion of the program has been described in its pages, and we have shared information about what our former colleagues are doing.

Follow-up interviews indicate that all but one of the faculty members who participated in career transition activities are now employed in positions that they enjoy as much as or more than their employment at the university. See Table 12.2, which lists some of the careers in which our former faculty are employed. As I indicated previously, 60 percent were employed within three months of leaving, and more than 90 percent were employed within six months. Although faculty staffing and dislocation problems have not been totally resolved at FDU, a significant impact has been made on these problems. Moreover, the university community is generally able to feel comfortable about our colleagues who have gone on to other areas of employment. Given the turmoil and litigation that often accompany attempts to resolve issues of overstaffing and dislocation, we feel that we have accomplished a highly workable solution to the problems.

Table 12.2. Careers Chosen by Faculty Buyouts.

| Academic Discipline | Career Transition |
|---|---|
| Biology (2) | Faculty member at another university. |
| Business (7) | Full-time consultant in industry (5); full-time accountant; full-time lawyer. |
| Construction technology (1) | Director of technical support services for a leading construction-contract law firm. |
| English (2) | English teacher to Chinese teachers of English in the People's Republic of China; faculty member at another university. |
| Fine arts (1) | Full-time painter. |
| Foreign languages (3) | Court interpreter for an attorney, interpreter of disability coverage for Social Security Administration, consultant to Educational Testing Service; full-time financial administrator for a religious order, of which she is a member; faculty member in another college. |
| Geology (1) | Full-time replacement for professors on sabbatical at other universities. |
| Mathematics (1) | Educational consultant. |
| Music (3) | Founder of school dedicated to the study of electronic music, specializing in computer and synthetic music; chair of the fine arts department in a high school known for its high academic standards; composer and leader of a jazz band. |
| Nursing (1) | Consultant for N.Y. Board of Regents, consultant for other nursing programs, author of community health book for professionals. |
| Physical education (2) | Manager of a racquetball club; owner of art-framing shop and sponsor of art shows. |
| Physics (1) | Real estate investor. |
| Political science (2) | Adjunct faculty member at FDU, part-time researcher and author; consultant, researcher, and author. |
| Psychology (8) | Full-time consultant (5); staff supervisor in market research at AT&T; faculty member at another university; real estate agent. |
| Social work (4) | Manager of a technical-training unit in a large financial institution; full-time consultant to a |

**Table 12.2. Careers Chosen by Faculty Buyouts, Cont'd.**

| Academic Discipline | Career Transition |
|---|---|
| | national philanthropic organization; contract administrator for a large county division of social services; part-time consultant to several social work agencies, training social workers in group dynamics, and part-time adjunct faculty member. |
| Sociology (1) | Adjunct faculty member and member of executive board in a large county social service agency. |
| Speech and drama (1) | Executive director of a cable television marketing company. |

## Duplicating an Organizational Development Approach in Other Colleges

Two major organizational development approaches, retraining of faculty in overstaffed departments for other positions within the university and a buyout and career transition program for faculty who will leave the university, have been described. These interventions or other possible organizational development strategies provide a means to address such difficult organizational issues.

Replication of an organization development approach requires the following: (1) strong support from the top level of administration; (2) integration of the work with the formal structure of an organization—that is, with the officials responsible for human resource planning and implementation (the president, vice-presidents, deans, academic chairs, personnel committees, and faculty leaders); (3) start-up funding, and continued financial support from the university when that money is used up; and (4) utilization of internal talent—namely, highly respected faculty who already possess organizational and human resource development skills.

## References

Baldwin, R., and others. *Expanding Faculty Options*. Washington, D.C.: American Association for Higher Education, 1986.

Bolles, R. N. *What Color Is Your Parachute?* Berkeley, Calif.: Ten Speed Press, 1988.

Brammer, L. M., and Humberger, F. E. *Outplacement and Inplacement Counseling.* Englewood Cliffs, N.J.: Prentice-Hall, 1984.

Brown, D., Brooks, L., and Associates. *Career Choice and Development.* San Francisco, Calif.: Jossey-Bass, 1984.

Burns, D. D. *Feeling Good.* New York: New American Library, 1980.

Clark, S. M., and Lewis, D. R. *Faculty Vitality and Institutional Productivity.* New York: Teachers College Press, 1985.

De Roche, F. W., and McDougall, M. A. *Now It's Your Move: A Guide for the Outplaced Employee.* Englewood Cliffs, N.J.: Prentice-Hall, 1984.

French, W. L., and Bell, C. H., Jr. *Organization Development.* (3rd ed.) Englewood Cliffs, N.J.: Prentice-Hall, 1984.

Furniss, W. T. *Reshaping Faculty Careers.* Washington, D.C.: American Council on Education, 1981.

Huse, E. F., and Cummings, T. G. *Organization Development and Change.* (3rd ed.) St. Paul, Minn.: West, 1985.

Kanter, R. M. "Changing the Shape of Work: Reform in Academe." In *Current Issues in Higher Education.* Washington, D.C.: American Association for Higher Education, 1979.

Krannich, R. L., and Banis, W. J. *Moving Out of Education.* Chesapeake, Va.: Progressive Concepts, 1981.

Lucas, A. "Academic Chair Training: The Why and the How of It." In M. Svinicki (ed.), *To Improve the Academy.* Lincoln: Professional and Organizational Development Network in Higher Education, Teaching and Learning Center, University of Nebraska, Lincoln, 1986a.

Lucas, A. "Effective Department Chair Training on a Low Cost Budget." *Journal of Staff, Program, and Organization Development,* 1986b, *4* (4), 33–36.

Lucas, A. "Strategies for a Team-Building Intervention in the Academic Department." *Journal of Staff, Program, and Organizational Development,* 1988, *6* (1), 21–32.

Morin, W. J., and Cabrera, J. C. *Parting Company.* San Diego, Calif.: Harcourt Brace Jovanovich, 1982.

Paul, C. "Buyouts and a Career Transition Program as a Response to Retrenchment." In J. R. Jeffrey and G. R. Erickson (eds.), *To Improve the Academy*. Lincoln: Professional and Organizational Development Network in Higher Education, Teaching and Learning Center, University of Nebraska, Lincoln, 1985.

Storey, W. *Career Dimensions I: Personal Planning Guide*. San Diego, Calif.: University Associates, 1986a.

Storey, W. *Career Dimensions II: Manager's Guide*. San Diego, Calif.: University Associates, 1986b.

Storey, W. *Career Dimensions III: Trainer's Guide*. San Diego, Calif.: University Associates, 1986c.

13

# A Consortial Approach:

## *The Great Lakes Colleges Association*

*Neil R. Wylie*

This chapter seeks to illustrate how a consortium of colleges—in this case, the twelve-member Great Lakes Colleges Association (GLCA)—can collaborate to promote faculty vitality. The message is that other institutions may well find that consortial arrangements can be an effective means for assisting faculty members.

Incorporated in 1962, the GLCA is one of the oldest higher education consortia. Its membership has never changed. The twelve members, located in the states of Michigan, Indiana, and Ohio, are Albion, Antioch, Denison, DePauw, Earlham, Hope, Kalamazoo, Kenyon, Oberlin, Ohio Wesleyan, Wabash, and Wooster.

The GLCA was not founded primarily to do faculty development. In 1962 such objectives as offering students the opportunity to study abroad and the possibility of forming a model athletic conference especially for small colleges had more salience than faculty development. However, some faculty development concerns were present early on, and such concerns have come to occupy a very important part of GLCA operations, especially in the past decade. Elkin (1982) has described the origins of the GLCA, including early faculty development efforts, in useful detail.

GLCA professional development programs serve a broad spectrum of individuals. In addition to sponsoring major faculty professional development programs, including a program in women's studies (Reed, 1982), the GLCA also encourages professional development meetings for institutional administrators and supports these through a program of collecting and disseminating comparative institutional research. With GLCA assistance, admissions and business officers, registrars, chief academic officers, and presidents regularly exchange management information.

The GLCA also conducts research on the outcomes of baccalaureate education (Fuller, 1986). Federal policy issues—especially federal tax policy—and student financial aid and faculty grant-support opportunities at liberal arts colleges are regularly monitored. We also sponsor or cosponsor over a dozen off-campus study opportunities enrolling over 500 students each year.

### Governance of the GLCA

To understand how faculty professional development is conceived of and promoted in the GLCA, it is necessary to understand something about how the organization is governed. Governance is achieved through a complex interplay among three constituencies—presidents, chief academic officers, and faculty members. Each constituency has a special role to play within the GLCA governance structure. The board of directors—composed of the presidents of all twelve institutions, one chief academic officer, and three faculty members—has legal responsibility for the operations of the consortium, direct responsibility for approval of the GLCA operating budget and maintenance of the consortium's reserve funds, and oversight responsibility for all GLCA matters. Although the board might occasionally be asked to approve major faculty professional development initiatives (giving direct financial support for our consortial Women's Studies Program or approval of grant applications, for example), it rarely becomes involved in ongoing faculty professional development matters. However, at each of its biannual meetings the board does receive a report of faculty professional development activities for questions or comment.

The GLCA board has delegated to the deans' council direct oversight responsibility for the faculty professional development program. The deans' council, which is made up of the chief academic officers of the twelve GLCA colleges, meets twice a year to review a wide range of GLCA programs and is especially concerned with program quality. It conducts regular evaluations of the GLCA student off-campus programs and receives the evaluation results of each of the GLCA faculty professional development conferences and workshops. To facilitate communication and ensure account- ability, the chair of the GLCA deans' council is a member of the GLCA board.

A faculty perspective on GLCA programs is ensured through the operations of the GLCA academic council, made up of twenty- seven faculty members from the GLCA colleges. Each college selects two faculty members each year to serve on the academic council; the three faculty members who serve on the GLCA board are also members of the academic council and serve to facilitate effective communication between the council and the board. The academic council has frequently played a role in the development of new faculty professional development initiatives, an important recent example being the encouragement of a GLCA commitment to un- dertake programs for the benefit of junior faculty. In addition to the formal channels, individual contact with GLCA faculty members and administrators is a normal part of consortial work, providing the opportunity for suggestions and feedback.

GLCA's professional development program is designed to supplement and enhance the faculty professional development op- portunities that are available to faculty members at our twelve member colleges. All of the colleges offer sabbatical leave programs and summer stipends to undertake small research or course/curricu- lum development projects, for example. In addition, a number of them offer other programs that are exemplary in their own right.

### Exemplary Faculty Development Programs at GLCA Colleges

Among the special programs at individual GLCA colleges, several offer generous start-up grants for research, especially in the sciences. These are often contingent on a new faculty member's submitting one or more grant proposals to outside agencies within a year. The grants may be from a fund made possible because of indirect-cost monies received from other grants, they may be funded by endowment income, or they may be funded from the regular operating budget.

The College of Wooster offers the possibility of a paid research leave every five years, in addition to sabbaticals. DePauw
University makes special funds available to permit a temporary reduction in teaching load for faculty returning from research leaves,
so that the research that was completed during the leave can be
prepared for publication. More than one GLCA college will now
permit a career exploration leave to be taken, in lieu of or in addition to a sabbatical.

Several of the GLCA colleges have designated a specific faculty member or administrator as a faculty development consultant
or coordinator, to ensure that faculty are informed about available
professional development opportunities and are encouraged to take
advantage of them. These consultants or coordinators often deal
with other professional issues as well, such as poor teaching evaluations, departmental or institutional politics, and the exploration of
career change opportunities. Such individuals are usually tenured
faculty members on multiyear appointments, often with only partial released time from other faculty responsibilities.

### GLCA Professional Development Conferences and Workshops

Although the GLCA offers a number of other professional
development opportunities for faculty—such as the opportunity to
be a resident director for one of seven different off-campus programs, to serve as a reviewer for or direct the annual GLCA New
Writers Award Program for poetry and fiction, to organize the annual GLCA Poetry Festival, or to serve on the GLCA women's
studies committee—most of GLCA's faculty professional development efforts are directed toward conferences and workshops for
GLCA faculty members. These meetings differ from the typical conferences offered by national or regional professional organizations
not only in size but also in focus. Although we always offer opportunities to share the results of one's scholarship and to increase
one's knowledge in the discipline, our emphasis on teaching issues
is far greater than is typical for most major professional meetings.
For example, at any conference we offer we usually organize discussion sessions centered on teaching the most common undergraduate
courses in that discipline.

An indirect benefit of our conferences, also distinct from the benefits achieved at the larger professional meetings, is the opportunity to reduce personal and professional isolation and to foster networking among GLCA faculty members with similar interests. The largest departments at GLCA colleges might have a dozen faculty members, but many departments employ four or even fewer people. The goal in the hiring of individuals who serve in the smaller departments is to minimize the overlap in specialty areas between departmental colleagues and to maximize the total coverage of the discipline. However, although GLCA faculty members rarely overlap in terms of academic specialty within any one of our colleges, specialties are frequently duplicated between them. Thus bringing together faculty members with similar specialties who teach at similar institutions makes it possible for them to share information at a variety of personal and professional levels. We know that professional interchanges frequently do take place following our conferences—exchange of papers in preparation for publication, exchange of guest speakers between two or more departments, and so forth. In addition, important comparisons about personal and professional life in small, selective, primarily rural, midwestern residential liberal arts colleges become possible.

Through its program of conferences and workshops, the GLCA supplements most on-campus faculty development programs, which tend to be oriented toward promoting faculty research and publication. Faculty members at our colleges are professionals who are expected to do a variety of things well in addition to publishing, including teaching undergraduates at both the beginning and advanced levels, providing effective academic and at least basic career and personal counseling, and contributing to the welfare of the institution through committee service, chairing academic departments, and maintaining the college's curriculum.

GLCA conferences and workshops can be organized into three semidistinct categories: conferences for the disciplines, interdisciplinary conferences on topical issues, and workshops or conferences for the development of special skills. Regardless of category, our programs typically reflect the liberal arts philosophy of our colleges, including a concern for the ethical dimensions of teaching and scholarship and an appreciation of the contribution each discipline can make to the overall college curriculum. Examples of conferences in the disciplines are meetings for GLCA music faculty members, computer scientists, and members of sociology and anthropology departments. Interdisciplinary conferences or conferences on topical issues have been held to bring together Africanists, Latin Americanists, people interested in women's studies, and people interested in finding more effective ways to teach about nuclear issues. Workshops for the development of special professional skills have included sessions on grant writing in the sciences and in the humanities, meetings for department chairs, conferences to orient new faculty members to our colleges, and the annual week-long GLCA Workshop on Course Design and Teaching (Nowik, 1983). Thus GLCA supplements the focus of most on-campus faculty development programs, which are primarily oriented toward involving faculty members in research, with a variety of activities that focus much more broadly on the role of faculty members as teachers and scholars.

A typical GLCA workshop might begin at noon on a Friday and conclude following lunch on Saturday. This Friday through Saturday schedule seems to work well: faculty need to be away from their classes for only a day, and they need to give up only one weekend day. A typical conference might include an outside speaker or consultant to whom an honorarium is paid, but GLCA faculty members often contribute and are usually not compensated for being a part of the conference program unless outside funding is available.

Because we normally use campus locations for our meetings, costs can be kept quite modest. A typical two-day conference for twenty-five to thirty GLCA faculty members might cost between $75 and $95 per person covering all on-site costs (including one outside speaker), costs for meals and overnight housing for participants, and costs for a one-day meeting with a conference planning committee. These costs are borne by the colleges in proportion to the number of faculty members sent by each college to the meeting.

For almost all of our conferences, a planning committee made up of faculty representatives from several of the colleges who are interested in the conference topic meets in advance to assist GLCA staff, especially in the areas of program development and program organization, and to make recommendations for outside conference speakers. More detail on one GLCA conference, this one in psychology, has been published elsewhere (McPherson and Wylie, 1983).

*The Development of a GLCA Conference.* An example of the process by which our conferences are developed is found in a recent meeting for GLCA faculty members with interests in Latin America. Faculty members from a wide variety of disciplines have Latin American interests, and we attempted in this meeting to serve faculty members having a variety of disciplinary perspectives. The theme for this conference, The Search for Identity in Latin America, had been suggested at one of the annual meetings of the faculty advisory committee for the GLCA Latin America Program. The Latin America Program is an off-campus program for students, administered by Kenyon College and located in Bogotá, Colombia.

A planning committee composed of five GLCA faculty members and the director of the Latin America Program met approximately six months before the planned conference date to make program recommendations. Prior to that meeting, a mailing to a list of GLCA Latin Americanists provided by the Latin America Program announced the planned conference, invited participation on the planning committee, and also invited conference suggestions. Suggestions from prospective participants as well as evaluation summaries from a previous Latin American conference were made available to members of the committee. During the planning meeting a preliminary framework for the conference was developed and responsibilities for follow-up were assigned. One committee member was responsible for selecting films to be shown in conjunction with the conference, while another with a personal connection agreed to contact one of the prospective outside leaders. As is typical, we in the GLCA office agreed to coordinate communications and handle all the mailings to prospective participants.

As a result of two additional mailings, our Latin American constituency was kept informed and involved in every aspect of the conference, from the early conceptual stages through actual conference participation. In addition to Latin Americanists, the GLCA chief academic officers received all conference materials and mailings and were invited to encourage their own faculty members to attend the meeting. Chief academic officers occasionally attend GLCA programs for faculty, but (there being no Latin Americanists among them) none did in this case.

*Program Accountability for Conferences and Workshops.* Because we are dependent on the GLCA chief academic officers for financial support, it is the responsibility of the GLCA to demonstrate that our conferences and workshops meet the needs of GLCA faculty members. Thus everyone who attends any of our conferences or workshops is asked to complete an evaluation form. Individual evaluation comments are combined with those of other participants, organized into a readable summary form, and distributed to the members of the GLCA deans' council and academic council. As I indicated above, the evaluation forms also provide useful information for the GLCA office should another conference on a similar or related topic be offered in the future.

Evaluations of our conferences are usually positive. Faculty who attend frequently rate them favorably in comparison with other conferences in their discipline, for example. One thing almost always mentioned among the best conference features is the opportunity faculty have to discuss the specific issues of the conference with other faculty members from institutions similar to their own. Through our programs the sense of isolation that many GLCA faculty members feel on their own campuses is reduced, and their understanding of the positive contributions that they can make as members of those institutions' faculties is enhanced.

## Factors That Influence Faculty Vitality

The GLCA recently undertook a more extensive evaluation of its own faculty professional development activities and of the activities sponsored by the individual GLCA colleges. We sought to discover which programs or professional development opportunities have made a significant difference to faculty members at GLCA colleges. This project, undertaken under the leadership of a former Denison University provost, Louis F. Brakeman, was designed to be illuminative; that is, it was designed as an attempt to identify those activities, either consortial or otherwise, that were perceived by faculty members as having had the greatest positive impact on their own professional lives and vitality (Brakeman and Loring, 1989).

Individual in-depth, hour-long interviews were conducted with a sample of 200 GLCA faculty members. All of them had been at their institutions at least three years, and all were full-time. Half of the faculty interviewed were selected randomly, and half were selected from a pool of individuals nominated by their chief academic officers or others at their institutions as being particularly vital, professionally alive, and somehow exemplary. The overall sample was selected so that the proportion of full, associate, and assistant professors and of men and women mirrored the total faculty in these categories present at the GLCA institutions. The interview results were supplemented by almost 900 responses to a mail questionnaire distributed to all 1,100 full-time faculty members at GLCA colleges with three or more years of service.

Several important findings are clear from the study by Brakeman. The first is that, rumors of a general faculty malaise notwithstanding, many GLCA faculty members are satisfied and some are even delighted with their careers. This is true of senior faculty members as well as junior ones, and of men as well as women. However, Brakeman did not find that all faculty members were alike, even at the same career stage, nor did he find that they all identified the same professional development activities as critical to maintaining vitality. He found that the sources of vitality and satisfaction for faculty were almost as variable as the faculty members themselves. Special sources of satisfaction and vitality included teaching, scholarship linked to teaching, traditional scholarly research, developing new disciplinary or interdisciplinary competencies, interacting with students, participating in curriculum development projects, chairing an academic department, and relationships with colleagues. Specific activities considered important were specific conferences and workshops, sabbaticals and research leaves, and course and curriculum development efforts. Women faculty members frequently cited the importance of the GLCA Women's Studies Program. (See also the work by Austin and Rice, 1987, for institutional factors that affect faculty satisfaction.)

A number of assumptions guide the GLCA as we make decisions about future directions in our faculty professional development program. Some of these relate to faculty members themselves, while others relate to the institutions in which they work. For example, we have learned not to assume that all faculty members—even those in a single discipline—have the same professional priorities. The Brakeman research confirms this. This means that even in a conference for a single discipline we must introduce a variety of topics and try to provide alternatives to meet various faculty members' needs. This often leads us to run concurrent discussion or paper sessions, for example.

We also assume that virtually all faculty members want to be good teachers, no matter how involved in research they are (substantiated, for example, by Ladd, 1979). We think it is appropriate to discuss how one teaches a particular subject at any of our disciplinary or interdisciplinary meetings. Because we view teaching as a craft that is in large part learned, we assume that everyone can become a better teacher than he or she is by working at it while receiving the appropriate encouragement and support.

### Faculty Burnout and a Renewal Strategy

Many faculty who are seen as needing renewal are referred to as being burned out. If by *burned out* we mean that the faculty member is no longer as effective in the classroom as he or she once was, we may be tempted to conclude that the faculty member needs a refresher course on teaching techniques. While retraining or review of teaching techniques may have some benefits, it may be far more helpful to the faculty member if these reminders are presented within a supportive context where other issues of concern are discussed.

It is helpful to consider that both faculty members and institutions change over time, and constant adjustments are normally needed to maintain the fit between institution and individual. If an institution changes and an individual does not, the dissonance created can be as great as if the individual changes and the institution does not. In either case it is important to look for the sources of the disparity and to provide faculty with the incentives necessary to explore options and bring their aspirations in line with those of the institution. Faculty renewal may result because an attitude change takes place to bring the individual's behavior more in line with institutional expectations. Thus renewal can be seen as the process of receiving the proper incentives so that individuals are encouraged to attend to and behave in accordance with specific institutional and/or disciplinary expectations.

(Please note that the above analysis is not applicable in cases where institutional changes rather than individual adjustments are more desirable. In such situations *burnout* is not the applicable term, and other organizational development strategies would be more appropriate.)

Burned-out faculty may still be involved in college governance, community affairs, family life, home renovation, church activities, or hobbies; they do not, in our experience, stop doing everything. The faculty member suffering from burnout has, however, lost interest in contributing to and doing well the activities most valued by the individual's colleagues and profession or institution. Because all faculty are not the same—because even faculty members at the same career stage differ so greatly even within the same discipline and specialty—a variety of approaches are necessary, and GLCA professional development activities may be seen as one subset of activities that may prove helpful when activities on the home campus do not.

## Faculty Career Stages

Burned-out faculty may be seen as a special constituency among all college faculty. However, there are a number of other special constituencies that we have identified as deserving special attention. A number of authors have developed theories of adult development, and several, including R. Eugene Rice (1985), have applied these general theories of adult development to college faculty members. Using a developmental rubric and combining it with our own empirical observations, we can identify some potentially difficult periods in the professional life of a faculty member (Wylie, 1986).

*New Faculty.* Because it involves so much uncertainty, the life of a new faculty member is especially stressful as he or she seeks to establish an individual identity and to be successful in a career at one of our institutions. With the support of the Fund for the Improvement of Postsecondary Education, the GLCA recently undertook a major program to assist new faculty to adjust to careers in liberal arts colleges. Several initiatives were undertaken, including two workshops for new faculty members and one for their department chairs.

The first of the new-faculty workshops focused on issues of the undergraduate curriculum, understanding the politics of teaching, and faculty career issues, including issues of time management and stress. As was also the case for the second workshops for new faculty, conference participants prepared a plan for appropriate follow-up activities to be conducted on their home campuses.

The second workshops for new faculty members took into account suggestions made in the evaluations of the first one and attempted to address more specific, practical issues. These included using evaluations to improve teaching, improving lecturing techniques while taking into account differences in student cognitive development and learning styles, developing an effective new-faculty organization on campus, and learning successful time- and stress-management techniques.

The workshop for department chairs who either had untenured faculty in their departments or were about to undertake a search for new faculty members focused on such issues as giving appropriate and constructive feedback to new faculty members, encouraging appropriate levels of professional productivity, effective time- and stress-management techniques, effective recruitment and hiring practices, and contemporary views of faculty careers.

To help reduce the isolation felt by new faculty members, we developed an interinstitutional mentoring program to match new faculty members from one of our colleges with tenured faculty members having the same specialty at another. The interinstitutional mentoring program has been successful and is continuing with funding from our colleges. While developing it, we discovered that the issues of greatest importance to new faculty members are not always related to their specific disciplinary specialty. For example, new faculty are very concerned with establishing professional priorities and understanding the politics and sociology of their institutions and departments, and many are concerned with dual-career arrangements. Recognizing that new faculty have a broader set of concerns than just teaching their own courses has permitted a greater variety of matches to be made.

Finally, tied in part to the recommendations for home campus activities derived from our workshops for new faculty, we provide assistance to permit individual GLCA colleges to develop their own new-faculty programs. The most common activity undertaken on a campus is some form of orientation program for new faculty members. Other activities include the development of an intrainstitutional mentoring program, the development of a faculty professional opportunities handbook, and the development of special library collections on teaching.

*Midcareer Faculty.* Faculty at midcareer—perhaps at about the time of promotion to full professor or the earning of a second sabbatical—face different sources of stress than do new faculty. For midcareer faculty the stressors tend to be personal—for example, doubts about whether to stay in the profession, and if so, whether to stay with the same discipline and specialty or to deliberately attempt to change directions. Faculty at midcareer can benefit from faculty development opportunities just as new faculty can, but different kinds of programs are more effective for them. We have offered a special workshop to encourage midcareer faculty to explore alternative careers, for example.

*Senior Faculty.* A third period of special stress for faculty may occur at about the time the individual nears the age of traditional retirement for faculty members. Now that the legal constraints for continuing in the profession have largely been removed, opportunities for self-assessment need to be provided to permit senior faculty to make informed decisions about whether to stay longer in their institutions and/or professions. (Financial considerations are often not the most important factor in this decision.) Institutional initiatives may be as important here as consortial ones. For example, Earlham has implemented a regular program of collegial self-assessment for tenured faculty members, to permit them to review their accomplishments and to make career plans for the subsequent five years.

In our conferences and workshops we encounter faculty at all three of the critical career stages described above, and at every stage in between.

### Faculty Development in Cooperation with Others

GLCA faculty professional development activities do not exist in a vacuum, and we have been able to enhance the diversity of our offerings by cooperating with other organizations and other consortia. Among them are the Associated Colleges of the Midwest (ACM), the Program for Inter-Institutional Collaboration in Area Studies (PICAS), the Midwest Faculty Seminar Program, and the Council for International Educational Exchange (CIEE). The ACM is a consortium similar to the GLCA, with a membership of thirteen liberal arts colleges located in Colorado, Illinois, Iowa, Minnesota, and Wisconsin. ACM faculty members are frequently invited to attend GLCA conferences and workshops, and recently the ACM and GLCA together developed a successful proposal funded by the National Endowment for the Humanities to undertake a major review of the history curricula within GLCA and ACM colleges.

The PICAS program is made possible by the three-way cooperation of the GLCA, the ACM, and the University of Michigan Non-Western Area Studies Centers. Three private foundations have provided funds for students and faculty to pursue summer language study and to undertake short research projects, and for faculty to undertake research projects lasting up to an academic year using the resources of the University of Michigan Centers. Other liberal arts colleges and major universities may find a useful professional development model in the PICAS program.

A number of GLCA colleges participate in the Midwest Faculty Seminar Program, operated by the University of Chicago. Recent seminars have been on student cognitive development and critical thinking, for example—topics that are not covered in depth in any of the GLCA conferences and workshops—and we have encouraged participation by GLCA faculty.

Finally, the CIEE sponsors a number of student academic

programs in various parts of the world. Through ACM and GLCA membership in CIEE's China Consortium, GLCA and ACM faculty members have an opportunity to participate in consortial decision making and planning and to serve as resident directors for the programs in China, as well as to serve on the China Consortium curriculum committee and its executive board. GLCA faculty members and directors of international education also regularly serve on the CIEE board of directors.

### Factors That Promote Consortial Cooperation

Some comments about the factors that have made the GLCA successful over the years are in order. These observations may prove useful to individual campuses as well as to other consortia. The first point has to do with the fact that the GLCA was actually founded by a group of college presidents who thought that there would be some advantage to each of their institutions if they all cooperated. What could have remained only a presidents' club did not, although our presidents continue to work closely together. Many different people now have a stake in the Great Lakes Colleges Association and benefit from its various programs, but at the beginning it was certainly important that the presidents of the member colleges actively participated in the organization's founding. Anyone planning to form a consortium to foster faculty renewal and faculty development ought to take this into consideration. It is critically important that the institutions' senior administrators and policy makers are aware of the program at its inception, and endorse it.

A related point has to do with communication. Even a successful consortium must continually work to remain visible and thus accountable (and countable) among all of the activities that are simultaneously being undertaken by each institutional member. Unless the senior administrators and policy makers are regularly informed of activities undertaken by the consortium, and unless they see a direct benefit to their institutions (their faculties, in this case), the program becomes vulnerable to budgetary exigencies or shifts in institutional priorities. Under the right circumstances consortia can actually assume leadership roles and test new program directions that individual colleges might find too risky (Fuller,

1988). But this can happen only if an atmosphere of trust and confidence exists between the consortial and the institutional administrations and if the institutions are aware of the consortium's current programs and successful and responsible track record.

There are also probably some limitations to what a consortial program in faculty professional development can accomplish. Because consortial programs respond to the consensus needs of a number of institutions, idiosyncratic institutional needs are difficult to meet. For example, it would probably be inappropriate for a consortium to undertake a program to train foreign-language faculty members to teach English as a second language if only one college in the consortium were interested in developing such a program.

It is also true that many of the successes we can document in our consortial approach to faculty professional development have to do with indirect attentional or motivational effects rather than with the imparting of specific skills. The GLCA faculty professional development program is therefore unlike the instructional development programs that exist at a number of large institutions. Except in a workshop on course design and teaching, we do not attempt to teach specific skills to improve instruction.

One advantage of a consortial approach is that it helps institutions take a long-range view of faculty professional development needs, sustain programs, and anticipate needs for the future. For example, a decade ago the GLCA undertook to promote women's studies scholarship at our colleges. Although many of the individuals who were present at the founding of our Women's Studies Program have since left the GLCA and the various GLCA colleges, the program survives and is still growing. It has moved from foundation funding to funding as a regular consortial program underwritten by college assessments, and it has overseen the development of specialized conferences and workshops for women's studies scholars in the GLCA that could not have been offered a decade ago. Biannual seminars in feminist theory and a workshop on integrating feminist perspectives into the arts curricula are recent examples of these developments.

We have recently undertaken another initiative, this time dealing with black studies and with the problems that minority students and faculty face at predominantly white institutions such as those in the GLCA. Although we cannot predict all of the directions that our minorities initiative will take, a wide variety of possible activities are being considered. Included are special cooperative research opportunities for minority college and high school students, to encourage them to consider academic careers, an organization for minority students and faculty members from all the GLCA colleges, to reduce isolation and provide a broader base of personal and professional support, new recruiting activities focused on promising minority students in junior high school and their families, special conferences and workshops for minority faculty members, teaching fellowships for minority graduate students, a standing GLCA committee to focus on minority concerns, and a GLCA staff member to deal with these issues. As a consortium we are able to consider a wider set of activities than many individual colleges could. Although we do not expect everything that we try to be successful, by involving twelve institutions rather than just one we can bring a greater variety of expertise to bear on the effort and have less likelihood of being discouraged by the lack of success of any one element in the program. We hope that we will be able to develop a successful program to improve the quality of life for minority students and faculty members on our campuses and expect that our institutions will ultimately be better for our having undertaken this initiative.

## References

Austin, A. E., and Rice, R. E. *Community, Commitment, and Congruence: A Different Kind of Excellence.* Washington, D.C.: Council of Independent Colleges, 1987.

Baus, F., and LaRocco, T. (eds.). *1986 Consortium Directory.* Washington, D.C.: Council for Interinstitutional Leadership, 1986.

Brakeman, L. F., and Loring, K. M. *What One Has Within, What the Context Provides: Sources of Faculty Professional Vitality in the Great Lakes Colleges Association.* Ann Arbor, Mich.: Great Lakes Colleges Association, 1989.

Elkin, J. L. *The Great Lakes Colleges Association: Twenty-One*

*Years of Cooperation in Higher Education.* Ann Arbor, Mich.: Great Lakes Colleges Association, 1982.

Fuller, C. F. "Ph.D. Recipients. Where Did They Go to College?" *Change,* 1986, 18 (6), 42–51.

Fuller, J. W. "Consortia as Risk-Takers." In D. C. Neal (ed.), *Consortia and Interinstitutional Cooperation.* New York: Macmillan, 1988.

Ladd, E. C. "The Work Experience of American College Professors: Some Data and an Argument." In *Current Issues in Higher Education.* Washington, D.C.: American Association for Higher Education, 1979.

McPherson, K. S., and Wylie, N. R. "Teaching Psychology at the Small Liberal Arts College: A Two-Day Conference." *Teaching of Psychology,* 1983, *10* (3), 144–146.

Nowik, N. "Workshop on Course Design and Teaching Styles: A Model for Faculty Development." In M. Davis, M. Fisher, S. C. Inglis, and S. Scholl (eds.), *To Improve the Academy: Resources for Student, Faculty, and Institutional Development.* Lincoln: Professional and Organizational Development Network in Higher Education, Teaching and Learning Center, University of Nebraska, Lincoln, 1983.

Reed, B. "Transforming the Academy: Twelve Schools Working Together." *Change,* 1982, *14* (3), 30, 35–37.

Rice, R. E. *Faculty Lives: Vitality and Change.* St. Paul, Minn.: Northwest Area Foundation, 1985.

Wylie, N. R. "Enhancing Faculty Vitality and Commitment to Careers." In M. D. Waggoner, R. L. Alfred, M. C. Francis, and M. W. Peterson (eds.), *Academic Effectiveness: Transforming Colleges and Universities.* Ann Arbor: University of Michigan Press, 1986.

Wylie, N. R., and Fuller, J. W. "Enhancing Faculty Vitality Through Collaboration Among Colleagues." In R. G. Baldwin (ed.), *Incentives for Faculty Vitality.* New Directions for Higher Education, no. 51. San Francisco: Jossey-Bass, 1985.

 *PART FOUR*

# Recommendations for Institutional Action

This final portion of the book is an effort at synthesis. It acknowledges the realities of the academic environment and the evolution of faculty development, incorporates the kinds of development-related activities that are emerging on various campuses, and builds on existing successful campuswide strategies. It provides, in effect, an inventory of methods for improving the quality of academic life through enhanced developmental activities.

# 14

# Building Comprehensive Programs to Enhance Faculty Development

*Daniel W. Wheeler*
*Jack H. Schuster*

Throughout this book a number of orientations and descriptions of programs have been presented for consideration. Certainly the world of higher education, with more than 3,400 diverse institutions, presents a complex scene. Recognizing the idiosyncratic nature of these varying settings, we do not presume to propose a single formula or program that can be used to initiate or to nurture programs for faculty renewal and development. A multitude of factors—among them, campus awareness of faculty developmental needs, the knowledge level and receptivity of the faculty and other key decision makers, and the extent of competing claims for scarce discretionary resources—influence the type of program that is best tailored to a given setting.

Given these realities, we believe that solid professional development programs can be fashioned by drawing on the ideas and activities described in the preceding chapters. Those ideas and activities can be blended with existing programs or can complement ideas proposed for a particular campus. Toward this end, we encourage a basic two-step strategy. First, one must recognize the importance of conceptualizing broadly. It is important to recognize early on that a truly effective program for professional development must span all three major developmental aspects—professional (including instructional) development, personal development, and organizational development. Thus it is important, even crucial, to recognize the long-term objective: a coordinated, systematic approach that embodies all three facets of development.

Next, the second aspect of an overarching strategy comes into play: planning for incremental program development. No campus is likely to be prepared to institute a full-blown program from the start. Perhaps there never has been—or can be—a comprehensive professional development program created whole. Professional development is an inherently evolutionary process, and movement toward a comprehensive program inevitably must be incremental. There are many models with different elements from which to choose. Campus support takes time to build and is best achieved through wide participation in identifying local priorities. Each campus obviously must set its own priorities based on indigenous circumstances and then move in progressive steps toward a comprehensive program.

In considering the creation and expansion of faculty development programs, we have attempted to synthesize the recommendations of our various chapter writers. We have clustered these strategic recommendations and principles under four main headings: general principles, strategies for new programs, strategies for established programs, and strategies beyond the campus. There is some overlap among these categories; that is because issues take a different form depending upon the stage of program development. We encourage those persons committed to faculty development to use these recommendations as a checklist in assessing the vitality of a campus's faculty development efforts and in developing more comprehensive, suitably tailored programs. First, however, we attempt to describe what we mean by *enhanced faculty development*.

## Enhanced Faculty Development

We have occasionally used the term *enhanced faculty development* in this book, and now is the time to focus on the properties of that concept. It represents our best effort to identify and label an approach to professional development that we believe is particularly potent. We do not claim that enhanced faculty development is unique. Indeed, we think that we have added few entirely new elements to the earlier conceptions of faculty development; for, in our view, the techniques of how to enhance personal and professional growth have been reasonably well understood for some years. We maintain, however, that an enhanced approach to faculty development transcends the traditional tripartite elements of faculty development, as described above, and that the resulting whole is greater than those constituent parts. We argue that this insight leads to a better integrated, and therefore more powerful, approach to developing and maintaining a vital faculty.

Thus, by way of summarizing what we intend by the concept of enhanced development, we discuss three key elements: career reconceptualization, career facilitation, and the fusion of professional and personal development.

*Career Reconceptualization.* Enhanced faculty development means thinking anew about faculty careers. It means breaking out of preconceived notions about bounded, limited faculty careers. It means, in short, a reconceptualization of what opportunities may lie within one's career—potentialities that extend even to abandoning one's academic career (for all the right reasons).

Thus enhanced faculty development necessitates the construction of bridges. Most of the time these linkages extend from the individual client to other opportunities for the client *within* the organization—that is, opportunities for different kinds of pursuits or new combinations of pursuits. Less often the bridge may lead to a destination outside the campus: possibly on a permanent, "bridge-burning" basis into an entirely new (though likely related) career, but more likely on a more cautious, exploratory basis to a search for renewal through a fresh, stimulating environment. Specifically, this reconceptualization means thinking boldly; it strives for liberation from an orientation toward the future that is hemmed in by the prevailing experience and socialization in academe of what constitutes a career.

In sum, enhanced faculty development envisions the widest array of possibilities. It means providing an environment conducive to faculty renewal and redirection through opportunities, mainly at midcareer, to explore retraining. And, when indicated, it may even mean acceptance of the desirability of moving away from academe. Put in other words, it means opening up the higher education system to new career models and arrangements.

*Career Facilitation.* Helping faculty members to alter their career objectives and to devise strategies for reaching new objectives goes hand in hand with career reconceptualization. This process is the implementation phase that follows the broadening of one's career horizons. An enhanced approach requires that the means to facilitate careers be available; it requires professional consultants or peers who understand how to provide the means for addressing change and transition. Much of the necessary expertise is grounded in adult development and organizational research literature. Fortunately, there exists today increasingly useful information regarding what organizations need to do to humanize and develop the organizational environment, as well as how to diagnose faculty needs and understand faculty issues. Better understood "technologies"—in the form of, for example, wellness programs, employee assistance programs, and career consulting—can provide the means to address personal issues that have too often been misinterpreted simply as lack of interest or motivation.

This aspect of enhanced development necessitates providing faculty with the tools for planning and effecting change. The facilitative process may reach as far as aiding a faculty member to repudiate his or her original career decision—to find the vehicles for changing, or significantly redirecting, the career.

Certainly the concept of enhanced development maximizes the usual definition of faculty development as a process that "enhances the talents, expands the interests, improves competence and otherwise facilitates the professional and personal growth of faculty members" (Gaff, 1976, p. 14). And the concept fleshes out the original sense of professional development described by Lindquist (1981), who spoke of the necessity of facilitating growth beyond merely helping faculty members to extend their knowledge of their academic fields.

In short, higher education no longer has the luxury of allowing faculty to become trapped in "professional cul-de-sacs" or to be governed by career decisions made long ago. Yes, some faculty members are still independent entrepreneurs and scholars who can and do move on, or back and forth, when they desire. But most faculty members are likely to remain on the same campus, or with perhaps two institutions, throughout their careers. Accordingly, it is all the more urgent that faculty and administrative leaders having responsibility for academic affairs understand clearly that faculty development means much more than honing research skills, and learning how better to obtain grants, and studying how to be a more effective classroom instructor. Faculty development must be understood to break through those how-to-do-better-what-I-am-doing-today boundaries and venture into the relatively unbounded realm of maximizing interests and possibilities.

**The Fusion of Professional and Personal Development.** A third key element of enhanced faculty development involves intertwining within an institutional setting the professional and personal aspects, thought too often to be only tangentially related. Much of the traditional strategy for faculty development has failed to integrate organizational expectations with the individual needs of individual faculty members. Personal development ordinarily has been separated from professional development, conceptually and in practice, on the mistaken grounds that personal issues have little or nothing to do with the professional domain and that attention to them would be irrelevant, even inappropriate, in the workplace. This standard approach is represented by the nearly separate domains depicted in Figure 14.1.

In any well-integrated, comprehensive program there is considerable overlap and integration of the various aspects of professional development with the *individual* career, thereby bridging more successfully the personal, professional, and organizational elements of development, as depicted in Figure 14.2.

With a better understanding of the proper relationship of the various spheres of development, faculty and administrators can address faculty career vitality more effectively. In short, individual and institutional vitality must be fused in order to enhance the careers of faculty members and, in so doing, to better ensure the ability of campuses to fulfill their institutional missions.

**Figure 14.1. A Traditional Model of Faculty Development.**

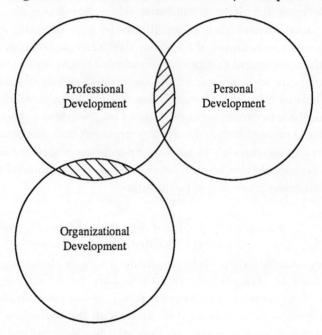

**Figure 14.2. An Integrated Model of Faculty Development.**

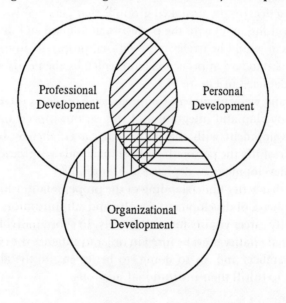

To recapitulate, an enhanced approach to faculty development is predicated on three clusters of issues: (1) assisting faculty to reconceptualize how they view their career; (2) providing the means to facilitate significant career shifts; and (3) blending or fusing personal and professional developmental agendas in efforts to revitalize faculty careers in an organizational context. These conceptual underpinnings lead to the next set of considerations—namely, what campuses can do to create a faculty development program, or to modify an existing one, that has a respectable chance of addressing effectively the wide range of individual and institutional needs.

The following strategies for renewal, drawn mainly from the preceding chapters, often synthesize the actions recommended by more than one contributor. As indicated at the outset of this chapter, these recommendations are organized into four categories: those that incorporate general principles, those directed toward the creation of new programs, those aimed at strengthening established programs, and those that draw on extracampus resources.

### General Principles

Whatever the setting for a program to assist faculty members in their professional and personal growth, a number of general principles derived from experience would seem to be applicable. These include:

1. *Emphasizing faculty "ownership."* Faculty development opportunities of whatever kind cannot be foisted upon the faculty. Administrators or faculty development professionals may well suggest ideas for programs; however, a particular program can succeed only if the corporate faculty is involved significantly in the decision to adopt it. Experience appears to show that more extensive faculty participation in shaping a professional development program will lead to wider faculty acceptance of that program (Eble and McKeachie, 1985).

2. *Using a faculty advisory committee.* In the same way that faculty ownership is crucial to launching a program, faculty involvement in the ongoing governance of a program is critical. This involvement would probably take the form of an advisory committee for the program or the campus unit that administers the pro-

gram. It would appear that the more substantive the advisory committee's role—consider, for instance, the committee's significant role at the University of Georgia (see Chapter Nine)—the more likely it is that the faculty at large will support and use the program.

3. *Obtaining administrative commitment.* Perhaps no factor is more potent in determining the success—or failure—of a faculty development program than the extent to which a campus administration shows itself to be committed to the concept. This commitment must involve far more than merely announcing the establishment of a program. Continual, visible demonstrations of support are essential—as is illustrated, for example, by the involvement of the dean in the University of Nebraska NUPROF project (Chapter Ten). Of course, budgetary support must be a central part of this effort; otherwise, administrative support is more hollow than substantial.

Beyond providing the resources for staffing (both professional and clerical), the administration needs to manifest its commitment in at least one additional way: symbolic support. Leading campus administrators need to be visibly involved in relevant recognition activities, including award ceremonies, retreats (where appropriate), campus newspaper/newsletter "testimonials" 'to the importance of such programs, and the like. There are plenty of opportunities for demonstrating support; resourceful, committed administrators—starting with the chief executive and academic officers—will readily find ways to do so.

4. *Creating an informed administration.* Few administrators track developments in the professional development field. They have other responsibilities and often fail to discern the relevance of these developments. Yet a supportive campus climate may hinge on the extent to which key campus administrators genuinely understand the relevant issues and their relationship to a vital, productive faculty.

Accordingly, consciousness raising must be an ongoing responsibility of those persons having direct responsibility for a campus's development program—both professionals and faculty advisers. Almost surely they should seek periodic opportunities to apprise key administrators of developments "in the field" and to engage in discussions about the accomplishments and needs of campus-based programs.

5. *Providing structural integration.* The effectiveness of faculty development activities may depend in some measure on how well those activities are meshed with the campus's organizational structure. If, say, an office of instructional development is administratively isolated or poorly placed in the organizational structure (perhaps its director reports to an administrator of middling rank who does not have ready access to top administration), its prospects for becoming a vital part of campus life may well be impaired. Moreover, administrative siting of the office wholly within one part of the organization—for example, a placement within one school/college of a university—may diminish its prospects for campuswide acceptance and impact. The symbolic importance of a manifestly *campuswide* effort should not be underestimated.

6. *Striving for comprehensiveness.* Most programs of professional development—very nearly all of them—start small. The authors know of no counterpart to Venus emerging full-blown from the sea. Gradualism is surely the dominant mode, and that is appropriate. However, a limited program should probably seek to expand its scope as soon as feasible into all three principal realms of development—professional, organizational, and personal. Though some risks surely attend premature expansion, the "beachhead strategy" recommended here can serve both to demonstrate the significance and interconnectedness of all three areas and to establish a base from which to expand gradually along all three fronts. This approach may lead sooner to the realization of a more comprehensive program than might otherwise be the case.

7. *Accentuating the positive.* Programs devised to foster professional and personal growth inevitably deal with a range of clients. Such programs help the strong grow stronger, but they also help the incapacitated to recover. Some activities focus expressly on faculty who are impaired in one way or another; faculty assistance programs (see Chapter Seven) are leading examples of primarily rehabilitative interventions. Such activities obviously must be conducted with utmost discretion. It is critically important, though, that campus professional and personal development efforts be perceived in positive terms—as a means of helping faculty to achieve

greater self-actualization rather than primarily a means of propping up the needy. Here again the role of administrative and faculty leadership is critical in conveying the legitimacy and positive orientation of a campus's development program.

8. *Demonstrating success.* Campus programs, with the assistance of campuswide administrative and faculty units, must seek opportunities to demonstrate to the wider campus audience that programs are achieving a measure of success—that is, that they are making a positive difference in the lives of faculty members. There are many ways to accomplish this. Promotional activities may include arranging for endorsements in appropriate campus publications. In addition, systematic evaluation of programs by participants—which are essential as a means of determining how well programs are working—*may* provide a basis for publicizing the effectiveness of, say, a workshop on retirement planning or a conference on team teaching or some other activity sponsored or facilitated by the campus professional development office.

9. *Assessing needs.* At least as important as determining how effective programs have been are efforts to determine what kinds of professional and personal growth activities are desired by faculty. (This harks back to the first recommendation about the importance of faculty ownership.) Faculty members need to be involved on an ongoing basis in conveying the kinds of activities that are most important to them.

10. *Responding to demographic imperatives: the age factor.* Assuming the validity of the demographic projections described in Chapter One, we can expect many campuses in the near future to deploy unusually large cohorts of both older (and old!) faculty and, simultaneously, younger faculty. The lifting of the mandatory retirement cap for faculty (beginning in 1994) injects a further variable destined to challenge academic personnel practices. Administrative and faculty leaders alike must deepen their sensitivity to the special needs of these cohorts and intensify campus efforts to respond to those needs.

11. *Responding to demographic imperatives: women and minorities.* In terms of what is expected of them for career advancement, women and minority faculty members—especially junior faculty—are much more like than unlike white male faculty members.

Nevertheless, minorities and women continue to be badly underrepresented on most faculties. This makes it all the more important to find ways in which they can be supported and helped to progress through the academic ranks. Possible strategies include, for example, seeking to reduce the pressure of role modeling, which often takes a toll, and providing relief from "relevant" committee assignments (such as affirmative action and status-of-women committees). Facilitating special peer support groups is another possible strategy.

12. *Conducting institutional research.* Better understanding of how and why faculty careers evolve is the beginning of wisdom in developing strategies designed to enhance those careers. Yet campuses often do a submarginal job of aggregating and analyzing information about their faculty and their careers. For example, many campuses know too little about patterns of faculty retirement—an increasingly important matter as the age for mandatory retirement moves upward and then disappears. What are the characteristics of those who are choosing to retire? What factors contribute to faculty members' decisions to retire or, conversely, to stay on? (Chapter Eight previews a tangle of retirement-related issues that will loom larger in the near-term future.) More generally, in what aspects of their work do faculty members feel most at ease, and in what areas do they most desire help or relief? These examples serve to illustrate the need to know more about the "clientele."

13. *Estimating benefits and costs.* The frugal and the skeptical will say that faculty development programs—especially new programs—are costly and politically risky at a time when discretionary resources are particularly scarce. True, exceptional resourcefulness may be necessary to locate and apportion the required funds. However, in contemplating the tangible costs of new or expanded programs, one must not overlook the intangible but invariably formidable costs of inaction. These costs will not show up on business office printouts, but they are ferociously real. Just what is the cost to the quality of the teaching-learning process of having 5, 10, or 20 percent—or more—of a campus's faculty disengaged or disengaging? How much is an institution's mission undermined, and faculty colleagues demoralized, by a faculty member or two who drink too much? What is the cost to an academic department of a senior

faculty member who desperately needs a radical career change but
does not know how to go about it—perhaps does not even know
that plausible career alternatives exist? And what is the cost to the
institution (not to mention the human costs) of faculty members
who take poor care of themselves physically—and in consequence
may well pay the price of temporary incapacitation, or worse?

Rhetorical questions? Yes. Imaginary issues? Of course not.
These are corrosive situations for which the organization pays
dearly; these are conditions that must be reckoned with in "real"
cost-benefit analyses—even though the costs cannot be isolated by
traditional accounting methods. In the final analysis, the hidden
costs of inaction will far outrun the concrete costs of new programming to promote faculty growth.

14. *Assuring institutional fit.* This section concludes with a
culminating observation about the importance of tailoring faculty
development programs to the idiosyncratic characteristics of a particular campus. Diversity is a theme that threads its way through
every chapter of this book. Not only do institutions of higher learning vary greatly one from another, but any given college or university is constantly in flux. Moreover, if the thesis advanced in
Chapter One is convincing—namely, that faculty conditions and
campus values are now in a period of accelerating change—then
campuses must be ever alert to shifting needs. It follows that programs that are congruent with the needs and values on one campus
may be wholly mismatched with the circumstances on another campus. What appears to work effectively at, say, Loyola University of
Chicago (Chapter Eleven) may be doomed to failure if grafted onto
Fairleigh Dickinson University (Chapter Twelve)—and vice versa.
This book has set forth a mosaic of models and strategies drawn
from campus settings of all kinds. In order for programs for professional and personal growth to succeed, their design and nurturing
must be matched to local conditions.

## Strategies for New Programs

Launching a new program entails some special considerations. The underlying philosophy and organizational principles
applicable for new programs are not essentially different from those

discussed either in the previous section or those described in the ensuing section on established programs. The difference here is in emphasis.

1. *Involving opinion leaders.* The prospects of a successful beginning will depend in some measure on the extent to which respected campus citizens—particularly faculty leaders—can be identified with the new initiatives. This process of legitimation will be necessary to develop an adequate base of support for a new program.

2. *Using a faculty advisory committee.* As indicated in the preceding section, the creation of a faculty advisory committee is critical. In fact, such an apparatus is probably a prerequisite for mounting a new program. Without visible faculty involvement at a policy level, there is always a risk that a new program may be perceived as an instrument of the administration for the purpose of doing *to,* rather than *for,* the faculty. Membership on such an advisory committee, especially in the program's initial stages, should include campus opinion leaders to the extent possible and should strive to draw faculty representatives from various sectors of campus life.

3. *Obtaining administrative commitment.* The commitment of a campus's administration, as suggested in the discussion of general principles, is crucial and must complement faculty support. For new programs the unequivocal endorsement of initiatives—underscoring their positive, constructive thrust—is all the more vital in order to gain faculty support.

4. *Developing a philosophical base and general plan.* Program initiators should early on draft a statement expressing the philosophical basis for professional development activities. Such a statement need not be an elaborate document; a succinct, straightforward explanation—a few pages, a few paragraphs—will suffice. The central notion here is that the rationale for such a program, cast in the most positive terms, should be clearly laid out. It might also be useful to develop at an early stage at least the outline of a general plan for future activities.

5. *Insisting on quality programming.* Experience suggests the importance of building quality into initial programs. In creating new activities inheres a special opportunity to demonstrate to

the faculty both the seriousness of the campus's commitment and the intent to make these activities succeed.

6. *Using in-house resources.* In some instances a campus may already have resources—staff and ongoing activities—with which to fashion an adequate program. Perhaps the staff at conventional instructional development offices have interests and competencies that would support additional activities. Perhaps faculty members in, say, counseling psychology (particularly in career counseling) or industrial psychology, or in student personnel services, can be useful (as described in Chapter Five). Further, faculty members in health, physical education, and recreation programs, as well as some health science specialists, may be ideally suited to help develop and oversee wellness activities (see, for example, Chapter Six). The fact is that many campuses—perhaps especially the larger, more complex institutions—have teaching and research resources that bear directly on human resource development. When the capacity already exists on a campus, perhaps it can be harnessed for these new or expanded ventures before program initiators look beyond campus boundaries. This strategy, besides being politically attractive, may prove to be quite cost-effective.

This is not to argue that outside consultants cannot be effective. Their experience may be indispensable in guiding the creation of a program, for instance. But outside consultants may well be at a disadvantage in some roles, and thus, where feasible, indigenous talent may be preferable (Eble and McKeachie, 1985).

7. *Maintaining traditional activities.* As we noted at the outset of this book (see Preface and Chapter One), many campuses have in place policies that are properly seen as traditional faculty support activities. Sabbatical leaves and summer stipends to support research or curriculum development are common examples. It will be important to retain such policies; for, like newer faculty development thrusts, they are highly relevant to faculty growth and organizational development. Accordingly, the early planning stages for fresh development initiatives almost surely should establish that contemplated activities will not displace existing ones. (This assumes, of course, that existing policies are regarded as being useful and reasonably cost-effective.) In other words, the campus commu-

nity should be assured that new ventures will not crowd out current activities deemed to be worthwhile.

8. *Evaluating programs.* Any new program ordinarily ought to be evaluated. Evaluation is important in faculty development to ascertain whether activities are perceived as being effective. Because there may be doubts about the value of programs before they are established, it is crucial that planners—including a faculty advisory committee—formulate general plans for program evaluation.

9. *Assuring confidentiality.* The identity of participants in therapeutic and rehabilitative activities must be protected. This is especially important for faculty assistance programs in which substance abuse may be involved. The tenets of confidentiality for therapist-client relationships need to be respected, and the campus community should be given assurances to that effect. (Toward that end, it may be preferable to conduct some activities off campus; see Chapters Seven and Eleven.)

10. *Leading with your strengths.* Different campuses have different resources and interests already in place. Play to those strengths in establishing programs. For example, if there is already a strong interest in wellness and some health resource people are on board, this may be the basis on which to establish a beachhead. Other aspects of faculty development may be added later. Building on existing strengths was particularly emphasized in the earlier discussions of career consulting (Chapter Five) and wellness (Chapter Six) but would be applicable to other program thrusts as well.

## Strategies for Established Programs

The "rules" for established programs should be understood to incorporate the principles endorsed in the previous sections. The challenge for established programs is to grow stronger and more comprehensive and to maintain the organizational suppleness to be able to adjust and make room for new techniques.

1. *Providing breadth in program offerings.* An established program to support professional and personal faculty growth must strive to offer a breadth of opportunities; that is, it must offer activities that span the normal spheres of developmental activity for fac-

ulty members in various stages of their careers and their adult development.

2. *Continuing to use in-house resources.* As with new programs, it is important that ongoing programs strike an appropriate balance between the use of campus capabilities and outside help. The wellness programs described in Chapter Six are a particularly good example of how resources on campus can be mobilized.

3. *Making adjustments.* People change. Organizations change. The environment is always in flux. Programs therefore need flexible boundaries. Thus mechanisms for ascertaining how well activities are meeting the needs of faculty are needed so that the campus can adjust its offerings accordingly. Adjustments may involve creating new areas of activity. And sometimes fresh technologies for attacking well-known needs may surface. Accordingly, a campus must be alert to identify unmet needs and must be prepared to fashion responsive new programs. Similarly, existing programs may no longer be effective. Periodic assessments of campus needs and program effectiveness should make it possible to determine when existing activities have overstayed their usefulness.

4. *Establishing solid funding for crucial programs.* Many programs have been established with grant money or other temporary funds. Often when this "soft money" ends, the program ends as well. Thus high priority should be given to commitments to have the institution make the program a part of ongoing, budgeted activities, possibly including line-item dollars as well as fees for services. (Fees appear to be a popular strategy in many of the wellness programs.)

### Strategies Beyond the Campus

The previous sections have focused on *intra*campus strategies for promoting faculty renewal. Other very important resources exist. The challenge to campuses is big and complex, and both *inter*campus and *extra*campus resources can be very important for initiating or maintaining a program.

Collaboration among campuses offers some attractive economies of scale, especially for smaller campuses. The creative efforts of the Great Lakes Colleges Association, as described in Chapter Thirteen, illustrate how intracampus programs can be effectively extended through consortial arrangements. Additionally, a number of statewide initiatives are now evolving. While no clearinghouse presently exists to identify all programs, several merit particular mention: among them are programs in Georgia, Kentucky, and Nebraska.[1] Such activities enable campuses with fully developed programs to have readier access to current thinking about how faculty development programs can be initiated and enhanced.

One of the most dramatic statewide developments is the faculty development initiative sparked by the New Jersey Department of Higher Education under the leadership of Chancellor T. Edward Hollander. It is a multifaceted program, cutting across all of New Jersey's campuses—public and independent, two- and four-year. It is an outgrowth of a series of Faculty Dialogues on Undergraduate Education, prompted by Governor Thomas Kean's commitment to increase the ability of the state's institutions of higher education to respond to future needs. The state has now funded a number of programs designed to facilitate faculty growth under the auspices of the department's Division of Faculty Development and Educational Policy (directed by Laurence R. Marcus).[2] These include the New Jersey Master Faculty Program, which is operated by the Woodrow Wilson National Fellowship Program and was initially directed by Joseph Katz, one of the nation's leading authorities on faculty development. Other elements of the state's ambitious faculty development effort include a Faculty Fellows Program, a Fellowship Program on the Academic Profession, a Minority Academic Career Program, and a Faculty Fellowship Program sponsored by Princeton University and the state colleges. A statewide Institute for Collegiate Teaching and Learning, under the direction of Martin J. Finkelstein, was launched in 1989. These New Jersey initiatives may

[1]For further information on these programs contact: Office of Instructional Development, University of Georgia, 164 Psychology Building, Athens, GA 30602; Kentucky Consortium for Faculty Development, Center for Faculty and Staff Development, 326 Strickler Hall, University of Louisville, Louisville, KY 40292; Center for Faculty Development, University of Nebraska, Omaha, 60th at Dodge, Omaha, NE 68160.
[2]For more information contact Department of Higher Education, State of New Jersey, 20 W. State Street, CN542, Trenton, NJ 08625, (609) 292-4310.

well prove to be a model of state support and leadership in the field of faculty development.

There are numerous other entities that influence, or can influence, professional and personal growth. Two organizations in particular exist expressly to bring together faculty development specialists and to stimulate the field. The Professional and Organizational Development Network in Higher Education (POD Network) is one of the leading professional associations. Begun in the early 1970s, the POD Network provides a network through which faculty developers can address a wide array of development issues. Its two major goals are to offer opportunities for the continuing professional and personal growth of its members and to provide services to others involved in faculty development. POD Network activities include an annual conference, various practice-oriented publications, and focused seminars and workshops.[3] In addition, the National Council for Staff, Program, and Organizational Development (NCSPOD) provides a similar networking function for community, technical, and junior colleges.[4]

Special mention should be made of the National Faculty Exchange (NFE).[5] Launched in 1983 with grants from the Exxon Education Foundation and the Ford Foundation, NFE was created to help provide revitalization opportunities for faculty members through faculty exchanges. Approximately 150 campuses across the nation pay modest membership dues to NFE, in return for which the NFE staff facilitates placement of faculty members seeking an exchange experience. NFE's "home campus" is State University of

[3]For more information contact POD Network, c/o Teaching and Learning Center, University of Nebraska, Lincoln, 121 Benton Hall, Lincoln, NE 68588-0623.
[4]For more information contact NCSPOD, c/o American Association of Community and Junior Colleges, One Dupont Circle, N.W., Washington, D.C. 20036.
[5]For more information contact Bette Worley, President, National Faculty Exchange, 4656 W. Jefferson Blvd., Suite 140, Fort Wayne, IN 46804, (219) 436-2634.

New York College, Buffalo. A counterpart to NFE for community colleges is the Community College Exchange Program.[6]

Foundations, too, have long played a major part in supporting faculty development; their involvement individually and as a group fluctuates over time. Among the most important over the years have been the Danforth, Exxon Education, Ford, Kellogg, and Mellon Foundations and the Lilly Endowment. Regional foundations, such as the Bush Foundation (which serves Minnesota and the Dakotas) and the Northwest Area Foundation have also been helpful on a regional basis. The federal government, too, is a player, especially through the Fund for the Improvement of Postsecondary Education (FIPSE); some FIPSE grants have been targeted to help faculty members improve their teaching skills.

Having suggested a number of strategies that we believe have particular merit, we turn our attention now to three remaining topics: the role of development specialists, the salience of organizational culture, and some concluding reflections.

### The Role of Development Specialists

Faculty development programs may be beautifully conceived, administrators genuinely committed, and faculty keenly receptive. But if the professionals responsible for delivering the services are not effective, all the other positives may well go for naught. The development specialists are a very critical link in the chain. Precisely what characteristics they need will vary from one setting to another and will depend, of course, on their particular tasks. Notwithstanding those variations, several generalizations can be proffered.

1. *Acquiring an appreciation for the culture of the academy.* Development specialists must understand and be sensitive to the perplexing peculiarities of academic organization and faculty culture. These pages are not the place to argue in detail that the academy is a distinctive workplace; it *is,* and the specialist who does

[6]For more information contact Gary L. Filan, National Coordinator, Community College Exchange Program, Maricopa Community Colleges, 3910 E. Washington, Phoenix, AZ 85034, (612) 267-4494.

not grasp the nuances of academic life cannot succeed. It is not essential that the facilitator embrace the academic life in all its sometimes bizarre ways, but if that development specialist does not place a high premium on understanding what forces propel the organization and motivate its faculty, he or she surely runs a high risk of failure.

2. *Being assertive, but not too.* Development specialists must be able to strike an elusive balance between assertiveness and deference. This may be true for any consultant, but it seems especially important when dealing with a faculty clientele. And this proposition holds with equal force in relationships with the administration from whom resources flow. Only by knowing when to push and when to give wide latitude can these specialists function effectively as facilitators and catalysts.

3. *Conferring status.* Whatever else may be said in praise or deprecation of academic organizations, surely they tend toward an obsession with credentials and status. Possessing faculty status may guarantee nothing, but the absence of faculty status tends to undermine a development specialist's credibility when he or she deals with faculty; it is unquestionably a significant handicap. This observation militates in favor of finding ways to accord status to faculty development specialists. Sometimes the status solution is rather simple; for not infrequently a current faculty member, status assured, doubles as a development specialist on campus. Development specialists hired from without often have the usual array of advanced degrees; for them, courtesy academic appointments may constitute an appropriate, if partial, response. This is not to suggest that the currency of faculty status be subject to cavalier devaluation. It is to suggest that status within the academy must be acknowledged and addressed resourcefully to better ensure effective programs.

4. *Making effective use of faculty development personnel.* These specialists need to be full-fledged partners in the process of institutional renewal and faculty growth. As increasing numbers of department chairs take on responsibilities for aspects of faculty development (Creswell and others, forthcoming), the role of faculty development specialists will change. New relationships and involvements will be needed. At their best, development specialists

can be a potent catalyst in helping faculty members to realize their fullest potential—thereby helping the campus to accomplish its basic mission.

## The Salience of Organizational Leadership

The culture and values of an organization are difficult to define and describe with any precision. What is needed for an effective faculty development program is a campus mindset, a commonly held attitude, that reflects a proactive commitment to professional and personal growth. This requires moving beyond rhetorical flourishes and general statements of principle. It means a commitment of resources. Above all, it means visible, consistent, persistent campus leadership. This leadership must emanate from the highest levels of the organization, including the campus's chief executive and academic officers. As we suggested earlier, substantial involvement of faculty leadership is likewise crucial. In sum, a positive attitude must be established and supported; a mutuality of commitment is vital. The core value is recognition of the importance of professional and personal growth as a high campus priority. That value is predicated on the proposition that faculty growth is fundamentally important, is indispensable to a campus's ability to perform its mission. For unless the campus value system is basically supportive of these objectives, a campus cannot expect significant faculty development activities to take root and flourish.

## Recapitulation

Enhanced faculty development requires that an institution be serious about the need for faculty members to understand and address their own growth and development. It requires, too, that the parallel objectives of continued renewal and development of the institution be respected. We are not speaking of an either/or situation (faculty versus institution); rather, both faculty and institution must make adjustments to ensure successful adaptation and development. The objective of a development program must be to attain adequate support for faculty members and appropriate linking of faculty members' activities to institutional priorities.

As our chapter authors have pointed out, different conditions will determine the kinds of developmental opportunities deemed to be necessary. When external factors threaten the health of the institution, more drastic measures to help make adaptations and new decisions will be necessary. On the other hand, when an institution is growing and needs to attract many new faculty members, strategies that focus on the needs of novice or new-to-the-institution faculty will be a priority.

The more common situation, at least for the proximate future, will be the need to address a range of issues involving a continuum of faculty and institutional circumstances: campuses with some parts that are prospering and expanding while other parts are stagnating, being redirected, or even withering. Enhanced faculty development is one approach—in addition to, for example, traditional, more narrowly focused developmental strategies—to maintain a human perspective no matter what trauma the institution and individuals may be experiencing.

Enhanced faculty development is not the only answer, but we believe that it can provide insight, support, and opportunities to enable faculty members to develop more fully even in difficult institutional settings. How potent a factor such an approach can be will depend upon the resourcefulness and commitment of members of the higher education community—and especially the community's leaders—to keep human development values prominent and to strive to build comprehensive programs to address the multifaceted needs of the campus and its faculty. We can imagine no better place to seek excellence in order to provide for a healthy future of the higher education enterprise.

## References

Creswell, J. W., and others. *Strategies of 200 Excellent Chairpersons: Building a Positive Work Environment for Your Faculty*, forthcoming.

Eble, K. E., and McKeachie, W. J. *Improving Undergraduate Education Through Faculty Development: An Analysis of Effective Programs and Practices.* San Francisco: Jossey-Bass, 1985.

Gaff, J. G. *Toward Faculty Renewal: Advances in Faculty, Instruc-*

*tional, and Organizational Development.* San Francisco: Jossey-Bass, 1976.

Lindquist, J. "Professional Development." In A. W. Chickering and Associates, *The Modern American College: Responding to the New Realities of Diverse Students and a Changing Society.* San Francisco: Jossey-Bass, 1981.

 Resource

# A Guide
# to the Literature
# on Faculty Development

*Carole J. Bland*
*Constance C. Schmitz*

We thought it advisable to preface the bibliography in this Resource with a few words about our experience in identifying the 315 references listed, and about what is not in the bibliography.

There are basically two kinds of review articles: descriptive and evaluative. A typical evaluative review analyzes past work in an area to ascertain the effectiveness of an intervention or innovation. A synthesis is made of only those studies that meet acceptable research standards set by the reviewer. A descriptive review, on the other hand, describes the total work in an area and synthesizes the literature into themes, areas of consensus, discrepancies, or other categories. The type of review conducted depends on the research questions, the subject, and the state of the literature.

This bibliography resulted from a descriptive review of the literature on faculty development. The questions that guided our search were descriptive, largely because the literature does not contain sufficient empirical studies to answer evaluative questions. This is not to say that the current literature has little to offer. As described in Chapter Three, these writings give strong testimony to the creative methods employed to promote vitality, and they serve as a valuable resource of knowledge on how to implement these methods. This literature is, however, uneven and scattered, reminiscent of Morgan's description of the medical literature—a "literature jungle . . . fast growing, full of deadwood, sprinkled with hidden treasures and infested with spiders and snakes" (p. 62).

For those of you treading this same ground, some advice on key words: as discussed in Chapter Three, the definition of what constitutes faculty development changed over the years we studied. Earlier writers equated faculty development with instructional improvement, while later authors included (under this rubric) all strategies that promote the vitality and productivity of individual faculty members, whole institutions, or the entire faculty corps. Thus articles on administrator development, faculty recruitment, and early retirement, for example, would probably be stored today under the terms "faculty development" or "institutional vitality" in computerized literature data bases. They might not have been stored this way, however, as little as five years ago. Therefore, readers searching the past for articles on specific strategies should search under specific strategy labels (for example, "outplacement") as well as under general terms (for example, "faculty development" or "institutional vitality").

One other significant phenomenon of computerized data bases is that the collections in the bases change. For example, when we returned to the computerized data bases in 1987 to update our 1965-1985 review, we used our 1985 terms and commands to search the most recent two years. Out of curiosity, we compared the printouts generated in 1987 for the years 1965-1985 to those generated two years earlier using the same terms and commands. The results, surprisingly, were not exactly the same. Articles from journals not previously found now appeared. This discrepancy was caused by the change in status of journals such as *Family Medicine,* which was one of the journals Medline added in 1987 to its index. Before 1987 many articles on family medicine faculty development programs did not appear on commonly used literature searching systems. Thus the persistent reviewer of faculty vitality literature might wish to periodically look again at previously searched years.

Now a few words about what is *not* in the bibliography. Although this is a comprehensive review of the literature, some of the activity that occurred in faculty development during the past two decades is not revealed in the citations. It seems that directors of faculty development efforts are more inclined to build and implement programs than to research or write about them. Thus, when wishing to know about the effectiveness of, or the frequency of use of, early retirement, for example, the reader would be wise to supplement a review of the written literature with phone calls to a few of the authors and to relevant associations, such as the Professional and Organizational Development Network in Higher Education, the Council of Independent Colleges, or the American Council on Education. The network among people in the field is good, and three or four phone calls would alert reviewers to other examples not in the literature.

Finally, the materials available only on microfiche in the Educational Resources Information Center (ERIC) are not included in this bibliography. The print and content quality of these materials varies tremendously. When looking for information on a specific strategy, however, the reviewer can uncover unexpected treasures by perusing this collection of project reports, meeting presentations, and evaluations.

## Bibliography

1. AAHE Task Force on Professional Growth. "Vitality Without Mobility: The Faculty Opportunities Audit." In *Current Issues in Higher Education*. Washington, D.C.: American Association for Higher Education, 1984.

2. Adams, C. C. "Faculty Awards Programs: Campus-Based and Systemwide." Long Beach: Center for Professional Development, California State University, 1977. (ED 136 725)

3. Alexander, D. R. "Case Study: The Wichita State University Experience." In G. M. Hipps (ed.), *Effective Planned Change Strategies*. New Directions for Institutional Research, no. 33. San Francisco: Jossey-Bass, 1982.

4. Alfred, R. L. "Organizing for Renewal Through Participative Governance." In R. M. Davis (ed.), *Leadership and Institutional Renewal*. New Directions for Higher Education, no. 49. San Francisco: Jossey-Bass, 1985.

5. Anderson, J., and others. "The Workshop as a Learning Sys-

tem in Medical Teacher Education." *British Journal of Medical Education*, 1972, *6*, 296–300.

6. Andrews, F. M. (ed.). *Scientific Productivity: The Effectiveness of Research Groups in Six Countries*. Cambridge: Cambridge University Press, 1979.

7. Argyris, C. *Integrating the Individual and the Organization*. New York: Wiley, 1964.

8. Armstrong, F. H. "Faculty Development Through Interdisciplinarity." *The Journal of General Education*, 1980, *32*, 52–63.

9. Arnst, D. "Improving Instruction: Reform the Institution, Not the Faculty." *Liberal Education*, 1978, *32*, 266–277.

10. Arreola, R. "Establishing Successful Faculty Evaluation and Development Programs." In A. B. Smith (ed.), *Evaluating Faculty and Staff*. New Directions for Community Colleges, no. 41. San Francisco: Jossey-Bass, 1983.

11. Arsham, G. M. "An Instructional Skills Workshop for Medical Teachers: Design and Execution." *British Journal of Medical Education*, 1971, *5*, 320–324.

12. Bailey, S. K. "Human Resource Development in a World of Decremental Budgets." *Planning for Higher Education*, 1974, *3*, 1–5.

13. Bakker, G. R., and Lacey, P. A. "The Teaching Consultant at Earlham." In W. C. Nelsen and M. E. Siegel (eds.), *Effective Approaches to Faculty Development*. Washington, D.C.: Association of American Medical Colleges, 1980.

14. Baldwin, R. G. "Adult and Career Development: What Are the Implications for Faculty?" In *Current Issues in Higher Education*. Washington, D.C.: American Association for Higher Education, 1979.

15. Baldwin, R. G. "Planning and Action on Campus." In R. G. Baldwin (ed.), *Expanding Faculty Options*. Washington, D.C.: American Association for Higher Education, 1981.

16. Baldwin, R. G. "Variety and Productivity in Faculty Careers." In J. W. Fuller (ed.), *Issues in Faculty Personnel Policies*. New Directions for Higher Education, no. 41. San Francisco: Jossey-Bass, 1983.

17. Baldwin, R. G. "Concluding Comments." In R. G. Baldwin

(ed.), *Incentives for Faculty Vitality*. New Directions for Higher Education, no. 51. San Francisco: Jossey-Bass, 1985.

18. Baldwin, R. G., and Blackburn, R. T. "The Academic Career as a Developmental Process." *Journal of Higher Education*, 1981, *52*, 598-614.

19. Baldwin, R. G., and Krotseng, M. V. "Incentives in the Academy: Issues and Options." In R. G. Baldwin (ed.), *Incentives for Faculty Vitality*. New Directions for Higher Education, no. 51. San Francisco: Jossey-Bass, 1985.

20. Baldwin, R. G., and others. *Expanding Faculty Options*. Washington, D.C.: American Association for Higher Education, 1981.

21. Barker, W. L. "Ripples on the Pond: A Teaching Fellows Program Examined." In P. A. Lacey (ed.), *Revitalizing Teaching Through Faculty Development*. New Directions for Teaching and Learning, no. 15. San Francisco: Jossey-Bass, 1983.

22. Barr, C. R. "Austin College's Experience." In D. T. Bedsole (ed.), *Critical Aspects of Faculty Development Programs*. Proceedings of Invitational Seminar in Faculty Development, Sherman, Tex., Apr., 1983. (ED 238 387)

23. Barry, R. M. "Career Development Program at Loyola University of Chicago." Paper presented at annual meeting of Professional and Organizational Network, Berkeley, Calif., Oct. 1980.

24. Bazuin, C. H., and Yonke, A. M. "Improvement of Teaching Skills in a Clinical Setting." *Journal of Medical Education*, 1978, *53*, 377-382.

25. Becker, W. H. "A Collegial Approach to Faculty Development." *Liberal Education*, 1981, *67*, 19-35.

26. Bedsole, D. T. "Preface." In D. T. Bedsole (ed.), *Critical Aspects of Faculty Development Programs*. Proceedings of Invitational Seminar in Faculty Development, Sherman, Tex., 1983. (ED 238 387)

27. Bedsole, D. T., and Reddick, D. C. "An Experiment in Innovation: The Faculty Career Development Program at Austin College." *Liberal Education*, 1978, *64*, 75-83.

28. Belker, J. S. "A Survey of California Institutions of Higher

Education." *Journal of Staff, Program, and Organizational Development*, 1983, *1*, 75-78.

29. Belker, J. S. "The Education of Mid-Career Professors: Is it Continuing?" *College Teaching*, 1985, *33*, 68-71.

30. Bennett, J. B. "Periodic Evaluation of Tenured Faculty Performance." In R. M. Davis (ed.), *Leadership and Institutional Renewal*. New Directions for Higher Education, no. 49. San Francisco: Jossey-Bass, 1985.

31. Bergquist, W. H. "Relationship of Collegiate Professional Development and Teacher Education." *Journal of Teacher Education*, 1978, *23*, 18-24.

32. Bergquist, W. H., and Phillips, S. R. "Components of an Effective Faculty Development Program." *Journal of Higher Education*, 1975a, *46*, 177-209.

33. Bergquist, W. H., and Phillips, S. R. *A Handbook for Faculty Development*. Vol. 1. Washington, D.C.: Council for the Advancement of Small Colleges, 1975b.

34. Bergquist, W. H., and Phillips, S. R. *A Handbook for Faculty Development*. Vol. 2. Washington, D.C.: Council for the Advancement of Small Colleges, 1979.

35. Bergquist, W. H., and Shoemaker, W. A. "Facilitating Comprehensive Institutional Development." In W. H. Bergquist and W. A. Shoemaker (eds.), *A Comprehensive Approach to Institutional Development*. New Directions for Higher Education, no. 15. San Francisco: Jossey-Bass, 1976.

36. Bevan, J. M. "Who Has the Role of Building in Incentives?" In R. G. Baldwin (ed.), *Incentives for Faculty Vitality*. New Directions for Higher Education, no. 51. San Francisco: Jossey-Bass, 1985.

37. Birnbaum, R. "Using the Calendar for Faculty Development." *Educational Record*, Fall 1975, *56*, 226-230.

38. Blackburn, R. T. "Academic Careers: Patterns and Possibilities." In *Current Issues in Higher Education*. Washington, D.C.: American Association for Higher Education, 1979.

39. Blackburn, R. T., and Baldwin, R. G. "Concluding Comments." In R. G. Baldwin and R. T. Blackburn (eds.), *College Faculty: Versatile Human Resources in a Period of*

*Constraint.* New Directions for Institutional Research, no. 40. San Francisco: Jossey-Bass, 1983.

40. Blackburn, R. T., Pellino, G., Boberg, A., and O'Connell, C. "Are Instructional Improvement Programs Off-Target?" In *Current Issues in Higher Education.* Washington, D.C.: American Association for Higher Education, 1980.

41. Bland, C. J. "Guidelines for Planning Faculty Development Workshops." *Journal of Family Practice,* 1977, *5*, 235–241.

42. Bland, C. J. *Faculty Development Through Workshops.* Springfield, Ill.: Thomas, 1980.

43. Bland, C. J., and Froberg, D. G. "A Systematic Approach to Faculty Development for Family Practice Faculty." *Journal of Family Practice,* 1982, *14*, 537–543.

44. Bland, C. J., Hitchcock, M. A., Anderson, W. A., and Stritter, F. T. "Faculty Development Fellowship Programs in Family Medicine." *Journal of Medical Education,* 1987, *62*, 632–641.

45. Bland, C. J., Reineke, R. A., Welch, W. W., and Shahady, E. J. "Workshops: An Effective Format for Promoting Faculty Development in Family Medicine." Unpublished paper, Department of Family Practice and Community Health, University of Minnesota, 1978.

46. Bland, C. J., and Schmitz, C. C. "Characteristics of the Successful Researcher and Implications for Faculty Development." *Journal of Medical Education,* 1986, *61*, 22–31.

47. Bland, C. J., and Schmitz, C. C. "Faculty Vitality on Review: Retrospect and Prospect." *Journal of Higher Education,* Mar./Apr. 1988, *59*, 190–224.

48. Bland, C. J., and others. "Effectiveness of Faculty Development Workshops in Family Medicine." *Journal of Family Practice,* 1979, *9*, 453–458.

49. Bland, C. J., and others. "A Study of Federally Funded Faculty Development in Family Medicine from 1978–1981." *Family Medicine,* 1985, *18*, 50–56.

50. Bogen, G. K. "Performance and Vitality as a Function of Student-Faculty Fit." In W. R. Kirschling (ed.), *Evaluating Faculty Performance and Vitality.* New Directions for Institutional Research, no. 20. San Francisco: Jossey-Bass, 1978.

51. Boice, R. "Reexamination of Traditional Emphases in Fac-

ulty Development." *Research in Higher Education*, 1984a, *21*, 195-209.

52. Boice, R. "The Relevance of Faculty Development for Teachers of Psychology." *Teaching Psychology*, 1984b, *11*, 3-8.

53. Booth, D. B. "Institutional and Disciplinary Ideas for Development." *Educational Record*, 1977, *58*, 83-90.

54. Booth, D. B. "Department and Chairperson Development." In J. G. Gaff (ed.), *Institutional Renewal Through the Improvement of Teaching*. New Directions for Higher Education, no. 25. San Francisco: Jossey-Bass, 1978.

55. Boozer, C. H., and others. "Innovative Approaches to Faculty Development at Louisiana State University School of Dentistry." *Journal of the Louisiana Dental Association*, Spring 1975, pp. 12-15, 18-19.

56. Borus, J. G., and Groves, J. E. "Training Supervision as a Separate Faculty Role." *American Journal of Psychiatry*, 1982, *139*, 1339-1342.

57. Bowen, H. R., and Schuster, J. H. *American Professors: A National Resource Imperiled*. New York: Oxford University Press, 1986.

58. Bowen, Z. "Retraining and Renewing Faculty in a Time of Retrenchment." In W. C. Nelson and M. E. Siegel (eds.), *Effective Approaches to Faculty Development*. Washington, D.C.: Association of American Medical Colleges, 1980.

59. Bowen, Z. "Faculty Incentives: Some Practical Keys and Practical Examples." In R. G. Baldwin (ed.), *Incentives for Faculty Vitality*. New Directions for Higher Education, no. 51. San Francisco: Jossey-Bass, 1985.

60. Boyer, C. M., and Lewis, D. R. "Faculty Consulting: Responsibility or Promiscuity?" *Journal of Higher Education*, 1984, *55*, 637-659.

61. Boyer, C. M., and Lewis, D. R. *And on the Seventh Day: Faculty Consulting and Other Supplemental Income Activities*. ASHE-ERIC Higher Education Report, no. 3. Washington, D.C.: Association for the Study of Higher Education, 1985.

62. Brakeman, L. "Designing New Roles in Off-Campus Set-

tings." In R. Baldwin (ed.), *Expanding Faculty Options*. Washington, D.C.: American Association for Higher Education, 1981.

63. Braskamp, L. A. "The Role of Evaluation in Faculty Development." *Studies in Higher Education*, 1980, *5*, 45-54.

64. Brookes, M.C.T., and German, K. L. *Meeting the Challenges: Developing Faculty Careers*. ASHE-ERIC Higher Education Research Report, no. 3. Washington, D.C.: Association for the Study of Higher Education, 1983.

65. Brown, D. G., and Hanger, W. S. "Pragmatics of Faculty Self-Development." *Educational Record*, 1975, *56*, 201-206.

66. Brown, G. A. "Two Days on Explaining and Lecturing." *Studies in Higher Education*, 1982, *7*, 93-103.

67. Brown, G. A., and Daines, J. "Creating a Course on Lecturing and Explaining." *Programmed Learning and Educational Technology*, 1983, *20*, 64-69.

68. Bruss, E. A., and Kutina, K. L. "Faculty Vitality Given Retrenchment: A Policy Analysis." *Research in Higher Education*, 1981, *14*, 19-30.

69. Buchanan, J. S. "Endowment Support." In D. T. Bedsole (ed.), *Critical Aspects of Faculty Development Programs*. Proceedings of Invitational Seminar in Faculty Development, Sherman, Tex., Apr. 1983. (ED 238 387)

70. Bucher, G. R. "Scheduling of More Frequent Sabbaticals." In D. T. Bedsole (ed.), *Critical Aspects of Faculty Development Programs*. Proceedings of Invitational Seminar in Faculty Development, Sherman, Tex., Apr. 1983. (ED 238 387)

71. Buhl, L. C. "Professional Development in the Institutional Setting." In J. Lindquist (ed.), *Designing Teaching Improvement Programs*. Berkeley: Pacific Soundings Press, 1978.

72. Buhl, L. C. "Empowerment in Academic Cultures: Whose Responsibility Is It?" In S. C. Inglis and S. Scholl (eds.), *To Improve the Academy: P.O.D. Resources*. Lincoln: Professional and Organizational Development Network in Higher Education, Teaching and Learning Center, University of Nebraska, Lincoln, 1982.

73. Buhl, L. C., and Greenfield, A. "Contracting for Professional

Development in Academe." *Educational Record,* 1975, *56,* 111-121.

74. Bumpus, J. F. "Career Vitalization and Stress Among Professors: An Attributional Model." Paper presented at annual meeting of American Psychological Association, Los Angeles, Aug. 1982. (ED 207 478)

75. Burke, P. J., and Fessler, R. "A Collaborative Approach to Supervision." *The Clearing House,* 1983, *57,* 107-110.

76. Caldwell, S., and Marshall, J. "Staff Development—Four Approaches Described, Assessed, for Practitioner Theoretician." *NASSP Bulletin,* Feb. 1982, pp. 25-35.

77. Cameron, K. "Managing Self-Renewal." In R. M. Davis (ed.), *Leadership and Institutional Renewal.* New Directions for Higher Education, no. 49. San Francisco: Jossey-Bass, 1985.

78. Cannon, R. A. "The Professional Development of Australian University Teachers: An Act of Faith?" *Higher Education,* 1983, *12,* 19-33.

79. Carlberg, R. J. "Faculty Development at Gordon College." Third annual report to the W. K. Kellogg Foundation. Wenhem, Mass.: Gordon College, 1978.

80. Center for Faculty Evaluation and Development. *Exchange.* Manhattan: Division of Continuing Education, Kansas State University, 1984.

81. Centra, J. A. *Strategies for Improving College Teaching.* Washington, D.C.: American Association for Higher Education, 1972.

82. Centra, J. A. "The How and Why of Evaluating Teaching." In J. A. Centra (ed.), *Renewing and Evaluating Teaching.* New Directions for Higher Education, no. 17. San Francisco: Jossey-Bass, 1977a.

83. Centra, J. A. "Plusses and Minusses for Faculty Development." *Change,* Dec. 1977b, *9,* 47-48, 64.

84. Centra, J. A. "Types of Faculty Development Programs." *Journal of Higher Education,* 1978a, *49,* 151-162.

85. Centra, J. A. "Using Student Assessments to Improve Performance and Vitality." In W. R. Kirschling (ed.), *Evaluating*

*Faculty Performance and Vitality.* New Directions for Institutional Research, no. 20. San Francisco: Jossey-Bass, 1978b.

86.  Centra, J. A. "Maintaining Faculty Vitality Through Faculty Development." In S. M. Clark and D. R. Lewis (eds.), *Faculty Vitality and Institutional Productivity.* New York: Teachers College Press, 1985.

87.  Chait, R. P. "Academic Management: What It Should Be." In R. H. Pearis (ed.), *Avoiding Conflicting Faculty Personnel Practices.* New Directions for Higher Education, no. 7. San Francisco: Jossey-Bass, 1979.

88.  Chait, R. P., and Gueths, J. "Proposing a Framework for Faculty Development." *Change,* May–June 1981, *13,* 30–33.

89.  Ciampa, B. J. "Fostering Instructional Improvement Through Faculty Development." *Planning for Higher Education,* 1980, *9,* 22–27.

90.  Clark, S. M., Boyer, C. M., and Corcoran, M. "Faculty and Institutional Vitality in Higher Education." In S. M. Clark and D. R. Lewis (eds.), *Faculty Vitality and Institutional Productivity.* New York: Teachers College Press, 1985.

91.  Clark, S. M., Corcoran, M., and Lewis, D. R. "Critical Perspectives on Faculty Career Development with Implications for Differentiated Institutional Policies." Paper presented at annual meeting of American Educational Research Association, New Orleans, Apr. 1984.

92.  Clark, S. M., Corcoran, M., and Lewis, D. R. "The Case for an Institutional Perspective on Faculty Development." *Journal of Higher Education,* 1986, *57,* 176–195.

93.  Clark, S. M., and Lewis, D. R. "Implications for Institutional Response." In S. M. Clark and D. R. Lewis (eds.), *Faculty Vitality and Institutional Productivity.* New York: Teachers College Press, 1985.

94.  Committee on Continuity in Academic Research Performance. "Research Excellence Through the Year 2000: The Importance of Maintaining a Flow of New Faculty into Academic Research." *Resources in Education,* June 1980. (ED 181 832)

95.  Connell, K. J., and others. "What Does It Take for Faculty

Development to Make a Difference?" *Educational Horizons,* 1976-77, *55,* 108-115.

96. Cooper, C. R. "Project PROF: A Professional Development Program for College Faculty." Unpublished paper, Agriculture and Natural Resources Education Institute, Michigan State University, 1976.

97. Corcoran, M., and Clark, S. M. "Professional Socialization and Contemporary Career Attitudes of Three Faculty Generations." *Research in Higher Education,* 1984, *20,* 131-153.

98. Creswell, J. W. *Faculty Research Performance.* ASHE-ERIC Higher Education Report, no. 4. Washington, D.C.: Association for the Study of Higher Education, 1985.

99. Crow, M. "The Future." *Journal of Teacher Education,* 1978, *29,* 34-35.

100. Cytrynbaum, S., Lee, S., and Wadner, D. "Faculty Development Through the Life Course." *Journal of Instructional Development,* 1982, *5,* 11-22.

101. Davis, R. H. "A Behavioral Change Model with Implications for Faculty Development." *Higher Education,* 1979, *8,* 123-140.

102. Desruisseaux, P. "Eleven Colleges Join New York University in a Network for Revitalizing Faculty Members." *The Chronicle of Higher Education,* June 1985, *6,* 21.

103. Diers, D. "Faculty Research Development at Yale." *Nursing Research,* 1970, *19,* 64-71.

104. Donnelly, F. A., and others. "Evaluation of Weekend Seminars for Physicians." *Journal of Medical Education,* 1972, *47,* 184-187.

105. Doyle, K. O. "Instructional Development and Faculty Development at a Large University." Paper presented at annual meeting of American Educational Research Association, New York, Apr. 1977. (ED 138 180)

106. Eble, K. E. *Career Development of the Effective College Teacher.* Washington, D.C.: American Association of University Professors and Association of American Colleges, 1971.

107. Eble, K. E., and McKeachie, W. J. *Improving Undergraduate Education Through Faculty Development: An Analysis of*

*Effective Programs and Practices.* San Francisco: Jossey-Bass, 1985.

108.  Edgerton, R. "The Need to Rethink Faculty Careers." In R. Baldwin (ed.), *Expanding Faculty Options.* Washington, D.C.: American Association for Higher Education, 1981.

109.  Elmore, J. E. "Peer Consultation." In D. T. Bedsole (ed.), *Critical Aspects of Faculty Development Programs.* Proceedings of Invitational Seminar on Faculty Development, Sherman, Tex., Apr. 1983. (ED 238 387)

110.  Elmore, J. E. "Intra-University Visiting Professorships for Faculty Renewal and Development." *Innovation Abstracts,* no. 6. Austin, Tex.: National Institute for Staff and Organizational Development, University of Texas, 1984.

111.  Evraiff, W., and Meshover, L. "Creative Management for Faculty Development." *Journal of Research and Development in Education,* 1981, *14,* 71–78.

112.  Farmer, C. H. "The Faculty Role in Administrator Evaluation." In J. G. Gaff (ed.), *Institutional Renewal Through the Improvement of Teaching.* New Directions for Higher Education, no. 25. San Francisco: Jossey-Bass, 1978.

113.  Farrell, R. V., and Seideman, S. "Role Swapping Can Work to Revitalize Faculty, Teachers." *Journal of Teacher Education,* 1979, *30,* 35–36.

114.  Fenker, R. M. "The Evaluation of University Faculty and Administrators." *Journal of Higher Education,* 1975, *46,* 665–686.

115.  Ferren, A., and Geller, W. "Classroom Consultants: Colleagues Helping Colleagues." *Improving College and University Teaching,* Spring 1983, *31,*82–86.

116.  Fessler, R., and Burke, P. "Interaction: An Essential in Developing Professional Growth Programs." *NASSP Bulletin,* Mar. 1983, *67,* 43–49.

117.  Fisher, C. P. "The Evaluation and Development of College and University Administrators." *Research Currents,* Mar. 1977, pp. 3–6.

118.  Foley, R. F., Lipetz, M., and Bussigel, M. "Rethinking Faculty Development." *Center for Educational Development Annual Report,* 1984, pp. 32–37.

119. Foley, R., and others. "A Department Approach for Improving Lecture Skills of Medical Teachers." *Medical Education,* 1976, *10,* 369-373.

120. Fontes, H. C., Schulte, J., and Brye, C. C. "Faculty Development: Three Programs Make the Grade." *Nursing and Health Care,* 1987, *8,* 153-155.

121. Francis, J. B. "How Do We Get There From Here? Program Design for Faculty Development." *Journal of Higher Education,* 1975, *46,* 719-732.

122. Freedman, M. "Facilitating Faculty Development." In M. Freedman (ed.), *Facilitating Faculty Development.* New Directions for Higher Education, no. 1. San Francisco: Jossey-Bass, 1973.

123. Friedman, M., and Stomper, C. "The Effectiveness of a Faculty Development Program: A Process-Product Experimental Study." *Review of Higher Education,* 1983, 7, 49-65.

124. Friedman, M., Tuckman, B. W., and Stomper, C. "Evaluating a Faculty Development Program in Terms of Student Achievement." Paper presented at annual meeting of American Educational Research Association, New York, Mar. 1982.

125. Frisch, S. R., and Talbot, Y. "Faculty Development in Family Medicine: A Survey of Needs and Resources." *Journal of Medical Education,* 1984, *59,* 831-833.

126. Froberg, D. G., Holloway, R. L., and Bland, C. J. "A Continuity Model for Research Consultation in Family Medicine." *Journal of Family Practice,* 1984, *19,* 221-224.

127. Fuller, J. A. "Institutional Resistance to Renewal." In R. M. Davis (ed.), *Leadership and Institutional Renewal.* New Directions for Higher Education, no. 49. San Francisco: Jossey-Bass, 1985.

128. Fuller, J. A., and Evans, F. J. "Recharging Intellectual Batteries: The Challenge of Faculty Development." *Educational Record,* Spring 1985, *66,* 31-34.

129. Fund for the Improvement of Postsecondary Education. *Resources for Change: A Guide to Projects.* Washington, D.C.: Education Division, U.S. Department of Health, Education, and Welfare, 1980.

130.  Furniss, W. T. "New Opportunities for Faculty Members."
      *Educational Record,* Winter 1981a, *22,* 8–15.
131.  Furniss, W. T. *Reshaping Faculty Careers.* Washington,
      D.C.: American Council on Education, 1981b.
132.  Furniss, W. T. "The Glorious Privilege of Being Indepen-
      dent." In D. T. Bedsole (ed.), *Critical Aspects of Faculty De-
      velopment Programs.* Proceedings of Invitational Seminar in
      Faculty Development, Sherman, Tex., Apr. 1983. (ED 238
      387)
133.  Gaff, J. G. "Faculty Development: The State of the Art." In
      *Current Issues in Higher Education.* Washington, D.C.:
      American Association for Higher Education, 1976a.
134.  Gaff, J. G. *Toward Faculty Renewal: Advances in Faculty,
      Instructional, and Organizational Development.* San Fran-
      cisco: Jossey-Bass, 1976b.
135.  Gaff, J. G. "Overcoming Faculty Resistance." In J. G. Gaff
      (ed.), *Institutional Renewal Through the Improvement of
      Teaching.* New Directions for Higher Education, no. 25. San
      Francisco: Jossey-Bass, 1978.
136.  Gaff, J. G. "Ongoing Development and Renewal." In J.
      Green and A. Levine (eds.), *Opportunity in Adversity.* San
      Francisco: Jossey-Bass, 1985.
137.  Gaff, J. G., and Justice, D. O. "Faculty Development Yester-
      day, Today, and Tomorrow." In J. G. Gaff (ed.), *Institu-
      tional Renewal Through the Improvement of Teaching.*
      New Directions for Higher Education, no. 25. San Francisco:
      Jossey-Bass, 1978.
138.  Gaff, J. G., and Wilson, R. C. "The Teaching Environ-
      ment." *American Association of University Professors Bul-
      letin,* Winter 1971, *57,* 475–493.
139.  Gaff, J. G., and others. "Project on Institutional Renewal
      Through the Improvement of Teaching." *Educational Ho-
      rizons,* Winter 1976–77, *55,* 97–103.
140.  Gaff, S. S., Festa, C., and Gaff, J. G. *Professional Develop-
      ment: A Guide to Resources.* New Rochelle, N.Y.: Change
      Magazine Press, 1978.
141.  Gale, J., and others. "Planning of Educational Courses: A
      Model of the Management of an Educational Workshop for

Teachers of Medicine." *British Journal of Medical Education*, 1974, *8*, 87-91.

142. Garbee, W. H., Strother, E. A., and Ferraro, E. "A Survey of Dental Faculty Development Programs." *Journal of Dental Education*, 1986, *50*, 728-730.

143. Gardner, J. W. "Self-Renewal." *National Forum*, 1987, *67*, 16-19.

144. Gerth, D. R. "Institutional Approaches to Faculty Development." In M. Freedman (ed.), *Facilitating Faculty Development*. New Directions for Higher Education, no. 1. San Francisco: Jossey-Bass, 1973.

145. Geyman, J. P. "Faculty Development and Evaluation of Teaching Performance." *Journal of Family Practice*, 1982, *14*, 987-988.

146. Gleason, M. "Ten Best on Teaching: A Bibliography of Essential Sources for Instructors." *Improving College and University Teaching*, 1984, *32*, 11-13.

147. Goldman, J. "Faculty Development and Human Resource Management in the Academic Setting." *Journal of Medical Education*, 1982, *57*, 860-865.

148. Graham, L. E. "A Faculty Research Development Project in a Baccalaureate Program in Nursing." *Nursing Research*, 1968, *17*, 321-326.

149. Grasha, A. F. "The Role of Organizational Development." *Journal of Teacher Education*, 1968, *29*, 27-30.

150. Gregory, I. D., and Hammar, B. "Case Study of First Course in Teaching Skills and Methods for University Medical Staff." *British Journal of Medical Education*, 1974, *8*, 92-98.

151. Gross, R. F. "Faculty Development at Gordon College." In D. T. Bedsole (ed.), *Critical Aspects of Faculty Development Programs*. Proceedings of Invitational Seminar in Faculty Development, Sherman, Tex., Apr. 1983. (ED 238 387)

152. Hagberg, J. "Reexamining Academic Careers as a Legitimate Process." In R. Baldwin (ed.), *Expanding Faculty Options*. Washington, D.C.: American Association for Higher Education, 1981.

153. Hahn, R. "Seeking Outside Help to Facilitate Renewal Efforts." In R. M. Davis (ed.), *Leadership and Institutional*

*Renewal.* New Directions for Higher Education, no. 49. San Francisco: Jossey-Bass, 1985.

154.  Hamill, P. J., Jr. "Faculty Incentives at the College of Charleston: A Case Study." In R. G. Baldwin (ed.), *Incentives for Faculty Vitality.* New Directions for Higher Education, no. 51. San Francisco: Jossey-Bass, 1985.

155.  Hammons, J. O. "Faculty Development: A Necessary Corollary to Faculty Evaluation." In A. B. Smith (ed.), *Evaluating Faculty and Staff.* New Directions for Community Colleges, no. 41. San Francisco: Jossey-Bass, 1983.

156.  Hammons, J. O., and Wallace, T.H.S. "Sixteen Ways to Kill a College Faculty Development Program." *Educational Technology,* Dec. 1976, *16,* 16–20.

157.  Harcleroad, F. F. "Escape Routes, Do They Exist?" In S. R. Hample (ed.), *Coping with Faculty Reduction.* New Directions for Institutional Research, no. 30. San Francisco: Jossey-Bass, 1981.

158.  Haywood, B. "Corporate Faculty Development: Enhancing Collegiality on Campus." In W. C. Nelsen and M. E. Siegel (eds.), *Effective Approaches to Faculty Development.* Washington, D.C.: Association of American Colleges, 1980.

159.  Heie, H., Sweet D., and Curlberg, J. *Professional Development Through Growth Contracts.* Wenham, Mass.: Gordon College, 1979.

160.  Heller, S. "Retreat for the Faculty Brings 'A Moment of Truth and Elevation' to Wilkes College." *The Chronicle of Higher Education,* Sept. 1985, *18,* 31–32.

161.  Helling, B., and Jorstad, E. "Faculty to Share Ideas." In W. C. Nelsen and M. E. Siegel (eds.), *Effective Approaches to Faculty Development.* Washington, D.C.: Association of American Colleges, 1980.

162.  Hipps, G. M. "Senior Faculty to Junior Faculty." In W. C. Nelsen and M. E. Siegel (eds.), *Effective Approaches to Faculty Development.* Washington, D.C.: Association of American Colleges, 1980.

163.  Hipps, G. M. "Faculty and Administrative Development." In G. M. Hipps (ed.), *Effective Planned Change Strategies.* New

Directions for Institutional Research, no. 33. San Francisco: Jossey-Bass, 1982.

164. Hipps, O. S. "Faculty Development: Not Just a Bandwagon." *Nursing Outlook*, Nov. 1978, *22*, 692-696.

165. Hitchcock, M. A., Lamkin, B. D., Clarke, C. M., and Kreis, S. R. "Skills for the Beginning Family Medicine Investigator." *Family Medicine*, 1987, *19*, 120-124.

166. Hitchcock, M. A. and others. "Affective Changes in Faculty Development Fellows in Family Medicine." *Journal of Medical Education*, 1986, *61*, 394-403.

167. Hodgkinson, H. L. "Administrators, Evaluation, and the Stream of Time." In J. Duley (ed.), *Implementing Field Experience Education*. New Directions for Higher Education, no. 6. San Francisco: Jossey-Bass, 1974.

168. Hoffman, C. "American Historical Association Faculty Development Program: Planning and Implementation." Paper presented at annual meeting of American Historical Association, Atlanta, Ga., Dec. 1975. (ED 120 041)

169. Holden, K. C. "Maintaining Faculty Vitality Through Early Retirement Options." In S. M. Clark and D. R. Lewis (eds.), *Faculty Vitality and Institutional Productivity*. New York: Teachers College Press, 1985.

170. Holloway, R. L., O'Brien, D. K., and Hyatt, M. J. "A Basic Research Seminar for Family Practice Faculty." *Family Medicine*, 1983, *15*, 143-146.

171. Howard, G. S. "A Program to Improve University Instruction: A Promising Area for Psychologists." *Professional Psychology*, Aug. 1977, *8*, 316-327.

172. Hoyt, D. P., and Howard G. S. "The Evaluation of Faculty Development Programs." *Research in Higher Education*, 1978, *8*, 25-38.

173. Inglis, S. C., and Scholl, S. (eds.). *To Improve the Academy: P.O.D. Resources*. Lincoln: Professional and Organizational Development Network in Higher Education, Teaching and Learning Center, University of Nebraska, Lincoln, 1982.

174. Irby, D. M. "Peer Review of Teaching in Medicine." *Journal of Medical Education*, 1983, *58*, 457-461.

175. Irby, D. M., and others. "A Model for the Improvement of

Medical Faculty Lecturing." *Journal of Medical Education,* 1976, *51,* 403-409.

176.   Jacobson, R. L. "New Carnegie Data Show Faculty Members Uneasy About the State of Academe and Their Own Careers." *The Chronicle of Higher Education,* 1985, *31,* 1-2, 25-28.

177.   Jason, H., and Westberg, J. "Microcomputers in Faculty Development: The Florida FAC-NET Project." *Journal of Family Practice,* 1984, *19,* 72-79.

178.   Kanter, R. M. "Changing the Shape of Work: Reform in Academe." In *Current Issues in Higher Education.* Washington, D.C.: American Association for Higher Education, 1979.

179.   Kanter, R. M. *The Change Masters.* New York: Simon & Schuster, 1983.

180.   Kapfer, M. B., and Della-Piana, G. M. "Educational Technology in the Inservice Education of University Teaching Fellows." *Educational Technology,* July 1974, *14,* 22-28.

181.   Kelly, R. E. *The Gold Collar Worker: Harnessing the Brainpower of the New Workforce.* Reading, Mass.: Addison-Wesley, 1985.

182.   Kirschling, W. R. "Concluding Observations and Suggestions." In W. R. Kirschling (ed.), *Evaluating Faculty Performance and Vitality.* New Directions for Institutional Research, no. 20. San Francisco: Jossey-Bass, 1978.

183.   Koen, F. M. "An Action Research Program in Faculty Educational Development" (in-house document). Detroit, Mich.: School of Medicine, Wayne State University, 1975.

184.   Koen, F. M. "A Faculty Educational Development Program and an Evaluation of Its Evaluation." *Journal of Medical Education,* 1976, *51,* 854-855.

185.   Koerin, B. B. "Teaching Effectiveness and Faculty Development Programs: A Review." *Journal of General Education,* 1980, *32,* 40-51.

186.   Kozma, R. B. "Faculty Development and the Adoption and Diffusion of Classroom Innovations." *Journal of Higher Education,* 1978, *49,* 438-449.

187.   Kruetner, L., and Godfrey, E. S. "Enrollment Management:

A New Vehicle for Institutional Renewal." *College Board Review*, 1980-81, *118*, 6-9.

188. Lacefield, W. E., and Kingston, R. D. "Relationships Between Faculty Evaluations and Faulty Development." *Journal of Nursing Education*, 1983, *22*, 278-284.

189. Lacey, P. A. "The Politics of Vitalizing Teaching." In P. A. Lacey (ed.), *Revitalizing Teaching Through Faculty Development*. New Directions for Teaching and Learning, no. 15. San Francisco: Jossey-Bass, 1983.

190. Lane, E. G., and others. "Faculty Development Activities." *Nursing Outlook*, Feb. 1981, *29*, 112-118.

191. Lanphear, J. H., and Cardiff, R. D. "Faculty Development." *Archives of Pathology and Laboratory Medicine*, 1987, *111*, 487-491.

192. Lawrence, J. H. "Developmental Needs as Intrinsic Incentives." In R. G. Baldwin (ed.), *Incentives for Faculty Vitality*. New Directions for Higher Education, no. 51. San Francisco: Jossey-Bass, 1985.

193. Levine, A. "Opportunity in Adversity: The Case of Bradford College." In R. M. Davis (ed.), *Leadership and Institutional Renewal*. New Directions for Higher Education, no. 49. San Francisco: Jossey-Bass, 1985.

194. Levinson-Rose, J., and Menges, R. J. "Improving College Teaching: A Critical Review of Research." *Review of Educational Research*, 1981, *51*, 403-434.

195. Linden, G. "Multi-Institutional, Multi-Level Faculty Development Programs." *Educational Horizons*, 1976-77, *55*, 56-63.

196. Lindquist, J. (ed.). *Designing Teaching Improvement Programs*. Berkeley, Calif.: Pacific Soundings Press, 1978a.

197. Lindquist, J. "Social Learning and Problem-Solving Strategies for Improving Academic Performance." In W. R. Kirschling (ed.), *Evaluating Faculty Performance and Vitality*. New Directions for Institutional Research, no. 20. San Francisco: Jossey-Bass, 1978b.

198. Lindquist, J. "The Challenge to Professional Development." *AAHE Bulletin*, Sept. 1980, 3-7.

199. Lipetz, M., Bussigel, M., and Foley, R. "Rethinking Faculty Development." *Medical Teacher*, 1986, *8*, 137–144.

200. Lortie, D. C. *Schoolteacher: A Sociological Study*. Chicago: University of Chicago Press, 1975.

201. Lubin, M. "Faculty Fight Burnout with Weekly Seminar." *American Psychological Association Monitor*, Dec. 1982, p. 24.

202. McGaghie, W. C., and others. "A Multi-Component Program to Increase Family Physicians' Faculty Skills." *Journal of Medical Education*, 1981, *56*, 803–811.

203. McGarrah, R. E. "Restoring the University from Within." *Educational Record*, 1980, *61*, 70–74.

204. Mackenzie, R. S. "Essential Features of a Faculty Evaluation Program." *Journal of Dental Education*, 1977, *41*, 301–306.

205. McLeod, P. J. "Faculty Development Practices in Canadian Medical Schools." *Canadian Medical Association Journal*, 1987, *136*, 709–712.

206. Maher, T. H. "Designing New Roles Within Academe." In R. Baldwin (ed.), *Expanding Faculty Options*. Washington, D.C.: American Association for Higher Education, 1981.

207. Maher, T. H. "Institutional Vitality in Higher Education." *Research Currents*, June 1982, pp. 3–6. (ED 216 668)

208. Mahler, S., and Benor, D. E. "Short and Long Term Effects of a Teacher-Training Workshop in Medical Education." *Higher Education*, 1984, *13*, 265–273.

209. Martin, R. E., Perrier, D., and Trinca, C. E. "A Planned Program for Evaluation and Development of Clinical Pharmacy Faculty." *American Journal of Pharmaceutical Education*, 1983, *47*, 102–107.

210. Martin, W. B. "Faculty Development as Human Development." *Liberal Education*, 1975, *61*, 187–196.

211. Mauksch, I. G. "The Socialization of Nurse-Faculty." *Nurse Educator*, July–Aug. 1982, *9*, 7–12.

212. Menefee, R. "Old Dog, New Tricks." In W. C. Nelsen and M. E. Siegel (eds.), *Effective Approaches to Faculty Development*. Washington, D.C.: Association of American Colleges, 1980.

213. Menges, R. J. "Career-Span Faculty Development." *College Teaching*, 1985, *33*, 181–184.
214. Merwin, J., and others. "Report of the Steering Committee to Facilitate the Scholarly Activities of the Faculty." Minneapolis: University of Minnesota, 1983.
215. Millman, J. "Improving Instruction Through Research." *Improving College and University Teaching*, 1983, *31*, 13–15.
216. Mills, W. C. "Orientation to Academia: The Socialization of New Faculty." *Nursing Papers*, 1983, *15*, 21–47.
217. Mitchell, M. M. "Professional Development: Clinician to Academician." *American Journal of Occupational Therapy*, 1985, *39*, 368–373.
218. Morrissy, J. R., and others. "Faculty Development at the Department of Family Medicine, University of Western Ontario." *Canadian Family Physician*, 1977, *23*, 80–94.
219. Mortimer, K. P., and others. *Flexibility in Academic Staffing: Effective Policies and Practices.* AAHE-ERIC Higher Education Report, no. 1. Washington, D.C.: Association for the Study of Higher Education, 1985.
220. Mulvihill, M. N. "Faculty Development and Resident Training in Epidemiology and Biostatistics." *Mount Sinai Journal of Medicine*, 1981, *48*, 350–352.
221. Munson, P. J., Mason, E. J., and Wergin, J. F. "So You Want to Try Faculty Development?" Richmond: Medical College of Virginia, Virginia Commonwealth University, 1975. (ED 105 801)
222. Neff, C. B. "Faculty Development Tug o' War, or Up a Tree with a Tuning Fork." *Liberal Education*, 1976, *62*, 427–432.
223. Neff, C. B., and Nyquist, T. E. "Faculty Retraining." Final report of the Faculty Retraining Project, State University of New York. *Resources in Education*, May 1980. (ED 180 418)
224. Nelsen, W. C. "Faculty Development: Prospects and Potential for the 1980s." *Liberal Education*, 1979, *95*, 141–149.
225. Nelsen, W. C. "Faculty Development: Perceived Needs for the 1980s." In W. C. Nelsen and M. E. Siegel (eds.), *Effective Approaches to Faculty Development.* Washington, D.C.: Association of American Colleges, 1980.
226. Nelsen, W. C. "Faculty Development: Applying What We

Have Learned for the Important Years Ahead." In D. T. Bedsole (ed.), *Critical Aspects of Faculty Development Programs.* Proceedings of Invitational Seminar in Faculty Development, Sherman, Tex., Apr. 1983a. (ED 238 387)

227. Nelsen, W. C. "Fifteen Plus One Low-Cost Faculty Development Ideas." In D. T. Bedsole (ed.), *Critical Aspects of Faculty Development Programs.* Proceedings of Invitational Seminar in Faculty Development, Sherman, Tex., Apr. 1983b. (ED 238 387)

228. Nelsen, W. C., and Siegel, M. E. (eds). *Effective Approaches to Faculty Development.* Washington, D.C.: Association of American Colleges, 1980.

229. Noonan, J. F. "Teaching Workshops for New Faculty Members: Aiding the Transition from Graduate School to Teaching." In W. C. Nelsen and M. E. Siegel (eds.), *Effective Approaches to Faculty Development.* Washington, D.C.: Association of American Colleges, 1980.

230. Nordvall, R. C. *Evaluation and Development of Administrators.* AAHE-ERIC Higher Education Research Report, no. 6. Washington, D.C.: Association for the Study of Higher Education, 1979.

231. O'Connell, C. "College Policies Off-Target in Fostering Faculty Development." *Journal of Higher Education,* 1983, *54,* 662–675.

232. Ost, D. H. *Explorations in Professional Development: The First Three Years.* Long Beach, Calif.: Center for Professional Development, California State University and Colleges, 1977. (ED 163 834)

233. Osterman, D. N. "What's Happening with Instructional Development and Media? A Research Project." *Resources in Education,* Dec. 1980. (ED 190 124)

234. Osterman, D. N., and others. "Improving Undergraduate Teaching Through a Faculty Development Program." Corvallis, Oreg.: Oregon State University, 1976. (ED 122 836)

235. Page, S., and Loeper, J. "Peer Review of the Nurse Educator." *Journal of Nursing Education,* 1978, *17,* 21–29.

236. Parker, C. A., and Lawson, J. "From Theory to Practice to

Theory: Consulting with College Faculty." *Personnel and Guidance Journal,* 1978, *56,* 423–427.

237. Patton, C. V. "Mid-Career Change and Early Retirement." In W. R. Kirschling (ed.), *Evaluating Faculty Performance and Vitality.* New Directions for Institutional Research, no. 20. San Francisco: Jossey-Bass, 1978.

238. Patton, C. V., and Palmer, D. D. "Maintaining Faculty Vitality Through Midcareer Change Options." In S. M. Clark and D. R. Lewis (eds.), *Faculty Vitality and Institutional Productivity.* New York: Teachers College Press, 1985.

239. Pelz, D. C., and Andrews, F. M. *Scientists in Organizations: Productive Climates for Research and Development.* New York: Wiley, 1966.

240. Perlberg, A., and others. "Microteaching and Videotape Recordings: A New Approach to Improved Teaching." *Journal of Medical Education,* 1972, *47,* 43–50.

241. Peters, T. J., and Waterman, R. H., Jr. *In Search of Excellence: Lessons from America's Best-Run Companies.* New York: Harper & Row, 1982.

242. Peterson, H. L. "Coping with the 1980s: An Organizational Response to Retrenchment." *Research in Education,* Nov. 1981. (ED 203 829)

243. Peterson, M. W. "Decline, New Demands, and Quality: The Context for Renewal." *Review of Higher Education,* 1984a, *7,* 187–203.

244. Peterson, M. W. "In a Decade of Decline: The Seven R's of Planning." *Change,* May/June 1984b, *16,* 42–46.

245. Phillips, S. R. "The Many Faces of Faculty Development." *College Management,* Nov./Dec. 1974, *9,* 14–17.

246. Plough, T. E. "Academic Leadership Development for Department Chairpersons." Paper presented at annual forum of Association for Institutional Research, San Diego, Calif.: May 1979. (ED 174 064)

247. Pochyly, D. F. "Problem-Oriented Faculty Development in a Medical School." *Educational Horizons,* Winter 1976–77, *55,* 92–96.

248. Ransom, J. "Learning with a Colleague." In W. C. Nelsen and M. E. Siegel (eds.), *Effective Approaches to Faculty De-*

*velopment.* Washington, D.C.: Association of American Colleges, 1980.

249. Reilly, D. H. "Faculty Development No: Program Development Yes." *Planning for Higher Education,* 1983, *11,* 25–28.

250. Reineke, R., and Bland, C. J. *Followup Evaluation Report for Workshops for Faculty Development in Family Medicine.* In-house report, University of Minnesota, 1977.

251. Rice, R. E. "Dreams and Actualities: Danforth Fellows in Mid-Career." In S. C. Inglis and S. Scholl (eds.), *To Improve the Academy: P.O.D. Resources.* Lincoln: Professional and Organizational Development Network in Higher Education, Teaching and Learning Center, University of Nebraska, Lincoln, 1982.

252. Rice, R. E. "Being Professional Academically." In D. T. Bedsole (ed.), *Critical Aspects of Faculty Development Programs.* Proceedings of Invitational Seminar in Faculty Development, Sherman, Tex., Apr. 1983a. (ED 238 387)

253. Rice, R. E. "Leaves and Other Institutional Resources for Maintaining Faculty Development." In D. T. Bedsole (ed.), *Critical Aspects of Faculty Development Programs.* Proceedings of Invitational Seminar in Faculty Development, Sherman, Tex., Apr. 1983b. (ED 238 387)

254. Rice, R. E. *Faculty Lives: Vitality and Change. A Study of the Foundation's Grants in Faculty Development, 1979–1984.* St. Paul, Minn.: Northwest Area Foundation, 1985.

255. Rice, R. E., and Davis, M. L. "Program Coordination of Academic Planning and Professional Development." Final report to the W. K. Kellogg Foundation, 1979. (ED 172 688)

256. Riggio, M. B. "In Praise of an Interdisciplinary Symposium." In W. C. Nelsen and M. E. Siegel (eds.), *Effective Approaches to Faculty Development.* Washington, D.C.: Association of American Colleges, 1980.

257. Rivage-Seul, D. M. "Preparing Faculty for Teaching Core Curriculum Courses." In W. C. Nelsen and M. E. Siegel (eds.), *Effective Approaches to Faculty Development.* Washington, D.C.: Association of American Colleges, 1980.

258. Rives, S. G., and others. "Academic Innovation: Faculty and

Instructional Development at Illinois State University." *Resources in Education,* Mar. 1980. (ED 178 020)

259.  Rodes, J. "Faculty Exchange: Overcoming Academic Calcification." In W. C. Nelsen and M. E. Siegel (eds.), *Effective Approaches to Faculty Development.* Washington, D.C.: Association for American Colleges, 1980.

260.  Romer, A. "The Role of a Faculty Committee in Facilitating Faculty Development." In W. · C. Nelsen and M. E. Siegel (eds.), *Effective Approaches to Faculty Development.* Washington, D.C.: Association of American Colleges, 1980.

261.  Rovin, S., and Packer, M. W. "Evaluation of Teaching and Teachers at the University of Kentucky College of Dentistry." *Journal of Dental Education,* 1971, *35,* 32-37.

262.  Rubin, I., and others. "Improving the Coordination of Care: An Educational Program." *Hospital and Health Services Administration,* Spring 1977, *22,* 57-70.

263.  Ruch, C. P. "HRD—An Organizing Approach to Faculty Development." *Improving College and University Teaching,* 1984, *32,* 18-22.

264.  Rutherford, D. "Developing University Teaching: A Strategy for Revitalization." *Higher Education,* 1982, *11,* 177-191.

265.  Scholl, S. C. "The Consortium Approach to Faculty Development: The GLCA Experience." In W. C. Nelsen and M. E. Siegel (eds.), *Effective Approaches to Faculty Development.* Washington, D.C.: Association of American Colleges, 1980.

266.  Schuster, J. H. "Faculty Vitality: Observations from the Field." In R. G. Baldwin (ed.), *Incentives for Faculty Vitality.* New Directions for Higher Education, no. 51. San Francisco: Jossey-Bass, 1985.

267.  Schwartz, L. L. "Nurturing an Endangered Species: A Constructive Approach to Faculty Development." *Improving College and University Teaching,* 1983, *31,* 65-68.

268.  Schwen, T. M., and Sorcinelli, M. D. "A Profile of Postdoctoral Teaching Programs." In P. A. Lacey (ed.), *Revitalizing Teaching Through Faculty Development.* New Directions for Teaching and Learning, no. 15. San Francisco: Jossey-Bass, 1983.

269.  Schwoebel, R., and Bartel, N. R. "An Alternative to Decline:

Revitalizing the Faculty." *Change,* Nov./Dec. 1982, *14,* 22–24.

270.  Seigel, H. "Expanding the Armamentarium for Faculty Development." *Journal of Nursing Education,* 1986, *25,* 126–129.

271.  Settle, T. J. "Excellence in Business and Excellence in the Academy." In R. G. Baldwin (ed.), *Incentives for Faculty Vitality.* New Directions for Higher Education, no. 51. San Francisco: Jossey-Bass, 1985.

272.  Sharp, L. J. , and Tschuden, M. S. "Nursing Faculty Research Development: Report of an Experience." *Nursing Research,* 1967, *16,* 161–166.

273.  Sheehan, T. J. "Faculty Development." *Journal of Medical Education,* 1979, *54,* 255.

274.  Sheets, K. J., and Henry, R. C. "Assessing the Impact of Faculty Development in Medical Education." *Journal of Medical Education,* 1984, *59,* 746–748.

275.  Shroyer, G. "Montana University System Faculty Vitality Project." *Resources in Education,* July 1984. (ED 240 924)

276.  Siegel, M. E. "Empirical Findings on Faculty Development Programs." In W. C. Nelsen and M. E. Siegel (eds.), *Effective Approaches to Faculty Development.* Washington, D.C.: Association of American Colleges, 1980.

277.  Sikes, W., and Barrett, L. *Case Studies on Faculty Development.* Washington, D.C.: Council for the Advancement of Small Colleges, 1976.

278.  Simerly, R. G. "Faculty Development in Higher Education: From Myths to Research Findings." Paper presented at annual forum of the Association of Institutional Research, Apr. 1975. (ED 124 069)

279.  Simerly, R. G. "Ways to View Faculty Development." *Educational Technology,* Feb. 1977, *17,* 47–49.

280.  Skeff, K. M. "Evaluation of a Method for Improving Teaching Performance of Attending Physicians." *American Journal of Medicine,* 1983, *75,* 465–470.

281.  Skeff, K. M., and others. "Assessment by Attending Physicians of a Seminar Method to Improve Clinical Teaching." *Journal of Medical Education,* 1984, *52,* 944–950.

282. Smith, A. B. *Faculty Development and Evaluation in Higher Education.* AAHE-ERIC Higher Education Research Report, no. 8. Washington, D.C.: American Association for Higher Education, 1976.

283. Smith, D. K. "Faculty Vitality and the Management of University Personnel Policies." In W. R. Kirschling (ed.), *Evaluating Faculty Performance and Vitality.* New Directions for Institutional Research, no. 20. San Francisco: Jossey-Bass, 1978.

284. Smith, I. H., and others. "Mobilizing the Campus for Retention: An Innovative Quality of Life Model." Iowa City: ACT National Center for the Advancement of Educational Practices, 1981.

285. Smith, R. B., and Ovard, S. F. "Professional Development: A New Approach." *Improving College and University Teaching,* 1979, *27,* 40-43.

286. Smith, R. V. "Developing a New Point of View." In W. C. Nelsen and M. E. Siegel (eds.), *Effective Approaches to Faculty Development.* Washington, D.C.: Association of American Colleges, 1980.

287. Smoot, J. G. "Faculty Development and Evaluation at a Small University." *Improving College and University Teaching,* Winter 1978, *26,* 87-90.

288. Smythe, O., and Jerabek, P. L. "Faculty and Institutional Development: Bridging the Experience Gap." In C. Taylor (ed.), *Diverse Student Preparation: Benefits and Issues.* New Directions for Experiential Learning, no. 17. San Francisco: Jossey-Bass, 1982.

289. Sorcinelli, M. D. "Campus Faculty Attitudes Probed." Bloomington University *Campus Report,* 1985, *9,* (special issue on faculty development), 1-10.

290. Sorcinelli, M. D., and Logothetis, L. "Faculty Development in Nursing Education: A Teaching Consultation Service." *Journal of Nursing Education,* 1982, *21,* 35-41.

291. "Special Report: The Year of the Faculty." *Change,* 1985, *17* (entire issue).

292. Spitz, L. W. "Humanistic Approaches to Faculty Development." *Liberal Education,* 1977, *63,* 529-536.

293.   Stauffer, T. M. "Academic Administrative Internships." In J. G. Gaff (ed.), *Institutional Renewal Through the Improvement of Teaching.* New Directions for Higher Education, no. 25. San Francisco: Jossey-Bass, 1978.

294.   Stice, J. E. "A Bargain at Any Price: A Steal at $1.24." *Educational Horizons,* Winter 1976-77, *55,* 80-85.

295.   Stordahl, B. "Faculty Development: A Survey of Literature of the '70s." *Research Currents,* Mar. 1981, pp. 7-10.

296.   Stritter, F. T. "Faculty Evaluation and Development." In C. McGuire, R. Foley, A. Gorr, and R. Richards (eds.), *Handbook of Health Professions Education: Responding to New Realities in Medicine, Dentistry, Pharmacy, Nursing, Allied Health, and Public Health.* San Francisco: Jossey-Bass, 1983a.

297.   Stritter, F. T. "Faculty Evaluation and Development." *Professions Education Research Notes (PERN).* Washington, D.C.: Division I, Education in the Professions, American Educational Research Association, 1983b.

298.   Sullivan, L. "Faculty Development: A Movement on the Brink." *College Board Review,* 1983, *127,* 21-30.

299.   Thompson, M. "The AHA and Faculty Development." Paper presented at annual meeting of American Historical Association, Atlanta, Ga.: Dec. 1975. (ED 120 040)

300.   Toombs, W. "A Three-Dimensional View of Faculty Development." *Journal of Higher Education,* 1975, *46,* 701-717.

301.   Toombs, W. "Faculty Development: The Institutional Side." In R. G. Baldwin and R. T. Blackburn (eds.), *College Faculty: Versatile Human Resources in a Period of Constraint.* New Directions for Institutional Research, no. 40. San Francisco: Jossey-Bass, 1983.

302.   Toombs, W. "Faculty Vitality: The Professional Context." In R. G. Baldwin (ed.), *Incentives for Faculty Vitality.* New Directions for Higher Education, no. 51. San Francisco: Jossey-Bass, 1985.

303.   Voekel, R. T. "Encouraging Faculty Learning: A Program of Study Leaves." In W. C. Nelsen and M. E. Siegel (eds.), *Effec-*

*tive Approaches to Faculty Development.* Washington, D.C.: Association of American Colleges, 1980.

304. Warburton, S. W., and others. "Teaching Physicians to Teach: A Three-Year Report." *Journal of Family Practice,* 1979, *9,* 649-656.

305. Webb, J., and Smith, A. B. "Improving Instruction in Higher Education." *Educational Horizons,* Winter 1976-77, *55,* 86-91.

306. Wergin, J. F. "Evaluating Faculty Development Programs." In J. A. Centra (ed.), *Renewing and Evaluating Teaching.* New Directions for Higher Education, no. 17. San Francisco: Jossey-Bass, 1977.

307. Wergin, J. F., Mason, E. J., and Munson, P. J. "The Practice of Faculty Development: An Experience-Derived Model." *Journal of Higher Education,* 1976, *47,* 289-308.

308. Whitcomb, D. B., and Beck, L. L. "Institutional Mission and Faculty Development." *Resources in Education,* Apr. 1981. (ED 195 198)

309. White, A. M. "Developing and Challenging Interdisciplinary Teaching-Learning." In W. C. Nelsen and M. E. Siegel (eds.), *Effective Approaches to Faculty Development.* Washington, D.C.: Association of American Colleges, 1980.

310. Whitman, D., and Schwenk, T. "Faculty Evaluation as a Means of Faculty Development." *Journal of Family Practice,* 1982, *14,* 1097-1101.

311. Winsted, P. C. "Foundation Support." In D. T. Bedsole (ed.), *Critical Aspects of Faculty Development Programs.* Proceedings of Invitational Seminar in Faculty Development, Sherman, Tex., Apr. 1983a. (ED 238 387)

312. Winsted, P. C. "Mini-Grants and Workshops." In D. T. Bedsole (ed.), *Critical Aspects of Faculty Development Programs.* Proceedings of Invitational Seminar in Faculty Development, Sherman, Tex., Apr. 1983b. (ED 238 287)

313. Worley, B. *National Faculty Exchange Materials* (program literature). Fort Wayne: Indiana University and Purdue University, 1984-85.

314. Wurster, S. H., and McCartney, J. F. "Faculty Development:

Planning for Individual and Institutional Renewal." *Planning for Higher Education*, 1980, *9*, 14–21.

315.    Wylie, N. R., and Fuller, J. W. "Enhancing Faculty Vitality Through Collaboration Among Colleagues." In R. G. Baldwin (ed.), *Incentives for Faculty Vitality*. New Directions for Higher Education, no. 51. San Francisco: Jossey-Bass, 1985.

## Reference

Morgan, P. *An Insider's Guide for Medical Authors and Editors*. Philadelphia: ISI Press, 1986.

# Name Index

# Subject Index